1963

CRITICAL ESSAYS
ON ROMAN LITERATURE

CONTRIBUTORS

A. W. Allen

H. F. Cherniss

J. P. Elder

A. G. Lee

R. G. M. Nisbet

K. F. Quinn

CRITICAL ESSAYS
ON
ROMAN LITERATURE

ELEGY AND LYRIC

Edited and with an Introduction by
J. P. SULLIVAN

HARVARD UNIVERSITY PRESS
Cambridge, Massachusetts

© Routledge & Kegan Paul Ltd 1962

Printed in Great Britain

CONTENTS

INTRODUCTION

A BOOK which purports to be a collection of *critical* essays on ancient literature has to face the misgivings of the sceptical reader, who is well aware that the study of Greek and Latin literature as *literature* presents peculiar difficulties in a way linguistic scholarship and textual criticism do not. Moreover, classical studies in England, whose three greatest ornaments are conventionally reckoned as Bentley, Porson, and Housman, have placed most emphasis on the philological side of classics and given that the place of highest honour in teaching. Vulgarization has been accepted merely as a way of spreading a little sweetness and light or of supplementing admittedly meagre academic salaries. Popular works and translations have always been regarded as the by-products of scholarship, not as 'serious' work. And rightly. Yet it is only in such publications that modern scholars have felt called upon to discuss the literary merits of the ancient authors in whom they are professionally interested. There is a feeling indeed that literary criticism has no place in a classical education, despite its importance in other humane disciplines, and this is not entirely due to the traditions of classical learning in this country or even to a distrust of those scholars who are, in Housman's phrase, 'tainted with literature'. There is a genuine pessimism about the very possibility of such activity in classical studies.

As a consequence, however, there are those who urge, not without justice, that the study of Greek and Latin literature, whatever its incidental pedagogic merits, has ceased to be a literary or cultural education. It does not promote, they argue, a lively and critical interest in literature, but rather an exclusively bibliographical or linguistic interest. One eminent critic even alleged that from studying Greek and Latin as we do, that is, as 'language divorced from experience', 'the resultant "taste", "judgement" and "sense of fitness" (usually so strong in the "classic") are almost insuperable bars to the development of critical sensibility'. Hence a training in one's own literature should be a prerequisite to a training in classics.[1] Almost every teacher of classics must sometimes be conscious of the truth in these remarks. And it may perhaps be held to our credit that some of us have made much the same criticisms.[2]

The grounds on which these charges are levelled and the quarters from which they come lend additional force to them. These are not the sneers such as those of John Bright ('people who talk about what they call *culture*! by which they mean a smattering of the two dead languages of Greek and Latin'), but serious and sympathetic offers of help. The day has happily long passed when, in Matthew Arnold's words, 'the culture which is supposed to plume itself on a smattering of Greek and Latin . . . is valued either out of sheer vanity and ignorance, or else as an engine of social and class distinction, separating its holder like a badge or title, from other people who have not got it. No serious man would call this *culture*, or attach any value to it, as culture, at all.'[3] The faults which our modern critics descry are much subtler deficiencies.

Nor is it the case that modern critics of our studies are repeating the charges made by Pope, for instance, who in the *Dunciad* did not hesitate to attack even Bentley:

> The mighty scholiast, whose unweary'd pains
> Made Horace dull, and humbled Milton's strains.
> Turn what they will to verse, their toil is vain,
> Critics like me shall make it Prose again.[4]

The allied objections of Wordsworth in *The Prelude*[5] and of Coleridge in *Biographia Literaria*[6] are, of course, too unbearably familiar to repeat. Their charges may be summarized in the less immortal lines of Courtenay:

> Let College verse-men trite conceits express,
> Trick'd out in splendid shreds of Virgil's dress;
> From playful Ovid cull the tinsel phrase,
> And vapid notions hitch in pilfered lays;
> Then with mosaick art the piece combine,
> And boast the glitter of each dulcet line.

But few would now claim for compositions anything more than a very ancillary status in a classical education, a useful, and for some enjoyable, method of learning the language.[7] The views of genuine lovers of literature such as Macaulay, who 'detested the labour of manufacturing Greek and Latin verse in cold blood as an exercise', and who wrote 'I have never practised composition a single hour since I have been at Cambridge,' have partially triumphed. More and more there has been a tendency to give up writing bad Greek verse in order to read good. And in particular the important new developments in classical studies (especially in the study of ancient philosophy and religion) blunt the edge of criticisms such as Pope's of exclusively linguistic and textual exposition—'*Words are Man's province, Words we teach alone.*'

What, however, concerns more recent critics is the nature and place of classics in a *literary* education. The health of an academic subject depends on the high standards of its scholarship and the vitality of its research, but its value as a medium of education depends also on the humane values it implants and the critical attitudes it inculcates. What is lacking, they feel, is not exact scholarship or research, for few liberal subjects have a better record, but the informed and serious discussion of *literature* among professional students of the classics, which is then re-flected in teaching. It is felt that this is not yet established as a 'respectable' pursuit. There is, for example, no classical periodical which is devoted to literary criticism similar to those that exist in all other literary studies. This is not to say that no attempts at literary evaluation are to be found in more technical journals, but these attempts are rare, scattered and disorganized, and if they are not to be regarded as disreputable, they must masquerade sometimes in a more workaday guise, parading an unnecessary show of erudition.

Many students of the classics share these feelings, but those who do not have reasonable grounds for their distrust of the desire to assimilate classical studies to the other literary studies in our universities. Their first objection is perhaps the most potent. Is criticism of the sort envisaged possible at all? A criticism, that is, which offers neither quirks nor prejudices nor conventional judgements, but which honestly concerns itself with understanding and *evaluating* such ancient works of art as have survived. After all, both the languages with which we deal are *dead*; they are 'languages that want the living voice'. How can we recover that inwardness which would allow us to feel as subtly as in our own language all the nuances, ironies, allusions, perhaps deliberate vulgarisms and so on, the delicate control of which may make up the *tone* of a given poem? It is true that by patient and laborious work we can attain an *external* appreciation of these, as, for example, Professor Axelson's work on 'unpoetic diction' in Latin poetry has shown, but how can we 'feel' this in the way we can feel it in *The Rape of the Lock* or *The Waste Land*? How can we feel the play of metaphor in a line of Aeschylus as we can in a line of Shakespeare? Perhaps we cannot. But despite this veil which is before our eyes the most important argument for the continued literary study of the best classical authors is the perception that here we are offered something of great value and significance, something of *patent* merit. This is, after all, the best reason for disregarding the *a priori* objection to literary criticism of the classics. Ignore tradition, ignore snobbery, ignore even the disinterested taste for learning, and we find that in spite of all the claims on our attention of more accessible literatures a vital and universal interest is still offered by the best classical authors. It is true that under their aegis many inferior authors are protected from harsh judgement and dismissal; it is also true that this merit can so overawe us by its sheer temporal endurance that we avoid the important task of discrimination between what is better and what is worse in them. Yet their ability to communicate to us seems undeniable and thus the basis for some sort of criticism and specifically literary study is established. Inaccessibility to criticism is inaccessibility to *any* sensitive reading or understanding, for what is criticism but the attempt to offer the fullest, most organized and most discriminating reading of a work in its literary context? And the very difficulty of this makes the need for it more urgent. If we regard the task as impossible, we must reconcile ourselves to the fact that the classics are dead as literature.

Of course, the patent difficulty of such an attempt inspires doubt in all of us, and often we turn with relief to the more laborious but easier tasks that abound in our studies—hence the twenty or so texts we have had of the *Dyscolos* and the paucity of literary comment on that play. We are, after all, aware of the deficiencies in our standard literary histories, which ought to be and allegedly are critical, but which on inspection seem only to purvey biographical material, summaries, and the stock judgements of status which are fixed all the more solidly for us because we know, as Pope and Dryden did not, the enormous complexity of the task of the literary historian. Yet the very fact that these standard works invariably parade a show of criticism, however feeble and conventional, is a tacit admission that criticism is what is needed and desirable.

What stands in the way of genuine criticism is plain. The literary historian is faced from the start with the brute fact that we cannot hope to enter into *living* relations with the whole of literature, since a taste so omnivorous, so catholic, would be no taste at all, but sheer indifferentism. But as a scholar, for no one else but a scholar could have the necessary equipment even to conceive a history of Greek and Roman literature, he feels that in his dealings with his chosen author or period his task is to suppress self-will and simply reveal to the reader the author he is dealing with. The scholar conceives his task as the honest, useful, perhaps to some even dreary, recovery of truth, whether the truth about a text or an age. To him questions of value, of the relations of literature to culture and life, are to be firmly set aside. All this strikes him as mere fireside chat, a *causerie* which would have to consist of his own personal reactions and judgements. And he may feel, as some have felt, that even the greatest critics were simply grinding an axe in the interests of their own poetry or their own view of life. This seems alien to the scholar, and it is natural for him to take refuge in all those necessary *preliminaries* to criticism, after which he must retreat to the accepted judgements of countless scholars before him. This unfortunately is not criticism, even if we disregard the obvious fact that these apparently objective judgements may be accepted inertly, copied out mechanically from predecessors and only dubiously connected with real conviction. For the most and the least we can expect from criticism is a view limited by the condition of being fully *alive* at this moment, by the vigorous exercise of *positive* taste, which arguably can only be acquired from a preliminary study of that part of our own literature which we can fully and intimately appreciate. But this is not the classical scholar's function nor his practice generally, and this, it is felt, is to be a literary critic rather than a scholar, or a literary critic first and a scholar second. On the other hand, only by being in some sense a literary critic can the literary historian adequately fulfil his task. He has to know what *literature* is before he can know what, say, *Latin* literature is. And all this seems to require a rare combination of talents and a wider than usual training. The combination, however, is absolutely necessary. For there can be no way of writing a history of Latin poetry in a *purely* scholarly way or of confining it to objective fact. A literary history is not a chronological list of literary events and summaries of plots, for poets are not discrete phenomena. A literary history would have to be criticism to be a *history* at all, and this requires scholarly and critical abilities of a fairly high order which have to be sharpened by hard critical and scholarly work which concentrates on neither to the exclusion of the other. Small wonder that we prefer, as did Bentley, Porson, and Housman, the pleasures of emendation or exegesis, which have all the limited finality of the limited problem with the occasional elegance of certain geometrical proofs to justify such phrases as *nihil verius hac emendatione*.

Some even more human motives are also at work. Scholarship is superseded, but the advance is steady, and classical scholars are especially generous in their acknowledgement of the work of predecessors. But criticism seems always a matter of dispute and is no sooner accepted than it has to be altered. It may be argued that the intangible pervasive effects of *bad* criticism colour unconsciously our literary views of classical authors and that it is therefore more pernicious even than the use of a defective text, yet the scholar is aware that though one may set out the reasons for preferring, say, Propertius to Tibullus with the same objectivity and disinterestedness as one states one's belief or disbelief in the evidence for Greek in the Mycenean archives, the grounds in each case are so very different, the ramifications of the question are so far reaching, that without a guiding precedent or an agreed method for tackling such questions, the chances of success in such an undertaking are small.

Nevertheless few would disagree that even in our more scholarly studies we cannot separate as easily as we would like the 'pure' scholar and the critic. The objective and scientific study of literature, we are painfully aware, is a chimera, unless we avoid anything that could be called studying literature in favour of *Ueberlieferungsgeschichte, Quellenforschung* and similar things, and we know that the establishment of a text raises many problems of literary tact and evaluation. Indeed, even in our division of labour among the classics, we realize that a critical judgement—good or bad—has been made by ourselves or our predecessors. As scholars we are constantly running into problems of literary discrimination, which are acutely different from the rest of our work. The more wary of us accept this and realize that ultimately we are attempting to achieve ourselves and give others a full apprehension of the work of art, and in doing this we try, as best we can, to discriminate the best and the worst elements of that work and so come as near as our alien sensibility allows to a *living* rather than a conventional regard for it. This, of course, is an ideal, as it is in most humane and literary subjects, nor would I have it thought that the state of criticism in subjects other than ours is entirely a satisfactory one. Convention, fashion, and an inert provinciality bedevil criticism of English literature, too. And literary histories of American literature sometimes seem to be dealing with a closed world, whose inhabitants, like the inhabitants of the ancient literary world, are only rarely brought to the test of comparison and analysis with *the best* in English and European literature, and are usually left to enjoy a status all their own. Nevertheless we do now know much more clearly what the ideal critic is doing and how he works. Classical literature, like American literature, has to enter the arena with him. In this way we will approach nearest, if we are fortunate, to something like genuine literary criticism. Of course, those who complain of our deficiencies frequently underestimate the sheer magnitude of the task and fasten for their derision on those who shirk it or fall short in it. But it is not that there is *no* critical activity in classical studies, but rather that it is carefully hidden almost shamefacedly among other things. But a really valuable edition and commentary may offer a *critical* revelation: settling the text, explaining the language, citing sources and parallels does not put us in possession of *the work of art*; these merely allow us to read in the most elementary sense a set of symbols on a page or a stone. It does not bring out the difference between Thucydides and the Athenian Tribute Lists or between Silius and Virgil.

It is true that those who call for a more literary bias in the study of the classics do not present us with more than the challenge: they offer neither a programme nor a demonstration of what they would like. And the shriller the voice, the more confused the demand is likely to be. But much though we may agree with some of them—and who does not?—both the educational changes required and the basic agreement about principles and method will require much time and labour of a sort to which we are unaccustomed. Of course, professional students of our native literature would like to have a common ground and interest from which they could widen their own literary range under our guidance and add to their common stock of appreciation the important Latin and Greek authors which have influenced modern literatures. But we have not yet evolved a critical discipline or critical principles which they could understand in order to gain entry into this world, which, as we are often aware, is a *closed world*. The literary tokens we employ have no purchasing power in live literary commerce. Most of us find regrettably that the very notion of close comparison with modern literary works is a suspicious one, for it seems to entail sciolism somewhere, a charge we are wary of incurring, even though we may realize the value of bringing our remoter literary concerns into contact with our own living literature and ensuring that our literary currency is backed by actual gold. Such literary controls would be invaluable. When a well-known Cambridge scholar saluted Sir Desmond McCarthy as the living representative of Horace, this was an illuminating comparison in many ways, though perhaps throwing more light on the scholar than on the poet. But the whole direction of our training has not encouraged this kind of sturdy self-commitment.

Occasionally these critics seem to be asking for something which above all they must not be given, that is, a mechanical attempt to apply to classical authors modern critical dicta (if there are any), modern techniques or principles—derived from the Chicago school, the New Critics like John Crowe Ransom, or *Scrutiny* or any set of modern critics whatsoever. Such attempts would be disreputable and disastrous. We do not deny that we may learn much from the practice of critics in our own language, but except in incidentals they can only help us to develop a critical taste and discrimination in our own language, and thus perhaps prevent us from importing unconsciously principles such as those of the 'romantic criticism' derived from our schoolboy reading into the study of classical literature. Perhaps critical instruction *should* start in one's own literature, for it is there that our taste is and can only be formed. And perhaps this is the way to make our study of classical works more alive, by bringing them into touch by comparison and contrast with works that are admittedly *living*. The principles of criticism for classical authors must be principles which are appropriate to them, and which emerge from the close literary study of them even if against a wider background of literature. This is not to deny our critics' plea for common ground, for such principles must also be comprehensible as *literary* principles. I protest merely against any such silly and uncritical attempt as the 'dethronement of Virgil', whose resemblance in certain respects to Milton might tempt the undiscerning to begin a controversy like that in English studies. And such a warning would not entail the acceptance of the conventional estimates of Virgil's merits.

We admit, of course, that we are, for good or ill, twentieth-century minds with twentieth-century attitudes and susceptibilities; that our taste—if it is an active, inquiring literary taste and not a philogical interest which masquerades as a cultural interest—is ultimately formed by our own milieu and our own literature; that it is from these that we know what the ultimate literary questions are which we have to pose to earlier literatures. But, of course, we must not expect the same answers, nor read back into Latin and Greek literature the features that impress us in our own literature. In effect, we must not be deceived into thinking that the first century A.D. is the twentieth-century, although this is possibly a more real danger for those who are not actively concerned with their own literature, for then *unconscious* assumptions have their greatest play. Naturally there will be much we cannot appreciate genuinely, however hard we try, and the study of these areas will exist simply for their ancillary or non-literary value. But the great gain in discrimination and critical appreciation from the acknowledgement of this fact should more than compensate for the loss of the inert and apologetic defences of authors that mean less to us. If we are ruthless about the inferior, we may give the superior and genuine classics a more discerning appreciation. The literatures of Greece and Rome were not doing something altogether different from all other literatures and they must therefore be judged by the same ultimate standards of art that we apply to all writers that command our critical attention. What other standards are there than the best we have, namely our own? This not to be unhistorical or unimaginative or provincial. Provincialism indeed is a more real danger if we refuse to allow our literary concerns to become involved with the literary concerns of other students of literature, if we protect our classics from the final test suggested long ago by Matthew Arnold—*are they adequate*? After we have expended our utmost in historical understanding and the patient reconstruction of their world, we are left with that final question. The effort of the historical imagination is only the preliminary to honest and un-flinching judgement, and though this effort of the understanding is a larger task than with any later literature of comparable size, we cannot shirk that judgement. Nor can we believe that each of our authors has an absolute worth which generations of scholars have inexorably established, even though the more fickle public, for which translators cater, has wavered in its allegiance—a belief recently stated at its most explicit by Professor H. J. Rose: 'Ovid's absolute worth is naturally unaffected by these fluctuations (of fashions in literature).'[8]

I have tried, as fairly as I can, to meet the objections which are or may be brought against classical studies at the present time, both as an education and a cultural discipline. I have also tried to make clear what unnoticed difficulties there are in the way of our joining immediately what our adverse critics in other humane subjects presumably consider the common pursuit. But there is one final question which is but rarely referred to in these democratic days, but which merits attention by all who are concerned more with high standards than financial rewards or mass culture, excellent things though both of these be. And that is the question of the audience to which our most earnest endeavours must be initially directed, and for which this book is intended. Some of our critics complain that classical scholars neglect their duty to the public. But this is far from being so, as a glance at any bookshop with its rows of popular translations and illustrated handbooks by reputable academics will show. But, as we know, these are not regarded as serious work, whatever good results they may have, financially or socially. Some, again, think that we neglect our duties to our pupils and devote ourselves to the production of good composers and textual critics, and after them to the production of second-, third- and fourth rate scholars of the same sort, who are debarred from the groves of Academe and find their half-assimilated techniques of little cultural value in later life. Both have in mind a more literary emphasis, but both avoid the highly important question of the Common Reader in Samuel Johnson's sense. As he puts it in the *Life of Gray*, 'by the common sense of readers uncorrupted with literary prejudices, after all the refinements of subtility and the dogmatism of learning, must be finally decided all claim to poetic honours'. Civilization is very different now from what it was in Dr. Johnson's day and the common reader is rarely to be found among the readers of popular translations—would that he were!

So it is not a move in the direction of more popularization that we require to bring about a more literary study of the classics. And it is doubtful whether in our teaching alone, which should reflect our more advanced research, the serious literary study of the classics could begin. Literary criticism has to be a co-operative endeavour and in classical studies it would have to begin first among the professional students of classical literature; it would have to be recognized as a respectable pursuit and vigorously pursued. Fortunately, there *is* a Common Reader for classical studies. He is every classical scholar who does not work on one's own author or period (for no man can keep up with all the advanced work done in classical literature), and also every student of literature in other languages who has the requisite basic knowledge and interest in ancient literature. This is an audience far wider than is realized, an audience too closely involved in the technicalities and minutiae of its own scholarship to take up ours, but which is, I know from experience, eager for adequate criticism, backed by, but not smothered by, the ever necessary scholarship. It is here that a start should be made and one would like our sympathetic critics to consider exactly how it might best be done.

This book, then, is an experiment. It does not offer a coherent critical examination of the particular areas of Latin literature which it covers, for the contributors have worked in isolation. Most of them have simply allowed me to reprint or accepted my invitation to write a general critical article on an author in whom they are interested as professional students of literature. No one of them should be held to subscribe to the critical views of any other contributor or to the opinions expressed in this introduction. Most of them would, I believe, agree that this volume is to be taken rather as propaganda for literary criticism than the definitive statement of a common critical point of view. Adverse critics of our studies may perhaps find in this not only a recognition of their requests for enlightenment, but also a willingness to attempt something which is more complicated and arduous than they sometimes realize. It says much for the atmosphere of sweetness and light which *can* prevail in the classical world that I had so little difficulty in gathering together this collection. With but a few unimportant exceptions, all who knew of or helped me in my task were constant in their encouragement and approval.

As an experiment this book may, of course, be a failure: the difficulties I have enumerated and the lack of a common critical point of view may prove too much for it. I would, however, count it as a failure principally if it were unable to stimulate critical discussion rather than because it failed to provide a definite critical conspectus of the poets it is concerned with. Its aim is to initiate rather than stifle such discussion.

I must stress this lack of a common point of view, because sometimes any critical essays which are bound in one volume are regarded suspiciously as the product of some new critical ortho- or heterodoxy. Already the *Times Literary Supplement* has spoken of 'neo-critical know-how' [*sic*] and 'New Critics', glancing at attempts similar to this. I shall not discuss the value of such inaccurate terms. And even the respected editor of the *Classical Quarterly* has spoken of 'the New Criticism', an indication that the habit is infectious. It would be a pity if a shadow school were invented. Certainly some of the critical principles exemplified in this book are respectably old and those who use *New Criticism* as a pejorative vogue-word for irresponsibility, critical ingenuity, verbal analysis, and symbol hunting will find little justification for that use here.

This volume and its successor, which will be devoted to Roman satire, were first conceived because I knew of a small number of articles, published and unpublished, which I wished to see given greater circulation in a specifically critical context, such as Professor Cherniss's still too little heeded warning against the biographical fashion in literary criticism, and Mr. H. A. Mason's discussion of Juvenal—*Is Juvenal a Classic*? I knew also of other scholars whose work had led me to hope that they might be willing to produce a more general critical essay on their chosen authors. I asked them to bear in mind not only classicists, but also professional students of other literatures who are interested in literature in general, but who are not adequately served by the popular handbooks which circulate for the general reader. For this reason also all the Latin passages quoted *in extenso* are translated.

My choice of subjects requires little explanation. Epic may well appear in a later volume, but despite the popularity of Virgil among students of English and the popularity of Homer with the general reading public, I realized that for what I had in mind Epic poses the most difficult and controversial problems. It seems a field pre-eminently reserved for the Heads of Oxford and Cambridge Colleges. With the possible exception of Greek Tragedy, it is the subject which offers least foothold for useful and enlightening criticism. Elegy and Lyric seem much more accessible to contemporary understanding and therefore to criticism. The importance of this sort of literature, and of satire, seems adequately vouched for by Quintilian's proud verdicts—*elegia quoque Graecos provocamus* and *satura quidem tota nostra est*. But besides bulking so large in Roman eyes, these poetic genres are also contiguous to the sorts of poetry most practised by twentieth-century poets. The representatives of these traditions thus speak most clearly to us. Neither epic nor narrative verse are now highly regarded by our current practitioners of poetry: perhaps the novel has replaced them. But personal poetry, lyrical or reflective verse, and that highly literary and ironic poetry which concerns itself with large moral questions and whose nearest ancient relation is satire: these are the kinds of poetry we appreciate and understand best today. The less *elevated* language which has been familiarized as the typical modern poetic manner may remind us of that Roman tradition which avoided the grandiloquent except for certain ironic effects in favour of something closer to ordinary speech—a tradition which gains in strength as we move from Catullus's self-deprecating *nugae* to the attack on mythological writing by Martial, whose boast is that *hominem pagina nostra sapit* (10.5). Some elements in this Roman tradition anticipate an attitude we might think characteristically modern, but, in fact, Carew's elegy on John Donne might also be used to paraphrase certain pronouncements of Roman satire:

> . . . of gods and goddesses, which in thy juste raigne
> Were banished nobler Poems, now, with those
> The silenc'd tales o' th' Metamorphoses
> Shall stuffe their lines and swell the windy Page . . .

My thanks are due to all who have helped me either by their encouragement or by their willingness to co-operate in this enterprise or by the many services which friends and colleagues so willingly give. W. W. Robson, H. A. Mason, and Mrs Mason were especially put under contribution, but A. G. Lee, L. D. Reynolds, and Miss S. Quennell helped in a number of ways. The patience in typing difficult MSS. shown by the Oxford Scriptorium was unfailing. Lincoln College exhibited its usual generosity with typing expenses. Acknowledgements are due to H. F. Cherniss and the Regents of the University of California for permission to reprint his article on *The Biographical Fashion in Literary Criticism* and to change the title to one which conformed with the plan of the volume. I am grateful to my pupil Howard Callas for the indices.

J. P. SULLIVAN

Lincoln College
Oxford

NOTES

[1] F. R. Leavis, *How to Teach Reading*, p. 135.

[2] E.g. C. O. Brink, who suggested in an Inaugural Lecture (*Imagination and Imitation*, 1953, p. 15) that 'the ancient and modern are now being studied too far apart from one another' and that 'a student of Classics can learn something from students of English and the modern languages'.

[3] *Culture and Anarchy*, ch. 1 *ad init.*

[4] Bk. IV. 211–14, but the whole attack begins at line 139. Cf. also the Epistle to Dr. Arbuthnot (159–62).

[5] 1805 edn. VI. 123–34; 1850 edn. VI. 105–12.

[6] Ed. Shawcross (1907), pp. 6–12.

[7] *Vide* H. J. Lloyd-Jones's Inaugural Lecture (*Greek Studies in Modern Oxford*): 'It is true that the old type of Mods. tutor grossly exaggerated the importance of this exercise, making it an end in itself instead of a useful instrument of elementary training' (p. 24).

[8] *Outlines of Classical Literature for Students of English* (1960), p. 277.

ME EX VERSICULIS MEIS
PARUM PUDICUM

H. F. Cherniss

SEVERAL years ago a professor of English literature was widely acclaimed for having made an important discovery in his field of research; he had found in certain English archives the record of sale of a house belonging to John Milton. This may seem like a parody of what I call the biographical fashion in literary interpretation rather than like a fair example of that fashion; but I suspect that few professors of Greek literature see anything comic in their scholarly debates concerning the number of Euripides' wives, the question of Sophocles' indictment of his son, Iophon, and the reasons for Aeschylus' removal from Athens. None of these questions, however, affects the works of these poets or our understanding of them. Neither has the discovery in the English archives elucidated a single word or line in the writings of John Milton; and yet that discovery, far from being taken lightly by any of the journals that announced it, was treated by all of them as an addition to our knowledge of the history of English literature. It *is* a detail added to our knowledge of the life and movements of an English author; and it is this that made the discovery impressive. It increases our knowledge not of any of the literary productions which made John Milton's name significant, but of the man himself. This is the reason why the discovery aroused so much interest; and it is because of the implied attitude toward the relationship between the author and his works that the event epitomizes the biographical interpretation of literature.

History itself, political and social, as well as that natural human curiosity which at its basest is scholarly scandal-mongering and at its best authentic interest in the human personality, must be distinguished from the study of literature. Certainly, the historian cannot with impunity refrain from employing literary monuments as instruments in his task of reconstructing and interpreting the character and activities of a people or period. Since the proper use of such materials requires comprehension of the peculiar nature of artistic production and recognition of the way in which it differs from documentary and material evidence, the historian, too, must have the capacity to understand and interpret literature. Since every truly artistic production is an historical anomaly, however, the historian applies his literary comprehension with a purpose diametrically opposed to that of the philologist. He is concerned to comprehend the individuality of a work of art only in order that he may eliminate it and so extract for use as historical evidence those elements which are not the private creation of the author. The student of literature, on the other hand, studying the same text is interested in it as a separate and unique phenomenon; his interest in the common elements which it contains is in turn a kind of interest of elimination, for he is concerned with the manner in which they have been individualized by the artistic form. The historian who uses Thucydides as a source for the study of the Peloponnesian War approaches the speeches with the problem put by Croiset: 'The difficulty then is to know in what degree it is Pericles or Cleon, in what degree it is Thucydides whom we are hearing'; [1] and his reason for drawing this distinction is his proper desire to recapture so far as possible the words of Pericles or Cleon. The attitude of the student of literature toward these same texts is admirably formulated by Mr. G. F. Abbott when he says:

'The question of the authenticity of the speeches . . . does not enter into the present criticism, which is entirely concerned with their literary treatment. In shaping them as he thought fit the historian made them his own, no less than a dramatist does when he reproduces a historical speech, even though he may give, wherever possible, the very words which had been used. The authenticity of some of the speeches in Shakespeare's historical plays does not affect their significance as specimens of Shakespearean art.'[2]

The book of Thucydides purports to be a history; it is at the same time a work of literary art, even though its author claimed for it only the value of 'usefulness' (I, 22). Consequently it presents an object of study to three different disciplines at least (for I omit the dubiously philosophical discipline of statecraft); the historian can use it as a source book of events, a repository of material from which, along with other evidence, to reconstruct a portion of the past; the student of historiography may treat it as an example of the recording and interpretation of human activity, criticizing the method which it exemplifies and testing wherever possible the accuracy of its records and the propriety of its interpretations; and the student of literature will study it not as a source of information about the Peloponnesian War or as an example of historical method, but as a piece of literature, a drama in prose more dramatic than Hardy's *Dynasts*. This does not mean that one should approach Thucydides by one of these disciplines to the exclusion of the others; it does mean that they should not be confused, that one should understand that the study of history is not the study of literature even when the same text is the object of both studies and even though the historian, in handling that text, employs the methods of philology. Into the old and rancorous debate concerning the relationship of philology and history it seems to me unnecessary to enter further. The historian from his own point of view is justified in considering philology an ancillary discipline. That does not mean, however, that it is in essence ancillary to history or any other study, any more than mathematics is deprived of its essential autonomy by the fact that it is ancillary to all the natural sciences; and those philologists who in the desperation of self-defence have insisted that philology and history are identical have transgressed the most elementary requisite of their own study, the distinction of differences of meaning.

Philology is ultimately the study of literature for its own sake, and everything that the philologist studies as a philologist must be directed toward this as toward its final cause. His purpose is to comprehend and to interpret —that is, to help others comprehend —as works of art the individual productions which comprise the literature of which he is a student, in the case of the classical philologist the works of Greek and Latin writers. This general formula can hardly be challenged in its generality. What is given to the philologist is books, the significant expression of thought in artistic form; only the value of this expression and this form has created philology as a study necessary to the spiritual life of man, and only this value justifies the continued existence of that study as an autonomous discipline. The works of literature are not hypotheses which the philologist uses like the rungs of a ladder on which to climb to some higher principle; they are the ἀνυπόθετοι ἀρχαί themselves, the clear and direct comprehension of which is the final purpose of the student of literature. Not the identity and biography of the artist, then, but the unique personality of the literary artifact is the proper object of his study. When we proceed to specify this general formula, however, to designate the practical procedure by which it is to be realized in particular cases, all that we have excluded as distinct from the study of literature and extraneous to it seems to require acceptance again as essential to the appreciation of each and every particular work.

If a work of literature is the significant expression of thought, to appreciate the work is to understand the significance of the thought which it expresses; and how is this possible without intimate knowledge of the physical and spiritual environment, of the political, economic, and social conditions in which the thought was formulated and to which its expression responded? A work of art is produced at a definite time, in a definite place, and for an audience which itself has certain tastes and conventions, accepted ways of thinking, and a common store of knowledge and belief, all of which the artist takes for granted. These are as much the material with which he works as is the language in which his thought is expressed or the marble from which his statue is carved. Must one not, then, in order to understand a literary production, make oneself a member of that original audience to which it was addressed, learning what they knew, thinking and feeling as they thought and felt, and therewith acquiring the ability to slough off one's own environment, knowledge, and tastes so far as they are at variance with those others? Really to appreciate a comedy of Aristophanes must one not first transform himself into an Athenian of the generation of Aristophanes? This should be the necessary conclusion of the historical interpretation; and Professor Wilamowitz drew it with *almost* complete thoroughness in the introduction to his edition of the *Lysistrata*. There, by way of explaining why no one had hitherto succeeded in making a satisfactory commentary on Aristophanes, he wrote as follows:

18

'One first becomes properly aware of it (that is, of what besides mere jollity there is in the poetry of Aristophanes) when with a historically trained eye one sees how this mad sport affected on that single day the thousands who were its audience, a whole people that still constituted a single society in which everyone knew everyone else and each felt himself to be a member of the community. One must also know the conventions of this people, its deportment, its thought and belief in work and leisure, in sorrow and joy. . . . And also it must have come to be felt as natural that Dionysus can appear as a comic character in his own sanctuary into which his holy statue has been brought in solemn procession, that his priest looks on and that the belief in the mighty god remains alive in the hearts of the people. Finally the poem that was designed for an hour must first be understood as that which it pretended to be at the moment, before it is considered with a view to its absolute worth. All this, however, was impossible as long as Athens was as good as unknown, so long as the earth covered the theatre and the innumerable monuments of Attic art and Attic life. Today one need hardly say that no one who is not intimate with vase-painting can understand Aristophanes from within. . . . Similarly the events and personalities of Athenian history must have been so thoroughly studied that one can enter into the transitory mood of each year and so that the forms of public life, which were immediate data for the poet and audience, remain ever present for us too without special reminder.'[3]

The Hindus, who excelled in epigram, put this theory more succinctly in their proverb: 'He who eats beef can never learn Sanskrit.'

Furthermore, the conventions and habits of thought, the political and social environment of the artist were themselves the result of long development, were determined by the events, the thoughts, the people that preceded them, and cannot be apprehended more than superficially without knowledge of these conditions whence they derived. Does not the rule of Aristotle hold here also: we know a thing only when we know its cause? The single literary artifact, too, did not spring ἀπὸ δρυὸς οὐδ'ἀπὸ πέτρης. The artist has employed, consciously or unconsciously, the form and expression of a definite tradition, and even his deviations from these and his innovations are intelligible only to those who know the course from which he has deviated. A long series of modern studies testifies to the assumption on the part of Hellenists that only knowledge of the origin and development of the form of comedy can explain—or rather, as they seem to feel, excuse—the position of the parabasis in the plays of Aristophanes.[4] So, in order to understand the structure and essence of Greek tragedy and comedy it is thought to be necessary to discover the original form of Greek drama whereby will be exhibited, as Kranz has put it, 'the truly constitutive element of these artistic productions, the character which decisively determined their development'.[5] The appreciation of a piece of literature, then, requires not merely the reconstruction of the environment in which it was produced, the ability to transform oneself into a contemporary of the author, but also historical knowledge, as complete as may be, of the processes by which all the elements of that environment were produced and of the origin and development of the artistic form in which the author has expressed his thought.

Yet even this does not suffice. The environment, physical and spiritual, the language and the traditional artistic form, developed to the point at which the artist found them, were there for innumerable men to use; but the work of art itself was produced by only one among all these men. To him alone, the individual author, is due the artifact in its individuality; and, since it is the product of an individual personality, since as effective influences and as significant constituents of the product all the elements of environment, convention, and tradition have been distilled through this personality which has gradually assimilated them to itself, the work of art can be understood and appreciated only as a moment of the personality which created it, a photographic exposure of a single, irretrievable instant in the organic development of the artist. The necessary consequence of this conception of literature, too, was drawn for philology by Professor Wilamowitz in the introduction to his study of Plato.[6]

'The philologist,' he there says, 'is once for all an interpreter, but not interpreter of the words alone. Them he will never completely understand if he does not understand the soul from which they come. He must be the interpreter of this soul also, for, since the whole art of biography is founded on interpretation, biography is, in the true sense of the word, the work of the philologist, only raised to a higher power. Yet the task stands no higher than to understand how this man has come to be, what was his intention, his thought, his effect.'

And a little later, in generalizing his own method in this book, he says:

'The biographer proceeds from work to work, from interpretation to interpretation, always seeking the author behind the book. If a human being stands out whom we can recognize as such, if the individual features unite themselves into a single portrait which as a unit is credible, the task of the philologist is accomplished.'[7]

The study of any literary work, then, must be based upon a study of the author's biography. In that biography the proper place of this work must be determined; only as an element in the biography can the word be understood. From this point of view, however, any and every detail of information concerning the activities, experiences, and habits of the author is of importance, since it is from the accumulation of these details that his biography must be constructed. The slightest external incident may have precipitated the mood which caused the poet to write a particular piece or may have been the impetus to a development of character by which the nature of all his subsequent work was determined. Even the sale of Milton's house, the number and character of Euripides' wives may have been important factors in the lives of the artists and so in the nature of their literary productions. As such details increase one's knowledge of the author himself, so even the student of literature, who is interested primarily neither in social, cultural, or political history nor in the personal history and psychology of this human individual, must address himself to these details, since it is only in the light of the author's biography that the author's productions can be adequately understood.

Without questioning the nobility and the psychagogic advisability of making the scholarly ideal as lofty and rigorous as possible, and even though subscribing to the doctrine that no detail of knowledge is useless or negligible, one may still properly wonder whether the requirements set up by the theories of literary interpretation previously outlined do not justify despair in the strongest and most ambitious spirits. Even a Wilamowitz, with all his knowledge of vase painting, Greek institutions, and Athenian history, cannot think and feel as did a contemporary of Aristophanes and could not do so were the monuments for study at his disposal a thousand times as many as they are. *Knowing* that Dionysus was a god to those who still delighted in his ridiculous antics upon the stage, and *feeling* that he is a god even while enjoying him as a clown—between these two states is a gulf that no erudition can bridge, a gulf not due to time and the absence of material evidence. It is most probable that for Professor Wilamowitz the thoughts and feelings of his own contemporaries in England were equally unassimilable when they, staunch supporters of throne and constitution, met with hearty laughter and loud applause—and without any consciousness of incongruity—the mockery of the House of Peers in *Iolanthe*, the parody of the royal prerogatives in the great duet of the *Gondoliers*, and the satirical *lèse-majesté* in the denouement of the *Pirates of Penzance*.

In the case of ancient literature there is not adequate material to enable the student to gain even a fairly complete *theoretical* knowledge of the environment in which were produced most of the works with which he is concerned; to believe that one can know the events and personages of Athenian history so intimately as to be able to detect the transitory mood of each year is to deceive oneself by taking for objective truth the tenuous phantoms of historical reconstructions. Yet quite apart from the practicality of this requirement, theoretical knowledge, however exact and complete, is not the immediate perception which only those can have who are themselves part of this environment. Furthermore, if the work of art can be properly understood only in this environment and from the point of view of the original audience, then it is a hindrance rather than a help to know the historical processes by which were developed the environmental complex and the artistic form, for in that environment and in the emotional and mental constitution of that audience the negative characteristics are factors as essential as the positive ones. It is certain that few if any of the original audience had this kind of knowledge, and it is at least highly improbable that the author himself knew the history of his art and was conscious of the place of his own work in that development. At any rate, as a means of reconstructing the environmental complex this method not only suffers all the disabilities already mentioned in connexion with the recovery of the period directly from its own monuments, but it also has to assume the object of its investigations, knowledge of that complex itself. When Professor Wilamowitz asserts that a knowledge of vase painting is essential for comprehending Aristophanes, he forestalls the objection that this vase painting represents principally the life of the generations preceding the appearance of Aristophanes by the statement that in essentials the life of his generation had altered very little.[8] This comparison itself, however, implies a knowledge of the environment of Aristophanes based upon evidence independent of the very vase painting which was asserted to be indispensable for understanding that environment.

The study of origins and development, social, political, and literary alike, consists in establishing hypothetical connexions among events or objects, the evidence for the existence and nature of which does not itself rest upon these hypotheses and the knowledge of which, being the premises from which the method proceeds, must always be more certain than any conclusion which can be drawn concerning their relationships. Moreover, as applied to literature itself this method considers the work from the point of view of neither artist nor audience. The poem or play becomes a single stage in a hypothetical historical development in which the author is only an accident or at most an agent of forces which transcend him and of which he is unconscious. The justification of this kind of literary history, its assumptions, and its limitations, need not be discussed here; it is enough to say that it is not concerned with the understanding and appreciation of any single literary production as such but with relationships and connexions which come to be taken for literature itself, whereas they are external to the essence of any particular piece of literature whatsoever. As an approach to literature it runs the risk of becoming the kind of method which has been characterized as

'. . . consisting in this: to speak not of the object but of the causes, not of the essence but of the relationships; not to intrepret the works, but to investigate the material, the environment, the influences; a method which ever remains in the sphere of the preliminary, the irrelevant, the extrinsic, and reduces true scholarship to erudition in what is not worth knowing.'[9]

To approach the literary work by way of the personality of the artist seems to be a more reasonable method, for in any artistic production this is the factor which is most important, in which all the others are subsumed, and through which they become operative. To this insight, I take it, is due the present-day popularity of the biographical method in the study of literature; if the work of a man must be interpreted as a manifestation of his personality, then we must address ourselves to the history of that personality, and this is biography. The origin and environment of the man, his associates, activities, and experiences, these are the determinants of the personality that is the author; surely it is only by the discovery and synthesis of these factors that we can restore the author as a human being and understand his works as the expression of specific moods and thoughts, the response to definite needs and influences. Nevertheless, even if the validity of this method be granted, its practicality is strictly limited. The *Iliad* and *Odyssey* we should have to abandon altogether; we have no knowledge of their author or even of the approximate date of their composition. And how many works of Greek literature could we hope to understand, if this were the sole means of understanding them? The champion of the biographical method in the interpretation of classical literature, Wilamowitz himself, asserted that 'for no Greek can we write a true biography, a history of the development of the individual within his environment'.[10] Even where we have a morsel of knowledge concerning the author's activity or experience, it is usually the merest conjecture by which this has been connected with some tendency or element of his literary expression, and yet it is this connexion itself which is the point at issue. So, for example, the fact that Plato left Athens for a trip to Syracuse in 367 cannot explain the difference in style between the first and second parts of the *Theaetetus*, even if it be granted that the composition of this dialogue is correctly dated in the year or two immediately preceding his departure. This explanation itself rests upon a critical assumption of a nonbiographical nature, namely that the second part *is* in an unfinished state, and requires a further hypothesis to explain why, if this is so, Plato failed to finish it after his return.[11] Since the connexion between Plato's departure and the *Theaetetus* is unknown, the knowledge of the date of his departure cannot facilitate our understanding of the dialogue.

Worse still, the validity of the method is itself dubious, for it is a method which rests upon the tacit assumption that the sum of biographical incidents constitutes the personality and that the essential meaning of the artistic expression can be identified with the environment and influences which have coincided to form a given moment in the personality of the author. This assumption is identical with Taine's theory which would make the study of literature a kind of psychophysical mechanics and against which even his admirer, Zola, protested that as soon as the spirit, the individual personality, strikes where and when it will, all influences are merely accidents, the results of which one may study and explain, but which act upon a natural element that is essentially free and that has not yet been reduced to any law.[12] Since the human individual is not a mechanical combination of events and influences, no reconstruction, however complete, of the external incidents of a man's life can reproduce or reveal the essence of the man himself. There is no such thing as an 'influence' in the abstract, and any particular 'influence', of tradition, of environment, or of personal experience, exists only in the individual influenced and is determined by his personality, which is passive only in grammar and in histories of literature but in fact is the active element in a complex in which the brute event is the passive material that gains form, significance, and efficacy only according to the way in which the particular individual fashions it. Even a phrase 'borrowed' by one poet from another does not have in the new poem the same significance that it had in the old one; and merely to identify the source whence the author 'borrowed' it is not even to begin to understand what it means in the context of the new production. Students of literature have given too little heed to the trenchant remark that it is not important what the poem is made out of but what it is made into; and so, too, the external incidents of the author's life have meaning only as they are assimilated to his personality and literary significance only so far as they have been transmuted by that personality into artistic form.

That the neglect of this fact renders the biographical method invalid has not gone unrecognized by certain critics who have understood that no personality can be comprehended by a compilation of isolated events and further that as an operative artistic entity it is manifested only in the artistic product. One group, the circle of Stefan George, accepting this axiom and identifying the artist with his work, has sought to reconstruct the figure of the author's personality in accordance with the 'inner form' which they reach admittedly from his work alone but by a kind of intuition. 'The works,' says Gundolf in laying down the programmatic principles of this school,

'. . . are not the tokens which indicate the life [of the artist] but the bodies in which that life is incarnate. . . . One has no scientific justification for investigating the life of the great artists outside of their art; nay, there is no possibility of doing so, for what is commonly called the life of an artist and more modernly his experience has from the very first been assimilated to his art and is the same impulse and force as his work.'[13]

From members of this circle have come a number of studies of ancient authors, notably works on Plato by Singer, Friedemann, and Hildebrandt, and on Posidonius by Karl Reinhardt; and these have exercised a large influence upon scholars in this country, most of whom are unaware of the tenets of the cult on which these constructions are based. For it is a cult of a semi-mystical kind, the object of whose reverence is the 'heroic individual'. With the nature and beliefs of this circle, however, I am not here concerned, but only with the elements of its method. The intuition which discovers in the writings of an author the 'natural law' and 'inner form' of his personality is proof against all objections, logical and philological; but, while one must admit that a certain native insight, call it direct intelligence or intuition as you please, is required for understanding any text, it is, all the same, a vicious circle to intuit the nature of the author's personality from his writings and then to interpret those writings in accordance with the 'inner necessity' of that intuited personality. Moreover, once the intuition of the individual critic is accepted as the ultimate basis of all interpretation, the comprehension of a literary work becomes a completely private affair, for the intuition of any one interpreter has no more objective validity than that of any other, and each interpreter lays himself open to the *peritropé*, like Protagoras in the *Theaetetus*. Yet in this regard the circle of George differs from most modern literary interpreters only in being conscious of its method, systematic in applying it, and outspoken in advocating it. Other scholars, not of this school, tell us that Plato's works must be comprehended as expressions of his life because he always continued to develop;[14] that Sophocles had the natural gift of remaining unaffected by anything foreign to his own nature and that the instinctive assurance of the characters of his dramas was an endowment of his own ego;[15] that Euripides felt himself more strongly impelled than Sophocles to take a definite attitude toward the actual problems of his country just because he took no active part in political life,[16] and that he was conscious of his own individuality and so felt it his highest duty to himself and his people to cherish that individuality.[17] Such statements refer only to the personality which the critic's intuition has seen in the author's works; they have no other authority, and they provide no means for understanding the text which is not in the texts themselves; they are the results of interpretation and cannot be used as the basis of interpretation without falling into a vicious circle.

To this extent Gundolf's contention is correct, that the artist *qua* artist exists only in his artistic productions; one need not follow him any farther to see that biography is nothing to the student of literature, to whom the only thing of significance in the life or personality of an author is his actual literary work. The potential poet may be a proper subject for psychological investigation, but the concern of the philologist is the actual poet and he is identical with his poems. So we are brought back to the texts themselves. If, then, we can never appreciate them as the original audience did and if, again, the reconstruction of the author's biography cannot lead us to understand them, are we to say that true understanding of a work of art is impossible? Consider first, for a moment, what reason there could be for studying a work which had no meaning except for a single audience in a single spot at a single moment in the past! The historian interested in the nature of that audience might use such a work, but only as a means of understanding the audience and without concern for the work itself. Only a madman would even wish to transmute himself into a member of that audience in order to appreciate what could have no meaning for men at any other time or place. If, again, a work of art should have significance only as a manifestation of an individual personality, it would be of interest only to a psychoanalyst. No one else would bother to read Sappho's poems if they were only exhibits in the individual history of a neuropathic case; but her poems remain unaffected by the question of her personal virtue, which for a century scholars have debated with blind ferocity, as if the import or beauty of her poetry depended upon their conclusions. One among these scholars, the most authoritative champion of her 'good name', confides in us that the poetess had 'an unquenchable intensity of feeling, a yearning of which she herself need not have been conscious'.[18] If she need not have been conscious of her feeling in order to write, still less need we have knowledge of her private life in order to understand her writing; and, if she was fully conscious of what she was feeling, then in her writing we have her most exact expression of what she intended to say.

When one reads a poem of Sappho's and reads it as a poem, one is interested primarily neither in Sappho of Lesbos nor in the particular audience to which her poems were originally addressed; one has no desire to transmute himself into a member of her circle or to gather psychological data concerning the author, but one does expect to find the poem itself directly significant. That this expectation need not be futile is due solely to the fact that a work of art exists independently of its author and of the accidental circumstances of its production, that its artistic qualities are entirely contained within itself and are not to be explained by anything outside of the work.[19] This alone is the reason that it can be understood and appreciated; it is only for this reason that it is worth considering at all, for this independent existence makes possible the direct approach of each individual to the work and makes this direct approach the only possible way of comprehension and appreciation. Those who have recognized the impossibility of attaining the point of view of the original audience or that of the author himself have tended to overemphasize the individualistic or relativistic nature of appreciation and to reduce interpretation to the anarchy of subjectivity. That appreciation of any work is ultimately an individual experience is certainly true; it is the chief reason why the study of art and literature remains ever new and ever interesting. Yet the same factor that enables each person to approach the work directly also limits the extent of the subjective element in interpretation. The term 'universal', so often applied to a work of art, means not that that work is not a unique individual, but that it has significance for all men as men in all times and places, and this, we saw, is a possibility only if the work has independent existence. But the basis of this universal significance is a set of ideas, emotions, and values which thus far in the history of the civilized world at least have always been recognized as having validity beyond the arbitrary taste of any individual or the customs of any locality.

This is not a counsel of indolence. It does not mean that anyone, by reason of his humanity alone, can understand any literary work that is set before him, or that because it is a work of art with which he is concerned he need not study assiduously to acquire every instrument that may help him to comprehend the significance of the text before him. It means that one must never forget that his ultimate purpose is to understand and appreciate particular works of literature, that the one means of accomplishing this purpose is intelligent reading, and that all other studies are meant to equip one with this means. It is rather a counsel of austerity, for it means that one must learn to distinguish the essence from the accidents and to eschew the easy mechanical combinations that explain nothing.

The insidious danger of the biographical method lies in its assumption that the essence is merely a combination of accidents, that literature is an automatic by-product of external forces, whence comes its tacit conclusion that no literary work has autonomous significance. Such an attitude will have fatal consequences for the study of the classics, for all justification of that study depends finally upon the value of the literary monuments of Greece and Rome, not their value as source books for the historian, the antiquarian, or the psychoanalyst, but their value for men as human beings. We pride ourselves mightily on our 'true historical sense', of which, says one famous modern classicist, 'Lessing and Gibbon had scarcely a notion, for they thought that man in all ages is essentially the same'.[20] Perhaps that is why the writings of Lessing and Gibbon can still be read with understanding today, while the books of the new scholarship are antiquated after a decade. When the Hellenist no longer believes in man as *man*, he may as well shut his books, for he has confessed that he can never understand them.

NOTES

[1] A. Croiset, *Histoire de la littérature grecque*, Tome IV (Paris, 1921), p. 147.

[2] G. F. Abbott, *Thucydides, A Study in Historical Reality* (London, 1925), p. 184, fn. 1.

[3] *Aristophanes, Lysistrate* erklärt von U. von Wilamowitz-Moellendorff (Berlin, 1927), p. 5.

[4] See the résumé by Harsh, T.A.P.A., Vol. LXV (1934), pp. 178–9.

[5] W. Kranz, *Stasimon* (Berlin, 1933), p. 1.

[6] U. von Wilamowitz-Moellendorff, *Platon* (Berlin, 1919), Bd. I, p. 4.

[7] Ibid., p. 8.

[8] *Aristophanes, Lysistrate*, p. 5.

[9] Quoted from E. R. Curtius (*Die literarischen Wegbereiter des neuen Frankreich*) by J. Körner, *Neue Jahrbücher f. d. klass. Altertum*, Bd. XXV (1922), p. 175.

[10] U. von Wilamowitz-Moellendorff, *Euripides, Herakles* (Berlin, 1889), Bd. I, p. 1; cf. *idem, Platon*, Bd. I, p. 6.

[11] U. von Wilamowitz-Moellendorff, *Platon*, Bd. I, p. 510.

[12] E. Zola, *Mes Haines*, M. H. Taine, *Artiste* (Paris, Bibliothèque Charpentier, 1902), p. 227.

[13] F. Gundolf, *Goethe* (Berlin, 1925), p. 2.

[14] U. von Wilamowitz-Moellendorf, *Platon*, Bd. I, p. 6.

[15] Max Pohlenz, *Die Griechische Tragödie* (Leipzig und Berlin, 1930), Bd. I, p. 160.

[16] Ibid., p. 168.

[17] Ibid., p. 164.

[18] U. von Wilamowitz-Moellendorff, *Sappho und Simonides* (Berlin, 1913), p. 78.

[19] Cf. J. Körner, op. cit., p. 168.

[20] U. von Wilamowitz-Moellendorff, *Sappho und Simonides*, p. 3.

DOCTE CATULLE

K. F. Quinn

THE more one reads Catullus, the more one feels how *special* the position is that he occupies in Roman poetry. The feeling is prompted first, of course, by the evident quality of the best that Catullus wrote; then it is sharpened by our recognition that, though there are clearly several kinds of poetry here, the poems all bear a characteristic, individual stamp.

It is better probably, to begin with, to leave the long poems on one side. Not because of disputes about their quality, but because the long poems are too long and too complex for reliable initial impressions. Thinking, then, for the moment of the short poems only, recall those pieces (a score perhaps) that we have all long known and liked. Let us take Poem 46 to represent them, for it is less hackneyed than some and because, if we begin here, we shall be reminded of something which Catullus' romantic biographers may have caused us to forget—that Catullus is not only a love poet:[1]

> Iam uer egelidos refert tepores,
> iam caeli furor aequinoctialis
> iucundis Zephyri silescit aureis.
> linquantur Phrygii, Catulle, campi
> Nicaeaeque ager uber aestuosae: 5
> ad claras Asiae uolemus urbes.
> iam mens praetrepidans auet uagari,
> iam laeti studio pedes uigescunt.
> o dulces comitum ualete coetus,
> longe quos simul a domo profectos   10
> diuersae uarie uiae reportant.

Today spring's gentle thawing warmth is back.
Today the madman equinoctial sky is dumb,
soothed to silence by the gentle west wind's charm.
O! let me leave this land of Phrygia,
leave Nicaea's fertile soil to sweat in summer heat.
Let me race to Asia and to cities rich in fame.
Today my mind's impatient at the prospect. Wanderlust
today adds eager happy resilience to my step.
Sweet friends, I bid our society adieu.
Together we left our homes to journey here.
Now various routes in different ways will take us back.

This little poem claims our immediate respect. Here is something worth making a poem about and here is a poem well made. And it reveals to our continuing attention a subtlety and a richness that will reinforce, and not dispel, our initial impression.[2] We note the careful symmetry of the layout: eleven lines, of which the first states the dramatic moment of the poem, the central line the decision to which the excitement of spring leads up, and the final line the conclusion of the episode the poem announces. It happens we can fix the episode precisely: Catullus has finished his tour of duty with Memmius, propraetor of Bithynia Pontus. It is the spring of 56 B.C. But these are things it is interesting to know, not essential. Into this framework is infused a pattern of legitimate emotional incitement: lines 1 and 2 begin with *iam* (to convey the excitement of spring); so do lines 7 and 8 (to convey Catullus' excitement at the prospect of his journey through the famous cities of Asia)—four *iam*'s in eleven lines, but the poem can stand it.[3] Now some details. Note the economy with which the magic of the past is evoked by the single word *Phrygii*, in order to prepare the ground for the right overtones in *Asiae*, out of which we might otherwise here take only the administrators' name for a Roman province.[4] Observe also the four polysyllables *egelidos, aequinoctialis, aestuosae,* and *praetrepidans*—words so bulky, so unemotionally precise in statement one does well to ponder how Catullus manages to make them reinforce the slender lyric fabric one might have thought they could not fail to destroy.[5] But part of the strength of this poem comes from the sinewy tension between excitement of feeling and sober precision of statement. The best example is perhaps the last line:

diuersae uarie uiae reportant.

The members of Catullus' *cohors* have various plans for sight-seeing on their way home: the routes they will take are quite different (*diuersus* is the strong word in Latin for 'different'), but in the long run it won't make all that difference, they'll all arrive back in Rome (*uarius* is the weak word in Latin for 'different'). What on first reading might have looked like otiose repetition is now seen as economically meaningful.

The conviction of quality acquired, or recovered, by the perusal of a score of the short poems, it is essential to look at the rest of the collection and think about its overall nature with some care. Too often those poems whose poetic quality is evident are treated as though they were fully typical. Yet it is so obvious they are not. A more subtle confusion, of which distinguished critics have been guilty, consists in talking as though this score of poems were representative of what Catullus *may have done* regularly in poems actually written but now lost; or *might have done*, perhaps, in poems he did not live to write. How unsound a basis this kind of talk provides for a critical discussion of the poems we have is apparent the moment one states precisely what those who indulge in it assume.

There are one hundred and ten short poems.[6] A careful, sympathetic reading of them all can hardly fail to lead us to three conclusions. The first is that here is poetry so fresh in Latin it is legitimate to talk of revolution.[7] The second, that the individual poems forming our collection vary so greatly in the poet's *level of intent*, in the degree of his devotion to the task of making poetry, that valid generalizations about the Catullan *oeuvre* as a whole seem hardly possible.[8] The conviction is inescapable that to talk of the whole corpus as 'the work of a lyric poet', as E. A. Havelock accustomed a generation of students to talk,[9] involves a use of the term 'lyric' too loose to serve any useful critical purpose.

What I am talking about, of course, is not the poet's intentions at the moment of the initial decision to make the poem. This is one reason why I chose the less usual word 'intent', with its etymological overtone of directed tension, and avoided the ordinary word 'intention'. By 'intent' I mean, then, partly the objective aimed at by the poem when finally made (a Catullan poem often gets out of control and ends up by becoming something more seriously poetic than the poet had in mind to begin with); and partly the process of screwing oneself up in order to attain that objective—in so far as this is reflected in the poem and becomes thereby our proper concern. By *devotion* to the task of making poetry I mean partly absorption, but also a hint at the poet's surrender to something mysterious. What we call 'inspiration', the thing that makes a real poem. Sometimes the poem, or a bit of it, is provided without effort in the form of a bolt from the blue; sometimes by touching off in the poet a nexus of unnatural excitement, concentration, and sensitivity. The extent to which the poet gets wrapped up in this process determines his degree of devotion to the task of making poetry.

But I spoke of three conclusions that a careful reading of Catullus would lead to. The third will be that a lot of the pieces, the majority even, cannot by serious present-day standards of poetic intent or achievement be called poetry at all. There are two reasons, I think, why this should be so. One is that the Catullan revolution is still in progress within the Catullan *oeuvre*—many of the poems, in other words, really precede the outbreak of the revolution. A conception different from ours of the function of poetry is the other reason: some of the evidence for this we shall have to consider presently.

It is important to understand why we must fill out our initial judgement about the first-rate quality of a few of the poems with these feelings that the collection as a whole (still leaving out of account the long poems) inspires. Our purpose is not to diminish the stature of the good poems by reminding ourselves that the surviving work of their author contains more trivial pieces than really good ones. That kind of criticism would be even more foolish than the usual kind, which tries to push back the trivial and obscene pieces so far into the background that we can manage to forget how large they bulk in the collection. The reason why the sensible critic will look at the whole of Catullus' work is that by doing so he may avoid misunderstanding in important respects the poems he values most.

He will gain some indication of the gulf that separates Horace (in the *Odes*) from Catullus, and of the progress Roman poetry made in the intervening quarter-century. Horace regularly sets out to write an ode in full awareness of his powers and the dimensions of his objective. Catullus does this very rarely. Poems 8 (*Miser Catulle, desinas ineptire . . .*) and 11 (*Furi et Aureli, comites Catulli . . .*) were probably intended to be poems in the strict sense from the beginning. Most of the other short poems that we prize soar somehow to this level in the actual process of their making. The reason for the differences of intent in Catullus and Horace lies partly, of course, in the very different make-up and age of the two men, but more perhaps in contemporary attitudes to poetry. Catullus' contemporaries were hardly disposed to treat the short personal poem as literature at all. Cicero, despite his active enthusiasm for most forms of literature, declared, we are told, that, were he given his life to live over again, he did not expect he would find time even then to read 'the lyric poets'.[10] This was obviously not the attitude of Augustus (to say nothing of Maecenas) to Horace's 'lyric' poetry. For this a lot of the credit belongs to Horace; yet his poetry, however individual, is the outcome of a status won for the short personal poem by the Catullan revolution.

We are, in fact, confronted in Catullus with a kind of writing where poetry, in our strict sense, is a marginal product of the enthusiastic practice by a writer of genius of an activity that, poetically speaking, is much inferior. Catullus himself describes that activity in Poem 50, where he tells us of the hours he and Calvus spent together absorbed in the production of what he calls *uersiculi*: scraps of verse, tossed off by talented idle young men stimulated by intimacy with literature and the exhilaration of outdoing one another in technical competence. Examples of such *uersiculi* abound in Catullus. Their themes matter a lot less than the dexterity and sensitivity with which the themes are handled. Most often they are the everyday incidents of dinner parties and the ironical curiosity of a sophisticated set about who is sleeping with whom. Or the ribald, often obscene, expression of personal dislikes and enmities made acceptable by the ingenuity and lightness of heart with which they are versified. Catullus delights in words hitherto considered too crude for literature. The abuse is seldom meant to be taken seriously, or at any rate the poems' main objective is not attack. Poem 32 (*Amabo, mea dulcis Ipsitilla* . . .) is surely meant to be funny, and in any case the impact of its irony is designed to fall as heavily on Catullus as it does on Ipsitilla. In Poem 23 (*Furi, cui neque seruus est neque arca* . . .) it is unlikely any real malice against Furius is intended. The poem is an elaborate legpull, an extravagant evasion of Furius' request for a loan.[11] A slick, light-hearted *reductio ad absurdum* of the Epicurean precept to live *paruo contentus*. The more violently abusive the *uersiculi* become, the more prone some scholars are to miss the point by approaching them in a spirit of serious literal-mindedness. Cicero's words in defending a member of the smart set in which Catullus moved should warn us that what has been taken as foul-mouthed and crude was actually intended as urbane exaggeration:

Sed aliud est maledicere aliud accusare. Accusatio crimen desiderat, rem ut definiat, hominem ut notet, argumento probet, teste confirmet. Maledictio autem nihil habet propositi praeter contumeliam: quem, si petulantius iactatur, conuicium, si facetius, urbanitas nominatur. (*Pro Cael.*, 6.)

It is one thing to slander, another to accuse. An accusation requires a charge, thereby making the issue precise, pointing to an individual and offering proof in the form of evidence and testimony. Slander has only one objective, abuse. If the abuse is mainly motivated by spite, we call it insult; if mainly by a desire to be witty, we call it sophistication.

Cicero's own practice (for example, in *In Pisonem*, which is contemporary with Catullus' *uersiculi*) shows the very free standards of the time.[12]

What Catullus calls *uersiculi* had become a common exercise for talent in Greek in Hellenistic times. The Anthology preserves hundreds of ingenious epigrams neatly poised between the flippant and the outrageous. This kind of writing in Greek started to spread to Rome once Rome's contact with the Hellenistic world began. A well-known representative of the genre in Catullus' day is the refugee intellectual Philodemus, who came to Italy about 75 B.C. and established his home there. Consider how much of what Catullus wrote might be summed up by an unsympathetic critic in these words that Cicero uses of Philodemus:

Ita multum ad istum de isto quoque scripsit ut omnes libidines omnia stupra omnia cenarum conuiuiorumque genera, adulteria denique eius delicatissimis uersibus expresserit. (*In Pis.*, 70.)

This man, then, wrote a great deal of extremely sophisticated verse addressed to the accused, relating in full the accused's lusts and debaucheries, the dinners and drinking parties of all descriptions that he gave and even his adulterous affairs.

In fact, what Philodemus wrote for his patron talented young Romans of independent means had begun to write for themselves, and about themselves, in Latin. Somehow—the novelty of what they were doing, the fact that they were writing about themselves and not for a patron, some emotional warmth in the Italian temperament that the more coolly rational Greek lacked (it is easy to suggest causes, hard to be sure one has the right ones)—this became soon at Rome something more than a game for talent. Sporadically, unpredictably the *uersiculi* climbed to the level of real poetry. This revolution in the function and stature of *vers de société* (a convenient modern equivalent of *uersiculi*) can be seen in progress in Catullus. Sometimes there is only a single phrase that climbs out of efficient persiflage to the level of genuine poetry. The initial impulse, for example, that set Catullus writing Poem 41 was clearly remote from anything that we today should call poetry:

> Ameana puella defututa
> tota milia me decem poposcit,
> ista turpiculo puella naso,
> decoctoris amica Formiani.
> propinqui, quibus est puella curae,
> amicos medicosque conuocate:
> non est sana puella, nec rogare
> qualis sit solet aes imaginosum.

> Ameana's a girl's been knocked about a bit,
> but ten cool thousand's what she's quoted me.
> That girl with the rather horrid nose,
> bankrupt Formianus' friend.
> Relations! on you the care devolves:
> call friends, doctors into conference.
> This girl is sick. She checks her looks no more
> against reflection-crowded mirror made of bronze.

Ezra Pound has done brilliant pastiches of this sort of thing in *Personae*.[13] The ironically solicitous note that caps the crisply enunciated, quadrupled blow of the first quatrain is excellent writing. We should, however, be only confusing ourselves by calling this poetry—let alone 'lyric' poetry—if it weren't for those last two words[14] (one of them again—recall Poem 46—an unusual polysyllable) and the image they capture of the sheet of bronze, filled with vertiginously shining, revealing reflections of an Ameana that Ameana does not want to see.

Occasionally the flavour of something achieved over and beyond the task attempted is more sustained. Take Poem 17:

> O Colonia, quae cupis ponte ludere longo,
> et salire paratum habes, sed uereris inepta
> crura ponticuli axulis stantis in rediuiuis,
> ne supinus eat cauaque in palude recumbat:
> sic tibi bonus ex tua pons libidine fiat,   5
> in quo uel Salisubsali sacra suscipiantur,
> munus hoc mihi maximi da, Colonia, risus.
> quendam municipem meum de tuo uolo ponte
> ire praecipitem in lutum per caputque pedesque,
> uerum totius ut lacus putidaeque paludis   10
> liuidissima maximeque est profunda uorago.
> insulsissimus est homo, nec sapit pueri instar
> bimuli tremula patris dormientis in ulna.
> cui cum sit uiridissimo nupta flore puella
> et puella tenellulo delicatior haedo,   15
> adseruanda nigerrimis diligentius uuis,
> ludere hanc sinit ut lubet, nec pili facit uni,
> nec se subleuat ex sua parte, sed uelut alnus
> in fossa Liguri iacet suppernata securi,
> tantundem omnia sentiens quam si nulla sit usquam;   20
> talis iste meus stupor nil uidet, nihil audit,
> ipse qui sit, utrum sit an non sit, id quoque nescit.
> nunc eum uolo de tuo ponte mittere pronum,
> si pote stolidum repente excitare ueternum,
> et supinum animum in graui derelinquere caeno,   25
> ferream ut soleam tenaci in uoragine mula.

Colonia, you want some games on your Long Bridge.
You're ready for a dance, but you have doubts in case
your patched-up bridge's game legs give way,
spilling bridge on back, marshy crater for his bed.
Shall I pray for the first-class bridge that you desire—
one to undertake Salisubsalian rites themselves upon?
Will you, Colonia, present me then with a monster laugh?
From your bridge I'd like a citizen whom I can name
shot down, head over heels, into the mud,
precisely at the point in pond and stinking marsh
where the ooze is deepest and vilest in appearance.

The man's an utter clot, with not the intellectual power
of a two-year-old asleep, rocked in his father's arms.
He's got a wife. A girl that's lush with youthful growth,
tenderer than a tiny baby kid. The girl you'd watch
with greater care than your ripest, darkest grapes. Well, all
the fun she wants she takes. He lets her. Doesn't give a hoot.
Without the sense even to retire, he lies like an alder log
hamstrung in the ditch the Ligurian axeman left it in—
no perception whatsoever of all that's going on.
He does not see, this stolid lump, he does not hear;
who he is he doesn't know nor whether he exists at all.
Well, it's him that, face first, off your bridge I want to throw,
hoping that the senile goon (waking with a shock) flat
on back in clinging muck will leave his spineless brain,
like a mule in sucking mud its sandal wrought of iron.

The transformation into genuine poetry is almost complete. In
part, it is brought about by repeating the formula of which Poem
41 provided a single instance. The last line of the Colonia poem,
too, breaks away from the business in hand to sketch a sharp,
bright image that lingers after our thoughts are no longer with
'what the poem is about'. This last line reminds me always of the
last line of Hopkins's 'Felix Randal':

> Didst fettle for the great grey drayhorse his bright and
> battering sandal!

The basis of the association, the sandal, is admittedly fortuitous,
yet in both we feel, I think, an image taking us away, really, from
what the poem is about (that sandal was not bright and battering
in Randal's forge but later, when it beat upon the cobbled street),
and yet making richer and stronger the experience that the poem
provides.

In Poem 17 the stimulus to poetic experience is not just in the
last line, but continually recurring. The two-year-old asleep in his
father's arms (line 14). The girl (lines 16–17) who's so slight and
fragile (and yet so frisky) she makes you think of a tiny baby goat;
so precious you think (thinking through Catullus with a countryman's thoughts—remember the poem is set in Colonia, not in
Rome) of some other possession you treasure and enjoy contem-
plating (can hardly keep your hands off, perhaps) and there flashes
up the image of rich black grapes. The alder log (lines 18–19)

sprawled in the ditch where the axeman left it (like a stuck pig—*suppernata* personifies the log and adds image to image, while keeping us in contact with the husband through a fresh train of overtones). All these images have little to do with the statements the poem overtly makes. And yet see how much they add to the poem's richness, how much we have to add, in interpreting them, to make explicit the trains of association touched off by the words the poet actually uses. Then there is the image of the rickety bridge, for which a kind of affection is built up by the diminutive *ponticuli*, and the sustained personification implied by *crura, supinus, recumbat*—the bridge is a little old man, shaky on his pins, liable at any moment to fall flat into the bog he is trying to straddle. The bog, too, is lushly described, its look and smell evoked with gusto:

> uerum totius ut lacus putidaeque paludis
> liuidissima maximeque est profunda uorago.

Bridge and bog stand a little closer to what the poem is about than the baby goat and the black grapes, but we should have to eliminate all the 'details' of both if we were setting out to make a prose paraphrase.

Of course, the tone (to which the poem's five ringing superlatives make their contribution) of ironical, exuberant, righteous indignation at the husband's failure to observe the pranks of his pretty young wife is as essential an ingredient of the poem as the superbly vivid description of the penalty proposed, or the associational imagery that the poem branches out into as it proceeds. But these are, as it were, three stages of poetic achievement, and perhaps the order in which I have stated them represents ascending standards of assessment of the poem's stature. Ironical exuberance of tone (coupled as here with exhilarating metre, but with little imagery) might have given us a poem at the level of Poem 42 (*Adeste, hendecasyllabi, quot estis* . . .). Tone plus more or less strictly descriptive imagery, but with little free associational imagery of the kind we have here, something like Poem 39 (*Egnatius, quod candidos habet dentes* . . .). The thing, unfortunately, is not as simple as this makes it sound. But perhaps what I have said may help the sensitive reader to feel how this poem provides in abundance what the Catullan *uersiculi* at lower levels of intent hardly provide at all.

A careful perusal of the whole corpus of short poems will persuade us, therefore, not only of the extraordinary range in level of intent, but also that we have to deal, not with a poet of the normal kind who occasionally descends to *vers de société*, but with a writer of *vers de société* whose genius occasionally wrenches the trivial up to the level of unmistakable poetry.

We shall then be better able to appreciate the real poetry of Catullus. Set against this background of an enthusiastic devotion to *uersiculi* that called for the maximum of concentration and ingenuity of layout, features of our original score of short poems we might otherwise have failed to discern, or hesitated (in our unsureness of feeling for things written in a remote language and a remote age) to recognize, become clear. On the other hand, the long poems assume a juster aspect. They are not accidental poetry, but poetry deliberately—some will say too deliberately—contrived. A long poem, particularly an epyllion,[15] was for the *poetae novi* a demonstration that its author was not a dilettante versifier, and not a writer of old-fashioned epic either. Far from being 'hackwork' (a term that has been used of some of the long poems of Catullus), the long poems represent Catullus' most concentrated endeavour.

All the same, for Catullus the difference between long poem and short poem was more one of degree than one in kind. The long poems contribute to the short ones an adult poetic sensibility beyond the capacity of the trifler with *vers de société*, for whom verse was never the passionate, absorbing occupation it became for Catullus. Poem 7, for example, has obvious affinities with the other short poems we have been discussing:

> Quaeris, quot mihi basiationes
> tuae, Lesbia, sint satis superque.
> quam magnus numerus Libyssae harenae
> lasarpiciferis iacet Cyrenis
> oraclum Iouis inter aestuosi   5
> et Batti ueteris sacrum sepulcrum;
> aut quam sidera multa, cum tacet nox,
> furtiuos hominum uident amores:
> tam te basia multa basiare
> uesano satis et super Catullo est,   10
> quae nec pernumerare curiosi
> possint nec mala fascinare lingua.

You ask me, Lesbia, how many kisses it will take
to make me really satisfied.
As many as the sands of Libya's desert
that lies round Cyrene where the silphium grows,
stretching between the oracle of sweltering Jove
and the holy tomb of Battos long ago departed.
Or as many as the stars that in night's quiet
look down on us mortals stealing love.
That is the total of the kisses that will make
your passionate Catullus really satisfied.
A sum like that the nosy couldn't reckon up,
or evil tongue weave spells around.

It is a love poem addressed to Lesbia and tense with crisply suggested feeling for her. At the same time its twelve lines contain as much *doctrina* deftly exploited as we are likely to find in any dozen lines selected at random from an epyllion.[16] In particular, the *recherché* forms *Libyssae*[17] and *lasarpiciferis* and the 'learned' guidebook geography of lines 5 and 6. Indeed, at first glance a quarter of the poem seems expended on *doctrina* remote from the poet's feelings and the poem's purpose. But see how adroitly Catullus' poetic sensibility, in fact, exploits this learning. Cyrene, surrounded by a desert studded with exotic shrubs, provides a vivid image that revivifies the saying 'countless as the sands of the desert'.[18] Cyrene, too, has a special place in the affections of disciples of Callimachus. Catullus, however, scorns to name the great Alexandrian overtly. He arranges instead for our memory to be jogged by the tomb of old Battos: what Callimachean does not know that the master spoke of himself as 'Battiades'? There are reasons, then, for the learned scenery. Note finally how the touch of irony introduced at line 5 by the suggestion of Jove sweating in his temple in the desert (overlaid with a verbal ambiguity if *aestuosi* can also mean 'lusty')[19] creates, as it were, a fresh dimension of the poem, which is carried on by the ironical reference in line 8 to the liaison between Catullus and Lesbia (they, too, are mortals stealing love),[20] by the use of *uesanus* (a word that is usually pejorative, but used here with a note of ironical self-praise), and in the final two lines by the suggestion of contempt for the nosy, coupled with half-fear of the mysterious power they might have over Lesbia and himself.

On the other hand, the short poems contribute to the long

ones the slick ironical note, the calculated flippancy—the *urbanitas* that in the long poems strengthens, by a sense of the poet's presence, the *outré* stylization of the grand manner of epic and tragedy. In Poem 64, for example, when Catullus first introduces Ariadne after a quick statement of scene and circumstances, he gives us an oddly detailed picture:

> quem procul ex alga maestis Minois ocellis,
> saxea ut effigies bacchantis, prospicit, eheu,
> prospicit et magnis curarum fluctuat undis,
> non flauo retinens subtilem uertice mitram,
> non contecta leui uelatum pectus amictu,
> non tereti strophio lactentis uincta papillas,
> omnia quae toto delapsa e corpore passim
> ipsius ante pedes fluctus salis alludebant.　　(lines 60–67)

> Sad-eyed, Minos' daughter watched him out of sight,
> Bacchant turned to stone on an algae-strewn beach. Alas,
> yes, watched, tossed on a heavy swell of grief.
> Her fine-meshed net was slipping from her flaxen hair;
> her flimsy garment left unconcealed the torso that it veiled;
> her rounded brassière bound her milky breasts no more.
> All she wore was edging everywhere from place,
> made sport of by the waves that played about her feet.

King Minos' daughter bears all the signs of a night of *furtiuus amor*. She is in danger of losing her brassière and perhaps her *mitra* too.[21] Catullus has gone out of his way to emphasize details of her appearance that at first sight seem stridently incompatible with the grand manner. He is prepared to risk destroying the epic stature of his heroine at the very moment of her introduction, in order to have his readers think of her as though she were a real girl—not an epic puppet—deserted on the morning after her elopement. It is a dangerous device, but worth while for the sympathy he secures for Ariadne if successful. The realistic touches are slyly sandwiched in between the simile of the marble Bacchant (whose function is to emphasize the legendary aspect of Ariadne, but with the detailed realism of Hellenistic sculptural art) and the stylized declamatory passage (69–75) that follows. The two worlds of legend and reality are for a moment nicely linked. There is here the germ of the ironic juxtaposition of legend and realistic treatment of trivial detail that Eliot exploits (with much the same material) in 'Sweeney Erect'.

We must add, then, to our feeling for the spontaneity and freshness that in the best of Catullus result in a sudden soaring to the highest level, as the writing bursts almost accidentally into poetry, a recognition of the poet's subtle, conscious craftsmanship. This is no boy genius, gauchely breaking into song. His grasp of the details, too, of technique is impressive. Take metre: here is a poet who can make metre impart to statement more than the overall shape and sound, the general air and tension of verse. Contrast these two hexameters from Poem 64:

caerula uerrentes abiegnis aequora palmis   (line 7)
sweeping sky-blue sea with fir-tree hands

immemor at iuuenis fugiens pellit uada remis   (line 58)
the youth in thoughtless flight beats sea with oars.

In both what the poet is talking about is essentially the same: a ship propelled by the movements of its oars. The reader, however, who is alert to catch the sound as well as the sense notices a striking difference that affects the whole phonetic fabric of the two lines. The swinging rhythm of line 7 forces itself upon us at first reading. Four coincidences of stress with initial syllables of the foot (the normal maximum) and the solid mass of seven long syllables stretched across the middle of the line do much to build up an image (the sound picture suggesting the visual picture) of the firm, powerful sweep of Argo's oars. At the same time, the contrasting, languid motion of the ocean through which the oars move is suggested by the words *caerula* and *aequora*—each occupying a complete dactyllic foot, and the two dispersed almost to the extremities of the line.[22] The mood of powerful, steady, resolute, confident progress that the sense requires is underlined unmistakably by the rhythm.

The other line is very different. Instead of the coincidences of stress and initial syllable in the fourth and fifth foot, which did much in the line we have just considered to create a rolling rhythm at a key point in the line, coincidence here occurs only at the beginning and the end of the line. Except for the weak coincidence in *at* in the second foot, obscured by the more prominent stress in *iuuenis*, coincidence is absent throughout the central part of the line, above all in the fifth foot, where one expects almost always to find it.[23] Instead of the solid block of long syllables that

44

we had in the previous line, this line opens with a run of dactyls, interrupted with a jerk in the fourth foot. Up to that point the line has consisted entirely of short vowels, nine of them. The three long syllables required by the metre are all long by position. The effect is magnificently suggestive of the sense: hasty, nervous sweeps of the oars, too much excitement to row effectively, and then jagged, floundering blows as the rhythm of the rowing is lost altogether. The more one thinks about this line, the more one realizes the artistic compression and economy of effect. Theseus is spoken of as though he were rowing the ship himself—hardly likely if we think in realistic terms, but by this simplification the supernumeraries (as undesirable in this stylized writing as in the picture on the *uestis* it purports to describe) are tactfully disposed of. At the same time Theseus' emotions are graphically externalized.

Or take Poem 63. The most striking thing about the metre of this poem is the frantic sequence of short syllables with which each line ends. A speed of utterance is built up that reinforces the tempo of the action. This rhythm is broken five times in the ninety-three lines.[24] In line 14 the metre stumbles as it were on *exules*, throwing that word into prominence in order to underline the first hint of pathos. In line 35 (*lassulae*) the pathos is heightened by the same metrical device and by the use of a diminutive. In line 73 (*paenitet*) emphasis is thrown on the upsurge of regret that dominates the second half of the poem. The effect in the other two places where the end rhythm of the line is broken is only a little less striking. In line 76 (*leonibus*) the rhythm underlines the surprise effect of the dénouement. In line 91 the rhythm serves to make even stronger the final strokes of the hammering d's that run through the line:

dea, magna dea, Cybebe, dea domina Dindymi.

The d's and the rhythm combine to produce a stuttering effect.[25]

In Poem 4 Catullus has been to some pains to develop for his yacht the personality of a garrulous old man. His problem is to deal with an essentially sentimental situation without indulging in sentimentality. This is largely achieved by a rambling report of remarks, themselves ramblingly reminiscent, swept along by a firm, vigorous metre. The regularly interpolated 'he says' discreetly achieves a distancing effect (lines 2, 6, 15 and 16). The frequent accusatives and infinitives contribute to the same end. There is a sudden run of them in lines 14–19. The poem develops a kind of somniferous, repetitious rhythm suggesting the way the yacht goes on and on about its achievements. The contribution of the rhymes in lines 15 and 17 is striking (a pair of rhymes— *origine, cacumine*—followed by a third near-rhyme, *aequore*, each in a word stressed on the antepenult; no other rhymes in this poem).[26]

As a final detail of the way in which Catullus welds sense to metre, instead of just framing metre round the sense, consider the concluding lines of Poem 7 (discussed above):

> quae nec pernumerare curiosi
> possint nec mala fascinare lingua.

Our ear guides us into understanding the words in a way we should probably not otherwise have understood them. Pretty surely in normal prose we should take *mala lingua* as ablative. What happens in the poem is a little hard to explain. As we read the line, the metre rejects the ablatival construction which our eye, running on ahead, had perhaps prepared us for. Now *mala lingua* becomes the subject and the words jump into a fresh meaning—rather like that type of optical illusion where the object represented suddenly appears to transform itself into a quite different object.

Curiously enough it used to be fashionable to call Catullus a slovenly metrist. Ellis, for example, in his note on Poem 64, line 58 ('a carelessness of which there is no other example in LXIV') can see no merit in *pellit uada remis*. R. G. C. Levens is presumably reflecting the common view when he opens his report on Catullan studies (in most respects an excellent one) with words that may seem surprisingly unmindful of the ideals of the *poetae novi*. Catullus' popularity in recent years, he says, is ascribable to a contemporary fashion which is prone to 'judge poetry more by the energy it transmits than by the polish of its surface'.[27] The charge of slovenliness is based most often on the elegiac poems, whose supposed crudity is contrasted with Augustan practice. Catullus is reproached particularly for excessive use of elision. But his detractors have been firmly answered by D. A. West who maintains that in most structural details Catullus' usage is not separable from that of the Augustans. An examination of poems or parts of poems where elision is frequent points to the 'conclusion that this feature is felt by Catullus to be particularly appropriate where he is discussing some intense emotion of his own'.[28]

We have, in short, to postulate a poet endowed with the kind of technical skill and virtuosity which the intensive study of the masterpieces of ancient literature, Roman rhetorical education, and the diligent practice of verse could produce. A poet determined, however, wherever reality is the subject, to make poetry as far as possible out of real contemporary speech. For the short poems Catullus has evolved a style that appears not just simple and direct, but frequently slangy and at times ostentatiously obscene. The consequent freshness of Catullus cannot fail to produce an initial impact upon us, however closely worked the fabric often appears when we later examine it more attentively. He possesses, too, an emotional responsiveness and a psychological subtlety that Roman poetry had not attained before. Yet it is only occasionally, under special stress of inspiration, that these qualities are present to a degree adequate for the production of permanently worthwhile poetry out of themes that are often slight, however dexterously handled. Our modern experience of exploiting emotion and our imaginative readiness are so much greater that Catullus frequently appears to stop short of what we can regard as genuine poetic achievement.

We find Catullus, therefore, allowing himself at times to draw too crudely (by our concept of the note of ironical restraint required) upon the grand style of the epic-tragic tradition and its grandiloquence. I think those who admire Poem 76 for its solemn religious note admire too readily.[29] I find the self-righteous tone, appropriate enough to Ariadne in Poem 64, distasteful in a realistic setting. Poem 76, in my opinion, is therefore inferior to the more disciplined Poem 8, where a trace of wistful flippancy varies, and strengthens, the prevailing bitterness of tone. There is misplaced grandiloquence again in Poem 68a, where a fairly trivial situation is dealt with in language so inflated that many have been trapped into supposing something really tragic had happened to Mallius. In fact, the tragedy appears no graver than that which has descended on Propertius in his first elegy. Neither can sleep at night for unrequited love. Mallius asks Catullus for a love poem to comfort him, whereas Propertius can write his own. Propertius, moreover, has learned how to apply slickly just the right degree of tragic despair. Catullus, who may be reporting the words of Mallius' *epistolium*, overdoes things rather badly.

Fortunately Catullus is seldom easily satisfied. More often the battle for expression is so intense we are caught up in it and can overlook the comparatively crude linguistic resources with which it is conducted. In Poem 63, for example, Catullus is trying to convey the turmoil of thoughts that crowded through Attis' mind when he woke and realized his isolation and the enormity of what he had done. Our comparative psychological subtlety enables us to express without effort concepts beyond Catullus' reach. He simply piles up all the words that in Latin signify mind, seat of intelligence, or emotion:

> ita de quiete molli rapida sine rabie
> simul ipsa pectore Attis sua facta recoluit,
> liquidaque mente uidit sine quis ubique foret,
> animo aestuante rusum reditum ad uada tetulit.

> (lines 44–47)

Then, when after soft repose, free from madness' grasp,
Attis himself in mind reviewed his situation,
and with intellect cleared perceived where he was and what he lacked,
thought once more seething, he returned to the water's edge.

The words *pectore, mente, animo* follow one another in successive lines. The device is crude, but it lends the passage a vibrant strength we can still feel. Catullus is leaning, of course, upon a characteristic of early Latin verse-style, a fondness for repeating synonyms, which we can see in its simpler, more archaic form in Poem 64, 69–70:

> illa . . . toto ex te pectore, Theseu,
> toto animo, tota pendebat perdita mente.

> But she was pining for you, Theseus, with all her heart,
> all her mind; there all her despairing thinking centred.

Here there is the same psychological purpose, but its expression, dependent ultimately on the same device, is more consciously 'epic' and archaic. The epithet is colourless, repeated simply for emphasis and alliterative effect.

In Poem 109 Catullus dismisses his mistress's proposal to patch up their quarrel:

Iucundum, mea uita, mihi proponis amorem
   hunc nostrum inter nos perpetuumque fore.
di magni, facite ut uere promittere possit,
   atque id sincere dicat et ex animo,
ut liceat nobis tota perducere uita
   aeternum hoc sanctae foedus amicitiae.

Darling, it is an attractive prospect for our love
that you propose to me. And everlasting too.
Gods, if only she'd the power to promise truly!
Speech clean from subterfuge, spoken from the heart.
Then might we perhaps, all life through, never broken,
affection's sacred treaty really keep.

What he wants she cannot offer or even understand, and he is
angry at her glib talk of 'everlasting' love (line 2). He wants loyal
mutual affection, not just passion, and he wants it genuinely to
last as long as they live. Again it is not difficult for us, but how
does Catullus go about expressing these ideas succinctly and
effectively in half a dozen lines of verse? Passion presents no
difficulty. Loyal affection is harder and he has to build up a heavy
legalistic phrase: *hoc sanctae foedus amicitiae*.[30] For genuine and
permanent he resorts to the device of repetition that we saw in
Poem 63: *uere, sincere, ex animo; tota uita, perducere, aeternum*. Each
concept is precisely rendered three times, so that there can be no
doubt left in her mind what Catullus means, or about the strength
of the emotion fighting to frame the words. It is impossible not
to feel the impact of each blow, as the poet strains to hammer his
meaning home.

We need reminding of Catullus' intellectual ingenuousness
precisely because of his sophistication in other respects. Even so
we are disconcerted by a poet who is at times primitive (in a
noble sense of the word), at other times so adult and so contem-
porary-sounding. It is hard to keep the need for an historical
approach in mind in dealing with a poet who can exploit irony
and ambiguity as dexterously as we saw him do in Poem 7. Or
take poem 5:

   Viuamus, mea Lesbia, atque amemus,
   rumoresque senum seueriorum
   omnes unius aestimemus assis!
   soles occidere et redire possunt:
   nobis cum semel occidit breuis lux,   5

nox est perpetua una dormienda.
da mi basia mille, deinde centum,
dein mille altera, dein secunda centum,
deinde usque altera mille, deinde centum.
dein, cum milia multa fecerimus,   10
conturbabimus illa, ne sciamus,
aut ne quis malus inuidere possit,
cum tantum sciat esse basiorum.

Let us live, my Lesbia, and let us love!
If old men murmur protest, stricter now than once they were,
let us not give a damn for all their mutterings.
The sun can go on quitting the bed he sank in,
but we, when our brief day's light is done,
must sleep through a night that will never end.
Give me a thousand kisses, followed by a hundred;
another thousand then, and a second hundred.
Then a further thousand, plus a hundred.
Finally, when we've accumulated many thousands,
please muddle all the accounts and forget the total.
Then no nosy nasty person will be able to be envious
through knowledge of such heavy transacting in kisses.

Note the gusto of the opening. A first line lyrically simple in its overt statement, and yet clear-cut and strong, sense and line framed by the two rich, warm words *uiuamus, amemus*, bound together by assonance. An emotional level is at once attained that can stand the easy colloquial vigour of the next two lines. They are followed by three lines of very real lyrical pathos. Just the right hint, too, of a night to be slept through that differs from those the lovers now await eagerly. Line 5 is made up of simple, short words,

> nobis cum semel occidit breuis lux,

yet how precise: *cum semel*, instead of the more usual *cum primum*, 'when the time comes, and it comes once only'. The tense, too, deserves attention. If Catullus had wanted us to think of the day of his death and Lesbia's, he would have used the future perfect. The present indicative is frequentative: *nobis* means not Catullus and Lesbia, but mortals in general.[31] Now line 6, with its two doom-laden polysyllables, comes crashing down:

> nox est perpetua una dormienda.

Consider here the effect of the antithesis *perpetua/una*, the words not merely juxtaposed, but linked intimately by elision and assonance. It is a doom from which the only escape lies in escapism, and the poem, its point made, bounds off into a joyful jingle of numbers which sounds like simple exuberance, until it rounds on the *senes seueriores*. For them, the implication is, the appraisal of all forms of happiness is reduced to a matter of accountancy. There is a neat hint of malice here, of course. The *senes* would consider their disapprobation had a moral basis (*seueriores*). Catullus manages to make it sound as petty as the envy of business men for a young rival, when they base their estimate of how well he has done on a reckoning of how much he has made.

It is hard, too, to remember that we and Catullus stand almost at opposite ends of the long tradition of the short personal poem when we see him lay out his poems with the slick efficiency that he shows, for example, in Poem 39 (*Egnatius, quod candidos habet dentes* . . .). This poem falls into three stanzas: 1–8, 9–16, and the final insult 17–21. The second stanza is welded to the first by a neat ambiguity involving the word *urbanus*. At the end of stanza 1,

> hunc habet morbum,
> neque elegantem, ut arbitror, neque urbanum,

> It's a complaint he suffers from
> and one that's neither smart, I think, nor sophisticated,

the context confines our reactions to the secondary meanings: 'sophisticated', 'well-bred', and so on. When the word comes again early in stanza 2, we realize gradually that Egnatius is going to be derided as a provincial.[32] The third stanza is linked to the second by a comparable ambiguity, inherent in our failure at first to grasp the full significance of *qui puriter lauit dentes*. Likely enough at the first reading we place no particular emphasis on *puriter* and take the words as a loosely recapitulatory *descriptive* relative clause, reminding us of Egnatius' standards of oral hygiene. But the phrase sticks at the back of our minds, waiting to contribute its effect to the final blow, and then we discover it is a *defining* relative clause, framed to exclude Egnatius.

It is important to stress the *personal relevance* of the short poems —another aspect of their *vers-de-société*-transcended character. To understand, for example, why Egnatius is being got at so savagely in Poem 39, we have to remember he figures in Poem 37. Similarly, the Gellius epigrams have to be taken together for us to get their intensity in proper perspective. The fact that some poems by sheer quality achieve the status of front-rank poetry must not cause us to lose sight of the fact that Catullus makes little attempt at that obliteration of the crudely personal element which a modern lyric poet feels obliged to aim at and which we can see in Horace's Odes. 'Personal', of course, in Eliot's sense of insufficiently universalized for a poem to stand properly on its own artistic feet. We must bear this in mind as an important corrective to our natural tendency to ascribe too seriously 'poetic' a character to Poem 46 (*Iam uer egelidos refert tepores* . . .) with which we began, or the famous (and usually too sentimentally taken) Poem 31 (*Paene insularum, Sirmio, insularumque* . . .).

We must not be too ready, in fact, to ascribe to any of the short poems the level of intent of the best of the long poems. A concluding word about these. Poems 63 and 64 (and, to a lesser extent, 66 and 68) are intended as *tours de force*: pieces where sustained technical virtuosity is pushed to the limits that cultivated taste can tolerate. This, as we have seen, is often true of the short poems too. The long poems present, however, two special artistic problems. Firstly, their technical brilliance must not stand in the way of a more substantial theme. Secondly, the poems being so long, the reader must not be overpowered by the concentrated wealth of what they have to offer.

The careful reader of the short poems will approach Poems 63 and 64 without misgivings about the solidity of Catullus' technical competence and the sure instinct that guides its use, and he will find plenty to admire. Let us consider a couple of closely-wrought passages from Poem 64. Take the beautiful picture of the innocent young princess (lines 86–90, especially the similes of 89–90) who falls violently in love with the fair-haired heroic adventurer who has come to her father's palace. The picture is filled out by an image of astonishing precision:

> non prius ex illo flagrantia declinauit
> lumina, quam cuncto concepit corpore flammam
> funditus atque imis exarsit tota medullis.   (lines 91–93)

She did not turn aside from him her burning
gaze until she had kindled in her heart a flame, deep-seated,
pervasive; in her innermost frame fire burst out and reigned.

The fire of love is the tritest of metaphors in ancient poetry.
Catullus gives the figure fresh life by taking it literally and in
detail. He thinks of the eyes of Ariadne fixed on her splendid
lover as burning-glasses (like the precious stones, perhaps, mentioned by Pliny).[33] Through them the fire he radiates pours into
her, her whole body catches alight, and in a moment conflagration
leaps up in every part of her. The effect is almost too studied.
There is the sense pattern linking *cuncto, funditus* and *tota,* and the
alliterative pattern of 'fl' linking *flagrantia* and *flammam.* Note,
too, how the heavy thud of *quam cuncto concepit pectore* is thrust
aside by the explosion of s's in *imis exarsit tota medullis* (reinforced
by the internal rhyme at the caesura) as Ariadne's passion suddenly
bursts into flame.

Or take the scene where the mortal wedding guests depart
upon the arrival of the gods:

> quae postquam cupide spectando Thessala pubes
> expleta est, sanctis coepit decedere diuis.
> hic, qualis flatu placidum mare matutino
> horrificans Zephyrus procliuas incitat undas,
> Aurora exoriente uagi sub limina Solis,
> quae tarde primum clementi flamine pulsae
> procedunt leuiterque sonant plangore cachinni,
> post uento crescente magis magis increbescunt,
> purpureaque procul nantes ab luce refulgent:
> sic tum uestibuli linquentes regia tecta
> ad se quisque uago passim pede discedebant. (lines 267–77)

After the youth of Thessaly had feasted their gaze on this
and had their fill, they began to make way for the gods.
Then, just as the west wind, blowing early in the morning,
ruffles the calm sea and drives the waves before it,
while dawn climbs the threshold of the journeying sun;
and slow at first, driven by a gentle breeze, they move
forward, the crisp waves' sound answering the wind's whine;
later, as the wind rises, the waves grow more crowded,
and the bright light plays on them as they move:
so the guests, as they passed from the palace hall,
each wandering off on his journey homeward.

First let us analyse the simile. A westerly wind, rising at dawn, drives the waves of the ocean with increasing force towards the sun that is ascending the eastern horizon. Pretty clearly, Catullus is thinking of the open sea, not the plashing of waves on rocks. It is the noise of the wind that *plangore* denotes (the word always implies a loudish, continuous sound, varying in volume—wailing women, *stormy* sea),[34] not the noise of the water, as is often supposed. The noise the water makes is denoted by *leuiter sonant*—a crisp splashing noise as the peaks of the wavelets (*cachinni*) topple over before the wind.

Now we may proceed to apply the simile. Certain points of contact are obvious: the wind corresponds to the continuous, rising-and-falling noise of conversation, growing louder as the crowd gets under way. The crisp contrapuntal splash of the toppling wave-tops corresponds to the ripples of laughter that break out over the buzz of talk. This second correspondence is reinforced by the verbal ambiguity in *cachinni*. The simile, however, is more exact than that. The crowd moving slowly from the comparative dark of the banqueting hall along the *uestibulum* towards the open door of the palace, through which the daylight floods in, is, in fact, strikingly like Catullus' picture of the early-morning sea, still in half-light, moving in gathering waves towards the rising sun. Moreover, I think Catullus has carefully worked in the words *sub limina Solis* in order to guide the imaginative reactions of the attentive reader in the right direction. The verbal echo *uagi* (271) and *uago* (277) is also intended, perhaps, to emphasize the two different kinds of movement across a threshold. This is simile on the epic scale, but integrated with the scene illustrated in a new precision of detail.

So much for technical brilliance. About the soundness of Catullus' taste, however, it is obviously less easy to form a judgement. The tricks cannot have upon us an impact identical with that upon Catullus' Roman contemporaries. We may underestimate the cloying effect of relentless brilliance. The cumulative effect of it all is not something that can be exemplified here. The test is not the quality of isolated passages, but our reaction to the whole poem. For, unlike other long poems, the long poems of Catullus, because of their intensely cohering nature, cannot be fairly sampled in purple patches.

Moreover, our judgement of taste is bound up with another

question on which it may be anticipated that our stand today is more stringent than in Catullus' time. We shall expect of a first-rate poem of these dimensions more than entertainment or art for art's sake. While avoiding talk of moral purposes, we can reasonably ask to be satisfied that in these poems the poet has something to say which is of consequence to him and to us. Again this is a question that cannot be demonstrated, convincingly, by anything less than a full study of a whole poem. I do not myself think the sensitive reader *needs* such a demonstration to feel the plaintive urgency of Poem 63. About Poem 64, however, he may be less sure. Evidence that the poet is trying to suggest something about human relationships and about the decline of society from a stage of wholesome, god-like simplicity is unmistakable. The poet's ideas are naïve, of course. The real question is: Are they artistically successful? It is not easily answered. Let us end our appraisal of Catullus by looking at an aspect of Poem 64, relevant to this kind of general assessment of the poem, which has not, I think, been hitherto appreciated.

Catullus' main objective, in terms of story, is obvious. It is to bring epic up to date. A heroine who looks like a real woman and a man in whom we can recognize the character of a real person. Hence the detailed realism, the contemporary note in the description of Ariadne on the beach. Hence, too, I think, an attempt to give Theseus a real character, to show that his behaviour springs from dominant traits of his personality. At first sight, Catullus juxtaposes episodes from the Theseus legend that do not fit. How is Theseus, the hero who braved the Minotaur for his country's sake, reconciled with Theseus, the heartless cad who seduced and deserted his benefactress? Legend offered a tangle of tales about Theseus whose inconsistencies were unimportant so long as the episodes remained disconnected. In any case, epic got round the problem of Theseus' moral irresponsibility very simply: a god forced him to forget.[35] The old epic poets lacked our interest in motivation and were content to let the intervention of gods and goddesses provide the springs of action that we would seek to explain in terms of character. It is a regular convention and we accept it because the interest in early epic lies elsewhere. Catullus, however, has looked at his story more critically. If a god has caused Theseus to forget about Ariadne, why should Theseus be punished and made to cause the death of his own father? Catullus, it seems to me, tries to show that the character of Theseus brought about both calamities.

Let us remember this is a problem that Catullus has chosen to deal with. In a poem so selective of detail he could easily have avoided episodes that clashed. If he chooses to stress Theseus the handsome hero (*e.g.*, lines 73–93), Theseus the cad, and Theseus punished by his father's death it should mean that these are in some way the significant episodes for the story as Catullus wishes to shape it. His plan seems to be an attempt, within a framework of technique stylistically consistent with the epic manner, to suggest a view of Theseus' character sufficiently rounded for us to feel him a real person.

His character is built up by a pattern involving two key words, *ferox* and *immemor*. He was brave, he faced danger without hesitation: Catullus sums this up with the word *ferox*, and, by using this adjective of him at the moment he steps ashore in Crete,

> ferox quo ex tempore Theseus
> egressus curuis e litoribus Piraei
> attigit iniusti regis Gortynia templa,
>
> > (lines 73–75)

> > when hard Theseus,
> setting out from Piraeus' curving walls,
> reached at Gortyn the palace of the unjust king,

he suggests the dashing bravado Ariadne fell in love with. Then at the end of the story the word *ferox* is used again of Theseus— at the moment when he has brought about his father's death:

> sic funesta domus ingressus tecta paterna
> morte ferox Theseus, qualem Minoidi luctum
> obtulerat mente immemori, talem ipse recepit.
> > (lines 246–8)

> So it was a palace gloom-ridden with his father's death
> that hard Theseus entered: the grief he had brought on
> Minos' daughter by his thoughtless ways descended on himself.

Observe how the circle of Theseus' story stands complete, even to the parallelism of *egressus* and *ingressus*. What Catullus is trying to say is that heroes like Theseus in real life, too, can be insensitive, ruthless, brutish. The word *ferox* in ordinary usage can mean these things, as much as it means courageous or intrepid.

The opening and the final scene are linked by a more complicated pattern involving the word *immemor*, each pattern being intended to support the other. The word *immemor* occurs at the first mention of Theseus in line 58,

> immemor at iuuenis fugiens pellit uada remis,

and occurs alongside *ferox* in the final Theseus scene (line 248). It covers a complicated nexus of meanings which may be summed up by the translation 'without thought for'. At epic levels of motivation, this is equated with forgetting: Theseus forgot about Ariadne. Or he forgot about changing the sails on his ship, because the gods answered Ariadne's curse and made him forget. Catullus does not expressly contradict the epic version. He goes to some trouble, however, to ensure that we shall read more into *immemor* than we might otherwise think of doing. He leads us to see in 'without thought for' an element of ruthless disregard for what happens to other people. As we have seen, the rhythm of line 58, when Theseus first appears and the word is first used of him, does not suggest someone who has forgotten about what he has done. For the moment no more is made of these overtones. When we come back to the beach scene at line 123 after the flashback to Crete,

> . . . immemori discedens pectore coniunx,

> . . . thoughtless, heartless, departing husband,

nothing is specifically added. Within a few lines, however, the word is caught up by Ariadne herself. She reproaches Theseus for being *immemor* in a context that leaves no doubt about the range of meaning Catullus wants the word to embrace:

> 'sicine me patriis auectam, perfide, ab aris,
> perfide, deserto liquisti in litore, Theseu?
> sicine discedens neglecto numine diuum,
> immemor a! deuota domum periuria portas?
> nullane res potuit crudelis flectere mentis
> consilium? tibi nulla fuit clementia praesto,
> immite ut nostri uellet miserescere pectus?'
>
> (lines 132–8)

'So, liar, transported from my country's shores,
you've left me, Theseus, on this empty beach?
So you go, regardless of what the gods have power to do,
thoughtless you carry home your cursed lies?

Could nothing turn aside your cruel plan's
intent? Was no resource of pity available to you,
to make your ruthless heart feel for me a little?'

And a few lines later:

'nunc iam nulla uiro iuranti femina credat,
nulla uiri speret sermones esse fideles;
quis dum aliquid cupiens animus praegestit apisci,
nil metuunt iurare, nihil promittere parcunt:
sed simul ac cupidae mentis satiata libido est,
dicta nihil metuere, nihil periuria curant.'   (lines 143–8)

'Let no woman any more trust a man's word,
nor hope a man will keep to what he says.
Their desiring thoughts intent on what they want,
they respect oaths not, make no promise reluctantly.
But the moment they've fulfilled the lust they planned,
with no regard for what they said, unconcerned, they lie.'

If we accept the view of many scholars that Czwalina's conjecture
meminere for *metuere* is a necessary repair to line 148, we have the
Leitmotiv once again.[36] It is against the same background of
thoughtlessness equated with cruelty that we must read Ariadne's
curse:

'sed quali solam Theseus me mente reliquit,
tali mente, deae, funestet seque suosque.'

(lines 200–1)

'but in what attitude of mind Theseus abandoned me,
through that attitude, Goddesses, let him undo his and him.'

On the epic level this means: let a god intervene again and, by
causing Theseus to forget, bring ruin on him in his turn. On the
level on which Catullus is actually operating it means: Theseus,
as a result of the brutish streak in his character which causes him
to disregard all except himself, is just the person, now he is pre-
occupied, to forget all about what his father said to him when he
left Athens. So that in

quo motu tellus atque horrida contremuerunt
aequora concussitque micantia sidera mundus.
ipse autem caeca mentem caligine Theseus
consitus oblito dimisit pectore cuncta,
quae mandata prius constanti mente tenebat,

(lines 205–9)

Whereat the earth and disordered ocean
trembled, the shining firmament of stars vibrated.
And so Theseus, a dark mist descending on his
thoughts, let slip into oblivion all that
he'd been told, that till now his mind had steady grip on,

the divine machinery is to be taken with the rational overtones
we would read into Euripides. There are echoes, too, of Lucretius.
Compare:

> illud in his obsignatum quoque rebus habere
> conuenit et memori mandatum mente tenere.

> Here's a point in this connexion it's necessary
> to keep locked in one's mind, entrusted to one's thoughts.

Indeed Catullus may have got much of his interest in mental
processes from Lucretius.[37]

I think we can be pretty sure Catullus intended his *Leitmotiv
ferox* and *immemor* to convey more or less what I have suggested,
though he might have been less able to resolve the ambiguities
inherent in *immemor* than we. His use of the word *mens* should also
be observed. To explain Catullus' intentions is not, however, to
assert their success. In fact, I think he fails, at any rate by our standards. The failure is due, perhaps, to wanting too much to have
the best of both worlds. He keeps the divine machinery of epic,
and at the same time suggests more human explanations of
Theseus' actions. But the balance between the two is upset by
trying to keep the stylistic conventions of epic as well. To do this,
Catullus has built his contemporary insight into character upon
two epithets, used apparently according to the stylistic conventions of epic, but endowed actually with much more than conventional force. The words by the pattern of their repetition are
intended to convey what could have been more naturally conveyed
by fuller and more explicit parenthetical comment. The device
is a little too wooden. It takes us too long to see what Catullus
is up to.

This is, of course, a judgement to which it would be wrong to
attempt to compel the reader's assent until he has made himself
familiar with the whole poem. All we have been able to do here,
really, is to probe a few details with a little more care than Poem
64 is usually considered to deserve. If the investigation has revealed qualities of craftsmanship and poetic insight that appeal

to the reader, let him battle with Poem 64—and the other long poems—until he has wrested from them, with some completeness, the wealth of poetic experience they have to offer.[38]

NOTES

[1] The score might include as well Poems 4, 13, 31, 34, 45, 50, 84, 96, 101 and, say, ten of the Lesbia poems—perhaps (one is tempted to suggest an order that will reflect the beginnings of the liaison, its decay, and then its final rupture) 51, 2, 3, 5, 7, 8, 76, 85, 11, 58.

[2] The poem is well discussed by J. P. Elder, 'Notes on some conscious and subconscious elements in Catullus' poetry', *Harvard Studies in Classical Philology* 60 (1951) 103–4 and 120–1.

[3] Compare Horace *Odes* IV. 12: *iam*'s begin the first and third lines and whip up a jubilant, excited note that falls flat immediately.

[4] For *Asia* with overtones compare Virgil *Aen.* III. 1:

> Postquam res Asiae Priamique euertere gentem . . .

[5] As far as one can gather from latish writers, *egelidus* is a prosy word for tepidness in wine or water—except for Columella (*uer*) and Ausonius (*hiemes*) (who may be suspected of imitating Catullus) and the notorious Ovid, *Amores* II. 11. 10. This is leaving out of account the curious fact that Virgil (*Aen.* VIII. 610) and some others use the word in the quite different sense of 'extremely cold'. *aequinoctialis* is a common word in scientific and astronomical writing. Hence Cicero, *Arat.* 285, but it is not cited by *TLL* for any other poet except Sidonius. *aestuosus*, in the sense of 'sweltering hot', is a common but obviously unpoetic word, favoured by the elder Pliny. Its use in poetry is interesting. It occurs a couple of times in Plautus. In both passages the primary meaning is perhaps 'addicted to drinking' (as suggested by the glosses quoted in *TLL*), but in *Bacch.* 470 ff. (*meretricem . . . acerrume aestuosam*) it looks as though the meaning is 'passionate', which would provide an interesting ambiguity for the other occurrence of the word in Catullus (7. 5). The compound *praetrepidans* is extremely rare, as is the form *praetrepidus*.

[6] The Mynors text makes it one hundred and ten: 1–60 = 60 poems—18–20 are not by Catullus; 2b, 14b, 58b are separate pieces. 69–116 = 50 poems —78b, 95b are separate pieces.

[7] The word 'revolution' has been used both of the social phenomenon (the emancipation of the individual) and the artistic phenomenon (the emancipation of the artist). The former is spoken of by E. Reitzenstein, 'Das neue Kunstwollen in den *Amores* Ovids', *Rh. Mus.* 84 (1935) 62–88: 'In der Generation des Catull erfolgt in der Poesie eine richtige Revolution gegen die bisher alleingültige römische Lebensnorm und das trotz mancher Auflockerung doch zäh festgehaltene Ideal des *civis Romanus* und seiner Aufgaben' (pp. 64–65). The latter by H. Patzer, 'Zum Sprachstil des neoterischen Hexameters', *Museum Helveticum* (1955) 77–95: 'Die nicht-dramatische Dichtung der Römer hätte mit

den Augusteern nicht klassisch werden können ohne die Revolution, die die neoterische Schule in der bis dahin sich gemächlich entwickelnden lateinischen Dichtkunst hervorrief' (p. 77).

[8] For illustrations of differing levels of intent see Kenneth Quinn, *The Catullan Revolution* (1959), Chapter III.

[9] *The Lyric Genius of Catullus* (1939), p. 75. Havelock's thesis, being founded on the short poems, involves, in dealing with the long poems, critical judgements such as the following: 'Even in his longer compositions, his writing becomes significant and important only in so far as it is lyrical' (p. 78). But even with the short poems it will not work.

[10] Admittedly this is only a piece of literary gossip reported in one of Seneca's Letters: *Negat Cicero, si duplicetur sibi aetas, habiturum se tempus quo legat lyricos* (*Ep.* 49. 6).

[11] Kroll says this: 'Der Schluss, der die Aufklärung über die Veranlassung des Gedichtes bringt, kommt unerwartet: die ganze Verhöhnung des armen Furius ist nur die Einleitung zur Ablehnung eines plumpen Borgversuches.'

[12] N. H. Watts in the Loeb edition says: 'The speech in general is full of a scurrility astounding even by the standard of ancient usage.'

[13] *E.g.* 'The Temperaments', where one can see clearly the influence of Catullus' Poem 113.

[14] The MSS. have *et.* Fröhlich's *aes* is undoubtedly right. Kroll is determined not to see poetry and rejects Fröhlich's conjecture because it introduces a 'zum Tone des Gedichts nicht passende Periphrasis für "Spiegel" '. His argument that *aes* would imply 'die Voraussetzung, dass eine den Spiegel nicht befragende Frau geisteskrank sei' is unusually fatuous. A pun is probably involved into the bargain in view of the talk of money before. See Ellis's view in his *Excursus* that 'there seems to be a legal allusion running through the whole of this poem'.

[15] To use this term for convenience. The propriety of the label is sometimes disputed. See W. Allen, jun., 'The non-existent classical epyllion', *Stud. in Philol.* 60 (1958) 515–18, and J. F. Reilly, 'Origins of the word "epyllion" ', *CJ* 49 (1953–4) 111–14. All the same, there undoubtedly existed a genre which Patzer, op. cit., p. 77, defines as 'eine bis ins Detail genau ausgefeilte mythische Kurzerzählung'.

[16] I have found J. P. Elder's analysis of the poem, op. cit., pp. 107–9, perceptive and convincing.

[17] As Kroll says, '*Libyssae* ist in der Sache nicht gelehrt . . ., da jedermann von der libyschen Wüste Kunde hatte, aber in der Form: *Libyssa* als Adj. ist rein griechisch.'

[18] The image, alas, remains imprecise for us. Silphium was a plant from Cyrene (and often featured in the city's coins) much prized for its medicinal properties. Pauly-Wissowa devotes a dozen pages to the mysteries of its nature and uses, without solving them.

[19] See footnote [5] above.

[20] See Kenneth Quinn, op. cit., p. 53.

[21] Compare the heroic imprecision with which Virgil describes Dido (*Aen.* IV. 136–9) as she emerges to set in train the events of the day that

primus leti primusque malorum causa fuit. In Greek στρόφιον in this sense really only occurs in comedy. As one might expect, Aristophanes makes great play with the garment in the *Thesmophoriazusae*, where it figures four times (139, 251, 255, and 638). It is just possible that Catullus had in mind the passage (255–7) in this play where στρόφιον and μίτρα occur within a couple in lines, during the scene where Mnesilochus is being dressed for his part. Latin *strophium*, prior to Catullus, only once in Plautus, once in Turpilius and once in Varro (all fragments). For full information see Pauly-Wissowa, *s.v.*

In Greek μίτρα is used to denote a variety of forms of headgear (*ibid.*, 7, 2133). There is some evidence the word denoted among other things something women wore on their heads at night (perhaps a 'hairnet'), as is asserted by Kroll and Friedrich. They are supported by Propertius 2. 29. 15–6:

> quae cum Sidoniae nocturna ligamina mitrae
> soluerit . . .

In that case, Catullus has perhaps taken a word that could be heroic and then, by coupling it with *strophium*, undercut the heroic associations deliberately.

[22] For details of typical line structures in Poem 64 see Patzer, op. cit. He distinguishes three main types. An important feature of all types is the way they are locked together by an adjective placed some distance from its noun (*gesperrtes Attribut*). The adjective normally precedes.

[23] The normal rhythm of the fifth foot is similarly broken for obvious effect in line 315. Otherwise, apart from spondiazontes (usually with bucolic diaeresis) and two or three pentasyllabic endings (with secondary stress on initial syllable), the only other cases of non-coincidence in Poem 64 are 20, 141 (in both the slight catch before *hymenaeos* is appropriate), 304 and 319.

[24] In Mynors' text, reading *gyminasiis*, not *gymnasiis*, in line 60.

[25] For further evidence of the metrical virtuosity of this poem, see J. P. Elder, 'Catullus' Attis', *AJPh* 68 (1947) 394–403.

[26] Catullus' occasional use of rhyme is well worth watching. The ten lines of Poem 1, for example, contain four rhyming pairs. Or consider the assonances in the opening lines of Poem 42:

> Adeste, hendecasyllabi, quot estis
> omnes undique, quotquot estis omnes.

See N. I. Herescu, 'L'assonance latine', *Lettres d'humanité* 5 (1946) 133–48 (a fairly detailed examination of rhyme and assonance in Catullus), and 'L'assonance dans l'art de Catulle', *Rivista Clasica* 13–14 (1941–2) 55–73.

[27] In M. Platnauer, *Fifty Years of Classical Scholarship* (1955), p. 284.

[28] D. A. West, 'The metre of Catullus' elegiacs', *CQ* 51 (1955) 102. *E.g.* Poem 68, where 'five strong elisions occur in one couplet [89–90] after thirty lines which had offered only nine elisions, so that either this is the work of chance, which is unlikely, or else the couplet with its four

Greek proper names and its five elisions is in rhythm as in sense a link between the declamatory poetry of mythology that precedes, and the plain poetry of personal sorrow that follows'.

It is very likely that the highly elided lines often represent everyday speech, as W. B. Sedgwick, 'Catullus' elegiacs', *Mn.* 3 (1950) 64–69, followed by West, suggests.

[29] G. Luck, *The Latin Love Elegy* (1959), is the latest recruit to their distinguished ranks.

[30] See F. O. Copley, 'Emotional conflict and its significance in the Lesbia poems of Catullus', *AJPh* 70 (1949) 22–40.

[31] For examples of frequentative *cum primum* with present indicative, see Kühner-Stegmann[3] II, § 206, 2(a).

[32] There is a similar trick involving *Amphitriten* in Poem 64, 11: we first assume Homeric pastiche and take the word merely as a synonym for 'sea'. Line 15 causes us to revise our thinking, to include the goddess.

[33] See M. H. Morgan, 'De ignis eliciendi modis', *Harvard Studies in Classical Philology* 1 (1890), 13–64, especially 48–50.

[34] A good example is Cic., *Phil.* II. 85: *Tu diadema imponebas cum plangore populi.*

[35] This is the version given by the scholiast on Theocritus II. 45, and assumed by Kroll in line 58.

[36] See G. P. Goold's review of Mynors' text, *Phoenix* 12 (1958) 105.

[37] Lucretius II. 581–2. *Cf.* also III. 304: *suffundens caecae caliginis umbra.*

[38] In addition to the commentaries, the reader will find much of value in Fr. Klingner's long and learned study, 'Catulls Peleus-Epos', *Sitzungsberichte der bayrischen Akademie der Wissenschaften* (1956) 6. Other recent studies of Poem 64 indicating that a revaluation of the poem is imminent are: C. S. Floratos, 'Ueber das 64. Gedicht Catulls' (1957)—like Klingner's a detailed commentary; Michael C. J. Putnam, 'The art of Catullus 64', *HSCP* 65 (1961) 165–205, which shows how much the poem implies attitudes expressed explicitly in the short poems; and Douglas F. S. Thomson, 'Aspects of unity in Catullus 64', *CJ* 57 (1961) 49–57, a study of the way in which the poem is held together by recurring themes.

TIBULLUS: *TERSUS ATQUE ELEGANS**

J. P. Elder

'EVERY established writer exists in the aura of his legend—the accumulated opinion that we cannot help being aware of, the image of his personality that has been derived, correctly or incorrectly, from what he has written'.[1] Lionel Trilling was writing about Jane Austen. I shall not argue that the legend in the case of the Augustan elegist is as compelling as that surrounding Miss Austen. But all the same the legend about Tibullus is an active one and, I believe, in many respects incorrect.

Here it is: a simple, unruffled and unruffling poet who, if not downright anaemic, at least lacked forceful creative talents.[2] The myth about Catullus grants him personal intensity, that about Propertius passion and rough realism, that about Ovid lively imagination and smooth brilliance. But what is said of Tibullus? 'The simple delicacy of Tibullus has a winsomeness of its own, which is totally distinct from the bold inventions of Propertius and the sparkling vivacity of Ovid'.[3] Why should Tibullus nowadays trail the other elegists?

Let me say at once that I am not proposing to contend that Tibullus should head the list. The myth about him, like all myths, contains some truth. But it also, in my opinion, hides part of the truth, and so I should like to try here to right the balance a bit.

Perhaps one reason for the unenthusiastic evaluation which the

* I wish here to thank Professor Georg Luck, for the constant help I have obviously had from his penetrating *The Latin Love-Elegy*, and Professors Wendell Clausen, Elizabeth Evans, and Michael Putnam for their comments on what I have proposed in this essay.

nineteenth and twentieth centuries—nor at all true of the eighteenth—have generally given Tibullus is that he deliberately cultivated the restrained manner of writing which the Alexandrians called the 'slender style', and the result of his self-discipline looks 'simple'. Well, it is simple, and perhaps today's judgement of Tibullus merely reflects the taste and disposition of our age. But in the forties, thirties, and twenties of the last century B.C. the 'slender style' was admired at Rome. Virgil had used it in his youth, in the *Eclogues*, written between 42 and 37 B.C. Tibullus published the first of his two books of elegies only a decade or so later, around 26 B.C. Subscribing to the poetics of the most influential of the Alexandrians, Callimachus (*c.* 305–*c.* 240 B.C.), Virgil in his sixth eclogue, which contains a kind of brief for his writing the first pastorals in Latin, has Apollo say to him, Virgil:

> . . . pastorem, Tityre, pinguis
> pascere oportet ovis, deductum dicere carmen. (4–5)

the sheep a shepherd tends, Tityrus, should be fat,
but his song should be FINELY-SPUN.

So, too, Horace generally adhered to the same doctrine in his *Odes*:[4]

> . . . mihi parva rura et
> spiritum Graiae tenuem Camenae
> Parca non mendax dedit et malignum
> spernere volgus. (2.16.37 ff.)

Fate, who does not deceive, has given me a few acres and the SLENDER inspiration of the Greek Muse and the power to scorn the spiteful mob.

The 'slender style' in any age is rarely, if ever, directed to the 'many', but rather to the 'cultivated', and Ovid could not have chosen a better epithet for Tibullus than *cultus*.

To go back to Horace and the 'slender style', we may now perhaps understand why Horace was benign, if somewhat fatherly, to Tibullus, but fairly acid to Propertius.[5] This might seem strange, since Virgil, Horace, and Propertius all belonged to the same literary circle, that of Augustus' unofficial Minister of Propaganda and Grand Patron of the Arts, Maecenas. Tibullus, on the other hand, was a member of the poetic circle of Messalla Corvinus, one of the few republicans who dared to be independent or at least neutral in the politically dangerous decade of the twenties of the last century B.C. Further, Tibullus and Propertius were certainly rivals in the same genre. Indeed, Propertius' first book of elegies, his *Cynthia Monobiblos*, so called because it is mostly about his love for Cynthia, proabably appeared only a very short time before Tibullus' first book. Horace must have seen clearly that his openly expressed preference would not be without its influence. Why, then, his different attitude toward these two elegists?

Propertius wrote in a style that was frequently turgid and sometimes tortured and bombastic. Words under his guidance are compelled to take on unusual meanings; the syntax is twisted; his mythological allusions are often involved, obscure, and almost always demand study. Tibullus is quite the opposite. Tibullus and Propertius—it is almost as if we were contrasting Wyatt and Surrey, or Schumann and Berlioz, or in our own age, though no parallel goes on all fours, the two Harvard classmates Frost and Stevens. No wonder that Horace, whose natural bent would incline him toward the quiet statement and the economical expression, paid no heed to 'party lines' in his estimate of the two.

Possibly Tibullus' error was that he never discussed his poetic theories, but simply practised them. In this respect he is unlike the other Augustan poets who, at times, can be quite self-conscious on this score.

At all events, to return to the usual picture of Tibullus and to question parts of the picture, mere 'winsomeness' and 'simple delicacy' do not seem enough to account for antiquity's estimate of this poet. Thus, to his tributes to Lucretius and Virgil, Ovid at once joins his praise of Tibullus:

> donec erunt ignes arcusque Cupidinis arma,
> discentur numeri, culte Tibulle, tui.
>
> (Amores, 1.15.27 f.)

as long as fires and the bow are the weapons of Cupid,
elegant Tibullus, then men will learn your rhythms by heart.

And upon the death of Tibullus in 19 B.C. Ovid wrote the moving elegy beginning:

> Memnona si mater, mater ploravit Achillem,
> et tangunt magnas tristia fata deas,
> flebilis indignos, Elegeia, solve capillos.
>
> (Amores 3.9)

If a mother bewailed Memnon, if a mother bewailed Achilles, and if sad fates touch mighty goddesses, then weep, Elegy, and loose your unwilling locks.[6]

Nor will just the Dresden-like virtues of 'winsomeness' and 'delicacy' account for the unequivocal comment of the critic Quintilian (*c*. A.D. 35–*c*. 100):

Elegia quoque Graecos provocamus, cuius mihi tersus atque elegans maxime videtur auctor Tibullus. Sunt qui Propertium malint.

(Inst. Orat. 10.1.93)

In elegy also we challenge the Greeks. Of our elegiac poets Tibullus seems especially to possess a pure and elegant style. There are those who prefer Propertius.

Ovid called Tibullus *cultus*, and a century later Quintilian calls him *elegans*. Both are trying to describe Tibullus' discreet style of writing: the purity of his diction, the straightforwardness of his syntax, the directness of his comparisons. To find the right word is harder now than it was in the Roman world. Our own eighteenth century's 'elegant' is still probably the best.

By now we may see some of the elements which helped form the legend about Tibullus. Let me continue with the legend by giving one more quotation. It gives an accurate summary of modern 'learned' interest in Tibullus. Professor T. E. Wright declared: 'Although, in the judgment of Quintilian, Tibullus was the best of the Latin elegiac poets, he has during the last fifty years been a comparatively neglected author. The slender bulk of his writings, the perspicuity of his Latin, and his simple themes of love and country life present no strong challenge to scholarship and offer but little scope for a new assessment'.[7]

Professor Wright is speaking of classical scholarship, and not about the authors whom classical scholars read when they read for pleasure. But we may suspect that the professional interests of classical scholarship indirectly affect the private inclinations of classical scholars, and that Tibullus is about as much neglected by the latter as by the former. At all events, it is correct to say that Tibullus offers few problems for scholarship, though we may hope that this conclusion does not rule out the possibility of a 'new assessment'. True, there is always the question of what poems in the collection which has come down to us under his name (the *corpus Tibullianum*) were actually written by Tibullus, and then of what authors wrote the other poems.[8] But this is no very worthy problem. We know fairly well what is genuinely Tibullan, and most of the other poems are not fit fare for the common reader and a hard diet even for the scholar.[9]

So we come back to Professor Wright's facts: Tibullus did not write much, he wrote clearly and we understand him, and he wrote about 'simple themes', such as his love for Delia or Nemesis, the Italian countryside which is really one of his 'loves', the rustic gods of old, his hatred of war, and his scorn of wealth and understandable fear of poverty—

> Content to live, this is my stay:
> I seek no more than may suffice.

'Simple' perhaps implies among other things 'clear', in the sense that the comprehension of his themes does not depend upon an almost Alexandrian grasp of recondite mythology. To understand the full scope of Propertius' themes, on the other hand, often means working one's way through the complicated careers, generally erotically complicated, of frequently minor mythological heroines. With him mythology is truly functional. With Tibullus mythological allusions are few and then mainly decorative. They offer no particular puzzles.

It was said above that the legend about Tibullus, like most myths, contains some truth. Let me first deal with this element of truth.

The correct part of the legend lies in the general implication that Tibullus is not a poet of 'classical' rank, no Virgil or Horace. His was not what Dr. Johnson called a 'mind of large, general powers'. The myth does not imply that he was mediocre, but that he lacked in his handling of diction, imagery, and mythology, and in his idyllic creations, the governed looseness, the tensile suggestiveness, and the fanciful inventiveness which make a poet deeply emotive. We may well believe that he was keenly aware of his own native limitations, and that he chose carefully to work within them—which is saying a good deal for anyone. The result is poetry that has many virtues, and that rightly has become part of the funded excellence of Augustan verse. But we shall look at his poetic merits and weaknesses later on. Right now I should like to continue with the legend about him, and move to what seems incorrect in the legend.

The untruthful part is the picture of Tibullus as weak and wishy-washy, a dabbler in winsome sweetness. Rather, on closer examination he emerges as a poet who knew what he wanted to write about, knew how he wanted to write it, and knew what ultimate poetic tone or colour he was aiming at. Toward this end, he determined his way, the Tibullan way. He chose for himself a purity of diction and a lucid syntax. He deliberately limited the allusive range of his similes and metaphors, and in conscious self-irony at times even 'undercut' the emotional effect he had been creating. He elected—surely his own, private, psychological reaction to the Augustan Revolution—to make his pastoral, idyllic world blurred and hazy, but also to make the actual world of the City equally indistinct. What he says of life in Rome is mostly 'selected bits and fragments'. The contrast between the clarity of his verbal expression and the mistiness of his two worlds of the countryside and of Rome provides, in its faint self-mockery, the tension which he sought for his verse and which makes it 'work'. Unlike Propertius, Tibullus set himself the task of weaving together in an elegy a number of different themes joined in an easy and unobtrusive fashion; he always avoided what might possibly seem to be an overstatement of any one topic or mood.

These facts suggest a poet of quietly firm and independent views, and they seem to deny most of the myth. To support this opinion, let me begin with the influence of politics upon literature.

Tibullus is the only major Augustan poet who mentions neither Augustus (Octavian) nor his chief advisers like Maecenas or Agrippa. Tibullus is the only poet of the times who does not laud aspects of imperial policy. He is the only poet who does not try to write works whose subjects might please the emperor, such as the *Georgics* or the *Aeneid*, Horace's *Roman Odes* (3.1–6), Propertius' fourth book of elegies, or Ovid's *Fasti*.[10] Indeed, unlike the others, he does not even bother to beg to be excused from such lofty attempts.[11] All in all, a remarkable silence.

To move on to letters, what does Tibullus have to say about other poets, dead or alive? Nothing. In fact, he is the only major Augustan poet who mentions neither literary predecessors who might be his professed models nor contemporary poets who might champion or at least support him. We think of Catullus, who lightly names earlier and living poets, good and bad; of Virgil, who even brings his living friend Gallus into the company of Orpheus, Linus, and Hesiod, a daring compliment indeed; of Horace, who a bit self-protectively lists the poets whom he admires and who are his friends, and the poets whom he and his friends despise; and of Ovid, who never can be too generous in hailing a host of fellow poets and the great ones now dead. Further, these poets, proudly but yet hopefully, name their ancient models. Thus Propertius, perhaps more concerned specifically himself with the Alexandrian tradition than any of the others, begins his third book with the impressive:

> Callimachi Manes et Coi sacra Philitae,
> in vestrum, quaeso, me sinite ire nemus.

Shades of Callimachus and holy rites of Philetas of Cos,
permit me, I pray, to enter your grove.

But from Tibullus, no ancients and no moderns. That he had steeped himself in the Alexandrian poets is clear, despite his best efforts to conceal the fact.[12] But he takes no shelter, no refuge, in an appeal to their names, let alone to their shades. That he had friends who were poets, and good poets, is also clear. Horace addressed two poems to him and, as we have seen, Ovid wrote a dirge on his death. It must be a matter of Tibullus' scorning the support which personal reference to the leading poets of his day might give him. This silence need not be owing to natural unsociability, for Tibullus strikes us as pathetically needing love and affection. Rather, it would seem to stem from a strong artistic independence.

This characteristic is apparent in his style of writing. Plainly he had determined upon it for himself. Catullus before him had used the lusty erotic vocabulary of the common folk, and intimate colloquialisms and warm diminutives. Most of these Tibullus, unlike Propertius, eschews as if they did not exist. Propertius was forcing words to take on extraordinary meanings and was cultivating a style that was exuberant and sometimes inflated.[13] Tibullus employs words in their usual sense and prefers the quiet way. Propertius so places one word next to another that the consequently complicated syntax effectively mirrors his complicated emotions. In Tibullus the word-order is as smoothly flowing as his gently shifting thoughts and feelings. The same radical difference marks the two poets' use of imagery. As for their feelings about the role of poet, Propertius devotes an entire elegy (3.3) to his own consecration as 'sacred poet' in the best High Church fashion, but Tibullus scorns to strike the dramatic posture —a relief—or to introduce the admittedly interesting rococo apparatus of dreams, holy springs, grottoes, and hallowing Muses. He merely calls Apollo 'the inspirer of my song' (*carminis auctor Apollo*, 2.4.13).[14] But let me illustrate his way, beginning with his diction.[15]

Roughly speaking, we may say that Hellenistic scholars elaborated what the classical Greeks had instinctively felt: that there were 'higher forms' and 'lower forms'. Under 'higher forms' the Alexandrians put at the head epic and tragedy. These noblest forms called for the 'purest' diction. Then came didactic poetry and pastoral, both themselves epical forms, and elegy, and such lyrics as Horace's *Odes* and perhaps parts of his *Epodes*. The 'lower forms' included Catullus' metrically diverse little poems 1–60, Horace's *Satires* and *Epistles*, Juvenal's *Satires*, and Martial's *Epigrams*. We are concerned here, of course, only with the 'higher forms', elegy falling in this class, and specifically with what words were sanctioned for use in elegy and what were forbidden or looked down upon. We are not, naturally, thinking of any such word as the earthy *futuere* of Catullus and Martial, decently defined by the lexicon as 'to have connexion with a female'. Such words belonged to the 'satiric-epigrammatic' style of the 'lower forms' and were automatically out of the question for the Augustan elgists who were intent upon raising the dignity of their form.[16] So now let us look at what was deemed proper diction in the 'lyrical-elegiac' style.

The elegists in their vocabulary aimed at steering something of a middle course between the elevated language of epic and that of everyday, polite conversation—I do not mean the vernacular of the gutter. It is as if they wrote with one ear ambitiously turned towards Virgil and Horace and the other realistically cocked towards the circle from which they sprang and whose love-affairs they depict. Thus on the one hand they shun epic's archaisms, the antique and hallowed words. For example, epic's *extemplo*, 'at once', is found ten times in Ovid's epical *Metamor-*

phoses, and *ceu*, 'just as', nine times, but neither ever occurs in Ovid's elegies. On the other hand, the elegists let in words not considered lofty enough for epic, like the somewhat vulgar *plorare*, 'to wail, to cry', instead of the more genteel *flere*. *Plorare* is never used by the epic poets Virgil, Lucan, Valerius Flaccus, Silius Italicus, or Ovid in his *Metamorphoses*, nor by Seneca in his tragedies. But *plorare* is acceptable for works written in the 'satiric-epigrammatic' style, like Horace's *Satires* and *Epistles*, and it has even made itself respectable in the 'lyrical-elegiac' style. Thus it is found in Horace's *Odes*, and as for the elegists, Tibullus uses it twice, Propertius four times, and Ovid no less than ten times, one being at the beginning of his lament for Tibullus (see p. 67).

Now Tibullus is 'purer' than the other elegists in keeping down the number of half-vulgar words like *plorare, lassus*, 'tired', instead of *fessus, portare*, 'to carry', instead of the more dignified *ferre*. But he reveals his stylistic independence even more in his avoidance of colloquialisms and diminutives. Catullus had used these verbal intimacies plentifully, and Propertius was following him in this practice. But not Tibullus. Similarly with diminutives. Catullus had employed them abundantly and effectively to express affection and love, and so, too, in his early poems had Propertius, who in many respects must have looked upon himself as the Augustan heir of the late Republic's 'new poets'. But Propertius becomes more chary of diminutives in his later works, and here we may suspect the 'purifying' influence of Tibullus at work upon him. One point, which bears on this matter of 'pure diction', should be noted about Catullus: most of his colloquialisms and diminutives are to be found in his first sixty poems, the *nugae*—'les petits riens'—written in a variety of metres. His poems in the elegiac metre, however, most of which are also brief, have noticeably fewer such expressions.[17] Obviously Catullus, like the elegists, realized that these familiar expressions smacked too much of everyday speech to be fit for the venerable elegiac metre. After all, this metre had behind it a dignified tradition of some six hundred years.

Tibullus is equally strict with himself in avoiding the erotic terms which Catullus had popularized,[18] such words as *ludere* 'to play around in verse' and 'to play around in love', *perire*, 'to die of love', *libido*, or *medulla*, 'marrow' in the sense of 'the fires of love burning the inmost marrow', and the immortalized *deliciae*. In banning this part of the Catullan erotic apparatus, Tibullus probably determined that these words, like the colloquialisms and diminutives, were unworthy of the sort of verse he wanted to write. He may also have concluded that by now these phrases had grown trite and stale; they had lost their original thrust. Similarly, while Catullus had called Lesbia *lux mea* and Propertius had addressed his Cynthia as *mea vita* or *vita*, Tibullus, scorning a wearied metaphor between Delia and himself, calls her simply *mea Delia*.[19] His contemporaries must have caught much more than we can of the refreshing power of such 'refined' language.

To pass on to Tibullus' imagery, this is as controlled and clear as his diction. His similes are direct and 'keep their feet on the ground'. His metaphors are neither blown-up nor drawn out; at no time do they seem to have run away with him so as to create within the poem a new little poetic world of their own. All in all, Tibullus' comparisons doubtless do the task he set them. But this was no very great task, for most of them we feel to be intentionally bounded and limited, as if the poet feared that they might get out of hand. They lack depth. They fail to suggest extensions. Whether a comparison be a simile or a metaphor, whether it be drawn from everyday life or from nature or from mythology, we are very much aware that Tibullus is consciously watching to see how far the figure may project the reader. We do not, I take it, ask for 'some secret meaning, some artful allegory, or some occult intimation' in comparisons. But if we do ask, as is reasonable, for free-ranging inventiveness in imagery, we shall be disappointed in Tibullus. He wanted no such emotional 'open spaces', but a language of clarity and control. A bit later I shall suggest why he may have preferred these qualities. But first let us look further into his comparisons. Perhaps as good a way to begin as any is to see what Propertius does in this respect.

Propertius' imagery is usually involved, extended, full of insistence, and genuinely functional. To be sure, it frequently seems to struggle along its way, and it is often obscure until one has worked away at it. But generally the point comes through, and it is fair to say that his imagery in the end is the key to his verse and the source of his muscular vitality. Let me illustrate.

To give a crude summary of 1.2, Propertius says to his Cynthia that she needs no rare raiment; her own glory is enough: 'Love himself goes naked and has no love for those who make a craft out of beauty':

Nudus Amor formae non amat artificem. (1.2.8)

Suggestive enough so far. Then he touches on the stories of four heroines who shunned costly adornment, who relied on the beauty that Nature had given them, and who were *chaste*:

Illis ampla satis forma pudicitia (24)

Sufficient beauty for them was their modesty.

When we have worked our way through the myths—it takes learning and effort to comprehend Propertius—we see what he is driving at. He has used these stories so that he might pass from the absence of expensive clothing to the presence of chastity.[20] Cynthia could hardly have missed the point—'chastity' for Propertius meant 'fidelity to Propertius'—but we may wonder whether she or Propertius remembered that in the end all these heroines were abducted.

Tibullus' imagistic practice stands in sharp contrast. It is not that his comparison and allusions are merely decorative. Surely that could not be said of any good poet. Rather, they are not at all so functional as those of Propertius, and this is so because their author neither asked nor allowed them to assume such a pivotal office. Take the beginning of 1.5:

Asper eram et bene discidium me ferre loquebar;
    at mihi nunc longe gloria fortis abest.
Namque agor ut per plana citus sola verbere turben,
    quem celer adsueta versat ab arte puer.
Vre ferum et torque, libeat ne dicere quicquam
    magnificum post haec: horrida verba doma.

I was bitter, and kept saying that I could bear our separation well, but such brave boasting is now far from my heart. For I am driven like a top spinning swiftly along the even ground before the lash, when a nimble lad who knows his business has once set it twirling. Brand the wild man and torture him, that he may never again wish to talk so mightily. Tame his rough speech.

Delia and Tibullus had quarrelled; he had spoken harshly; now he cannot stand the separation. Everything is easy and straight-forward in the first couplet. The only image is the slight one in *gloria fortis*, 'courageous boastfulness', with its military overtones —the old figure of 'the lover as warrior'.

It has often been noted that Propertius, in a similar situation, began the second elegy of his second book:

> Liber eram et vacuo meditabar vivere lecto;
> at me composita pace fefellit Amor.

I was free, and was thinking of living without a mistress; but though the truce was settled, Love deceived me.

Whether or not Propertius was deliberately recalling Tibullus' couplet and recalling it in an attempt to surpass it, a comparison of the two is instructive. *Liber eram* is as simple as Tibullus' *Asper eram*, but after that Propertius packs a good deal more into his lines. Tibullus' plain statement 'I was saying that I could bear our separation well' now is changed to 'I was thinking of living in an empty bed'. The result is a stronger, more vivid line, achieved through the verb 'to live' and the figure of the 'vacant bed'. The second line in each case begins with a parallel: *at mihi* and *at me*, 'but from me' and 'but me'. Once again Propertius puts more into his line; a peace or truce had been made when Love—note the personification—deceived him.

Now let us go on with the remaining four lines of my quotation from Tibullus. The next couplet, lines 3–4, presents a comparison in the direct form of a simile. Tibullus in his helpless misery is driven along like a top. A mere boy, with the flick of a whip, makes the top spin from spot to spot. The simile is excellent for Tibullus' immediate purpose: Tibullus, the top, is powerless to resist; his passion for Delia, the lad's whip, whirls him along. The simile also illustrates what was meant above when it was said that Tibullus carefully limits the suggestiveness of his comparisons. Not only is the figure, drawn from a children's game, an old figure and not likely to move any reader by its novelty, but in itself it says what it is meant to say and no more. This kind of homely, flatly proportioned simile is not apt to set our imagination to work and induce us to go on to muse about other things. It is essentially practical and limited in its dimensions.

Lines 5–6 give us the same kind of familiar and controlled

image, this time in metaphor. Tibullus is a slave, the slave of love —again an old figure—and has been rebellious. He boasted and spoke harshly, too, but he has been caught, and now must be punished. Brands and tortures for him; he will be marked as hers and she will punish him. Again the comparison effectively does its work, but it will not extend our thoughts and feelings into deeper levels of poetic intent.

Finally, to bring these comments on Tibullus' imagery to a close, we might look at one mythological comparison. Propertius' complicated and functional use of mythology has already been touched upon. Now we should see how Tibullus handles mythological allusion.

In the same elegy we have been looking at (1.5), Tibullus says that he tried with strong drink to forget Delia. But the wine turned into tears—a pleasant conceit. He tried to make love to another girl. But just as he was about to reach the climax of pleasure (*sed iam cum gaudia adirem*), he thought of Delia, and Venus deserted him. The girl he was with, understandably indignant, declared that Delia had bewitched Tibullus. Tibullus artfully disengages himself from the question of the comparative efficacy of witchcraft and beauty in love-affairs by saying of Delia:

> Non facit hoc verbis, facie tenerisque lacertis
> devovet et flavis nostra puella comis.
> Talis ad Haemonium Nereis Pelea quondam
> vecta est frenato caerula pisce Thetis. (1.5.43 ff.)

It is not by magic charms that my girl does this. It is her beauty and soft arms and golden hair that bewitch me. Such was sea-blue Thetis, the Nereid, when in days of old she rode her bridled fish to Peleus of Haemonia.

The marriage of Peleus and Thetis was a popular and well-known myth, and whatever be the exact version that Tibullus has in mind here, the point would be clear to all readers.[21] It was Thetis' beauty that enchanted Peleus: thus does the Mermaid lure the mortal.

The whole passage is interesting from many points of view— the fact that he easily tells Delia all this, the delicate turn from wine to tears, the briefly sketched picture of the other girl and her reaction, and the skilful way Tibullus turns the argument of

77

magic versus beauty to his own purpose. Our immediate interest is in the mythological allusion that terminates the passage. Once again the comparison is admirable in that it does just what the poet wanted it to do. Thetis was beautiful—*caerula*, 'sea-blue', is enough—and she had charms. So has Delia. In both cases the magic *is* the beauty. Once again, too, we note that the image does not draw us on and on with suggestive powers, but keeps our thoughts just where Tibullus wishes them kept. Thetis is, in fact, an illustration, and appears after Tibullus has made his point: *non facit hoc verbis*, 'she does not do this through magic charms'. Hers is not the expansive role of Propertius' four heroines, who not only anticipate but actually make Propertius' point that 'chastity is enough for the beautiful'.

Now it is time to return to the legend about Tibullus, to the usual picture of an amiable but spiritless poet. The evidence is against the legend. What we have found, on the contrary, gives us quite a new picture, a picture of a man of gently tough independence who, paying little heed to the tastes of previous or contemporary Latin poets—individual elegies of Propertius must have appeared publicly while Tibullus was going his way—carefully determined what he wanted to treat, how he wanted to treat it, and what effects he sought. Let me speak for a moment about each of these three matters.

Most of his themes appear in his first elegy and so we might look into that poem. It would not, perhaps, be too much to say that he intentionally placed this elegy first in the book because it is, in fact, a very fair representative of his interests and methods. This first elegy would at once tell the reader what to expect in the volume. The poem moves effortlessly from theme to theme: scorn of wealth—dread of war—the Italian countryside—the countryside's antique gods—contrast between the olden days and the present—Delia and his wish that she and he were together in the country—war again—death—his own death and Delia's grief—so 'let me enjoy love now while I am young and financially well off.'

It will at once be seen that these themes belong to two worlds: his private idyllic pastoral world, and the actual world of Rome where men face war, the fight for wealth, and infidelity or at least frustration in love. As for why he chose these themes, I can only repeat my suggestion that they must somehow, in their combination and tone, have made up for him a satisfactory expression of his own reaction to the violent shifts and upheavals of the Augustan world and its heterogeneous society.

His manner of writing we have already examined in some detail. From this examination it seems obvious that he deliberately and carefully worked out a style that would be wonderfully clear and precise, and which would express just what he wanted said and suggest no more. This style would have delighted the purist Julius Caesar. Only fit and proper words are allowed, the words are used in their ordinary sense, the word-order itself is straightforward, the syntax is easy, and the images are reasonable and functional within their immediate context. The price of such disciplined artistry may be a lack of depth and internal movement, but the reward is lucidity and harmony of emotional colours.

Now, why *these* themes, and why *this* manner of writing? What effects was Tibullus aiming at? What impression did he wish finally to leave upon his reader?

To find the answer, we should begin with the world in which most of his themes lie, that is, with *his* brand of the pastoral. The pastoral, as everyone knows, is a most difficult genre; the dangers of inanity or silliness lie all about the pastoral poet. He must extract from our world, from the real world, what measure of goodness and innocence we have, and compound his bucolic world out of these qualities of purity. His bucolic world, then, will be Utopian, but all the same it must have the features of reality. We must be able, by suspension or what you will, to give credence to it. The countryside and its shepherds must be painted in strong, clear lines. They must seem real, if only for a moment.

Virgil succeeds at this task. In his *Eclogues* the countryside may usually be rich and sunny, but we believe in it. His rural folk are solid, substantial people. Stroke and movement are firm and sharp. It may be Arcadia, but Arcadia must seem likely either to have existed somewhere sometime, or even to be not too far away from us now—if only we could find it.

This 'pastoral realism' is indispensable, since the key to pastoral poetry lies in the implied or suggested contrast between the created Arcadian world of goodness and our own actual world of virtues and vices. To make the contrast, each world must be convincingly sketched. The mind knows, of course, that the idyll is impossible.

It is the heart that has been at work. Yet, though the mind knows there is no Arcadia, the mind gains a measure of expanded freedom within our own world merely by having looked at Arcadia. We see what our life *could* be like. Herein lies the moral quality of good pastoral poetry.[22]

But what of Tibullus' pastoral world? Unlike Virgil, Tibullus, as we have noted, draws his pastoral world and its folk with indistinct lines and misty hues. Generalization and wish mingle with description. We have no clear idea of specific landscape, nor of season, nor of weather, nor of the people—their work and their aspirations. There are too many verbs in the subjunctive mood—the indicative is the mood of strict reality—and most of these subjunctives express Tibullus' hopes. For example, in that same first elegy he says:

> Ipse seram teneras maturo tempore vites
>   rusticus et facili grandia poma manu;
> nec Spes destituat, sed frugum semper acervos
>   praebeat et pleno pinguia musta lacu.
> Nam veneror, seu stipes habet desertus in agris
>   seu vetus in trivio florida serta lapis,
> et quodcumque mihi pomum novos educat annus,
>   libatum agricolae ponitur ante deo.
> Flava Ceres, tibi sit nostro de rure corona
>   spicea, quae templi pendeat ante fores,
> pomosisque ruber custos ponatur in hortis,
>   terreat ut saeva falce Priapus aves. (1.1.7 ff.)

May I myself become a peasant and with easy hand, when the time is ripe, plant the tender vines and the sturdy fruit trees. May Hope not leave me but always grant me heaps of grain and rich new wine in full vat. For I reverence the gods, whether a deserted tree-trunk in the fields or an ancient stone at the cross-roads holds their flowery garlands,[23] and the first fruit that the new year brings forth for me I lay as an offering before the farmer's god. Yellow-haired Ceres, grant me from my land a wreath of grain to hang before your temple's doors. And may red Priapus be set up as a protector in my fruit-filled gardens, to scare off the birds with his cruel pruning-hook.

The pastoral apparatus is here. The softly romantic mood is set ('tender', 'deserted', 'ancient').[24] But Tibullus' prayers keep coming in, and thus the total effect is blurred. The result, unlike

Virgil's, is that his countryside is neither robust nor clear. Mistiness hangs low over it, and people, gods, shepherds, shrines, fields, trees, and fruits all quietly merge in muted tones. It is a world of mood and not of place, a world of past and present commingled, a dreamlike world of escape, located somewhere between Arcadia and the forum.

But now, what of the world of Rome? How clear is that in his verse? If anything, it is even less distinct, or rather less complete, than the bucolic world. Elements from life in the City appear, but not in any detailed, descriptive manner. Rome enters in the theme of war, but only in the most general terms. We recall that Tibullus spent many years in the army, journeying to such far-away spots as Palestine and the Nile. He was even decorated! But he gives us no specific items about his soldiering, not even about the exotic cities and kingdoms he visited, save at the start of 1.7. What he says about warfare and military duty mostly consists of his loathing for this way of life. Then, too, Rome comes into his elegies in the form of her national passion, the greed for wealth. But Tibullus, unlike most Roman poets, is no satirist;[25] he gives no concrete description of this madness, though he shares the satirists' moral or supposedly moral disapprobation of covetousness. Finally, Rome appears in the theme of love, for love in Tibullus' countryside is not love as the peasants knew it—whatever that might have been—but the complicated and refined business of a wealthy and largely idle urban class.

There had developed in Alexandrian poetry the stock theme of the lover shut out by his mistress, the *exclusus amator*.[26] The theme was passed on to Roman poets, and no doubt to a measure the theme actually reflected a not uncommon situation in Roman society as it probably had in Alexandrian. Either the mistress is prevented by the agents of the prophylactic man who maintains her from letting in another lover, or she thinks it good psychology to keep a lover waiting, or she is indulging in the age-old ploy of deliberately lingering over her make-up, or she has another lover inside, or is expecting another lover. Since frustrated or unhappy love is the standard fare of the elegiac poets—they could never have written whole elegies about successful love—this urban theme of the 'excluded lover' is bound to recur in the Latin elegiac poets again and again in one form or another. Thus Tibullus in his very first elegy:

me retinent vinctum formosae vincla puellae,
et sedeo duras ianitor ante fores. (1.1.55 f.)

I am a captive held fast by the bonds of a lovely girl, and I sit a doorkeeper before her unfeeling portals.

Or in the fifth, when things have grown even worse:

Heu canimus frustra, nec verbis victa patescit
ianua, sed plena est percutienda manu. (1.5.67 f.)

Alas, I sing in vain. The door will not be won over, will not open to words. It is only a well-filled palm that should do the knocking.

So love as it is realistically conducted at Rome—*la dolce vita*—sounds a strident note every now and then in Tibullus' idyllic symphony.

To sum up the matter of 'realism' in Tibullus, his pastoral world has a dreamy indistinctiveness about it. As for the hard life of the actual world of Rome, on the other hand, his references here are too general and too few to give us any very precise picture. What happens, then, when one world in his poetry confronts the other?

We said before that the success of pastoral poetry depends upon presenting Arcadia so clearly and so sharply delineated that, if only for a moment, it seems 'real' to the reader. Then, but only then, we inevitably contrast Arcadia with New York City. The pastoral poet, through delicate references, may recall the actual world, or he may stick entirely to his bucolic realm and leave the real world entirely up to the reader. Virgil follows the first method in his first *Eclogue*. Tityrus lives secure in the pastoral enclave, while Meliboeus, the other shepherd, has been ejected from his farm so that a war-veteran might take it over under the the land assignments made after Philippi (42 B.C.). But in his second *Eclogue* Virgil confines himself wholly to the pastoral domain, and the reader must evoke for himself the actual world and then make his comparisons.

Now what of Tibullus' two worlds? Why these occasional intrusions of the real world into the bucolic scenes? Plainly Tibullus cannot be aiming at just what Virgil sought. Tibullus wanted to invite us, as did Virgil, to make a contrast for ourselves, but another sort of contrast. At this point we should pull ourselves up short and remember that Tibullus was not primarily a pastoral poet, but a love-elegist writing about his own love-affairs. Virgil must make his bucolic world solidly clear and convincing because only such clarity will induce the reader to oppose Arcadia to reality. This comparison, general for the general reader, is Virgil's goal. But for Tibullus the countryside may be blurred and indefinite, because it is merely his own, private, personal background for the analysis of his own private, personal love-affairs. The reality of life in Rome may suddenly appear here and there upon the scene because it literally did so appear in his relations with a Delia or a Nemesis. Tibullus is not inviting the reader to contrast the world as it might be and the world as it is, though he himself often makes such a contrast. His real purpose, rather, is to invite the reader to enter into his, Tibullus', life, and to see what Tibullus dreamed of and what actually happened to his dreams—love as he wished it were and love as it turned out to be, and the consequent effects upon himself.

Hence it is that when Rome enters Tibullus' idylls, it generally 'undercuts' the wishes and hopes that had made up his dream. It is as if he is determined not to leave his dream alone, undisturbed, but to burst in upon it and scatter it. This, we may be sure, is what Rome did to Tibullus, and therefore his elegies mirror his own psychological reactions to the Augustan society and that society's values.[27] War and campaigning had actually taken him away for years from what he really cared for—pure love in an innocent countryside, or so he thought. Similarly the threat of poverty—the wholesale redistribution of land in the settlement after Philippi had grave economic consequences—seemed to him another potential attack upon his happiness.

These are the ominous Roman chords which enter into his counter-point. Or Death, for which the Augustan world could hardly be called responsible unless through wars, suddenly rings through to affect all that the poet has said and felt. No sooner in the first elegy has he declared to Delia 'only let me live with you' (*tecum dum modo sim*) than he proceeds to 'undercut' his dream by at once adding:

> Te spectem, suprema mihi cum venerit hora,
>   et teneam moriens deficiente manu. (59 f.)

May I gaze upon you when my last hour comes, and as I die may I hold you with failing hand.

This may be—indeed it is—sentimentalism,[28] but it too can under-mine the dream-fantasy. This dread of death, strong and morbid, owes its origin to some arcane psychological source, perhaps partly to be located in the contending forces of a large urban centre. At all events, this fear, this theme, functions like the themes of war and lack of faith and covetousness to knock down the idyll that has just been carefully and lovingly created.

This emotional 'undercutting' is especially frequent in the case of his hopes for a happy love. For example, to go back to the elegy we looked at before (p. 75 ff.), the fifth of the first book, Tibullus there bares to Delia what he had yearned for—and the result:

> At mihi felicem vitam, si salva fuisses,
> fingebam demens et renuente deo. (19 f.)

But I used to dream of a happy life for myself, if only you were spared. I was mad, and God said No.

Despite this strictly realistic start, the poet then devotes the next fourteen lines to his idyllic aspirations: Delia in the country with him, Delia watching the threshers, Delia counting the flock, Delia sacrificing to the rural divinities, and finally Delia humbly entertaining the great Messalla with sweet fruit. But at once Tibullus sweeps the spell away:

> Haec mihi fingebam, quae nunc Eurusque Notusque
> iactat odoratos vota per Armenios. (35 f.)

These were my dreams and my prayers. Now the East wind and the South wind toss them over all of perfumed Armenia.

And there follows the passage which we quoted above, in which he almost flauntingly declares that he had tried to forget Delia with strong drink and other women.

The instinct to 'undercut' his idyll must originate in large part from life at Rome as he found it. That life drove him to his dreams, and that same life made him masochistically snap the dream-thread. Both instincts reflect the urge he must have felt somehow to try to come to a conscious definition of what he was and should be in his actual circumstances, that is, these instincts are intimately connected with the necessity he felt for making his own judge-ments upon himself in terms of the reality of life in Rome. To say that he did not succeed is virtually to say that we have his poems about his unresolved problem. For us, the readers, the final result is the pull we feel between his two worlds, and it is this tension beneath the quiet exterior of his verse that gives it an arresting emotional vitality.

To close this section on Tibullus' artistic methods and aims, let me pick up the words 'tension' and 'quiet exterior'. The ultimate tension in Tibullus, the hidden clash that makes him an interesting and at times even dramatic poet, lies in the contrast between the amazing clarity of his manner of writing and the obscurity of what he actually wanted in life. Nothing could be clearer than his vocabulary, imagery, and syntax; nothing more limpid than the flow of his rhythms. But nothing could be more unclear than the effect which the impingement of the real world had upon his pastoral world of dreams. This confusion, felt by a sensitive man living in Augustus' materialistic metropolis, would seem to have every stamp of validity. We may be sure that in Tibullus' elegies we have an authentic picture of a personal struggle between an individual and society.

Now that we have examined the legend about Tibullus and questioned a good deal of the 'accumulated opinion' about him as an artist, it is time to see what in fact we know about his life and about the people to whom he addresses his elegies.

The external sources for Tibullus' life are few and brief. We learn even less from his poems, since what is personal in them is the expression of their author's feelings. He was not interested in telling us where he was born or lived, or at what hour he generally arose, or how he revolted against his father, or the like.

The outside sources of information about his life consist of references made to him by other poets—Horace wrote *Odes* 1.33 and *Epistles* 1.4 to him and Ovid not only mentions Tibullus several times but composed a poem on his death (*Amores* 3.9)— and we also have preserved a truncated medieval *Life* and four quite elegant but not very helpful lines of an epigram upon Virgil and Tibullus, written by a minor Augustan, Domitius Marsus.

The epigram suggests that he may have been born in the late fifties—we do not know where—and tells us that he died early, in fact in the same year as Virgil, 19 B.C. Hence the genesis of the epigram. The *Life* gives us a few more shreds. He came of an equestrian family, which in our terminology would mean that he belonged to the upper middle class. He was handsome and elegant in manner. He was deeply fond of Messalla Corvinus, and served on his staff in the war against the Aquitani in 27 B.C.

From Horace's *Epistle* we learn more about Tibullus, and something, too, about Horace. Tibullus, says Horace, has everything one could ask for: the gift of criticism, the gift of poetry, fame, beauty, wealth, and the art of enjoyment. Is Tibullus, asks Horace, even now writing verse that will outdo a recent success, or is he strolling in the woods and pondering what befits a man who is wise and good?

> Non tu corpus eras sine pectore: di tibi formam,
> di tibi divitias dederunt artemque fruendi.
> (Epist. 1.4.6 f.)

You were never a body without mind and heart. The gods have given you beauty; the gods have given you wealth and the art of enjoyment.

The implication is obvious. Don't waste your time, Tibullus, moping, but use your talents and think thoughts worthy of you—which you're not doing. Equally clear is what is intended by the omission of any mention of love, let alone of Tibullus' current love-affair—which surely is what indeed Tibullus is languishing over. Yet Horace's whole tone is affectionate and warm. It is easy to see that he liked Tibullus, and admired his poetic abilities, though not his elegiac subjects. These are unworthy of him. All this Horace says pleasantly but more directly in his *Ode*:

> Albi, ne doleas plus nimio memor
> inmitis Glycerae neu miserabilis
> decantes elegos, cur tibi iunior
> laesa praeniteat fide. (Carm. 1.33.1 ff.)

Albius, do not grieve overmuch, thinking of heartless Glycera, and do not keep droning out your piteous elegiacs that ask why a younger rival now shines brighter for her and why she has broken her pledge.

This, says Horace pretty bluntly, is Venus' way! A girl turns from man to man, and a man from one girl to another, and Venus enjoys it all. I know, confesses Horace sympathetically, from my own younger days. Though Horace's ending is charity itself, the point about Tibullus' melancholic brooding over unsuccessful love is plain. His elegies confirm Horace's innuendos.

So much for what we learn from outside sources about the 'facts' of Tibullus' life, and about his 'temperament'. Horace's remarks about the latter we can check from the elegies themselves, and we need not spend time proving him right or wrong. As for the total number of 'facts', their very scantiness may in the end prove to be a blessing, for they are too few in number to give us any very substantial help in reconstructing for the poet a hypothetical 'life', upon the basis of which we might then arbitarily interpret the elegies. The biographical approach to Latin elegy ignores the truth that this kind of poetry is at once highly personal and also highly general. It is personal in that the poet, analysing the psychology of love, treats love as he *himself* helplessly feels its power. The experiences out of which he writes are deeply private. But the material he handles, the concept of love and the motives, are all traditional and well known. In this sense elegy is general. If we had an extended biography of Tibullus handed down to us, it would only lead critics to read a reference to this or that 'fact' into the Tibullan text. The result would be that we should not be hearing Tibullus but the biography. It has been well said of Propertius—the same would be true of Tibullus—that: 'It seems fair to assume that an understanding of the elegies requires no more information on the part of the modern reader than it did in the case of the contemporary public'.[29] We ought to be able to agree that probably all the data which we need for understanding what Tibullus meant to tell us lies within a particular elegy itself. In trying to comprehend Tibullus we cannot, thank heaven, be led very far from our main concern, which is what he himself says, by what others have told us about the 'facts' of his life.

The elegies themselves add little about this life, save to tell us of his *paupertas*, to give us a few remarks about his military service (1.7) and his patron Messalla, and apparently to say quite a deal about two women he loved.

As for the fairly unimportant business of his *paupertas*, he himself claims to have suffered loss of property (1.1.19), and doubtless his income had been reduced, perhaps like that of other poets after Philippi. It is not, it should be quickly added, that poets in those days were particularly singled out to suffer confiscation of land, but that they are the chief ones who tell us of their financial plights. Still, we should not think of Tibullus as having become a poor man. He himself tells us that he really wasn't:

> . . . . . ego conposito securus acervo
> despiciam dites despiciamque famem. (1.1.77 f.)

As for me, safe on my collected pile, I shall look down on wealth, look down on hunger.

The Augustan 'classicists', Virgil and Horace, came of genuinely humble stock, but all the elegists—I do not know whether a Marxist has noticed this fact—were of equestrian rank and, if their property had been diminished, they were still well off. Indeed, an Augustan elegiac poet had better be, if he were adequately to play about town the expensive role of a gallant and idle gentleman of intrigue.

His patron, Messalla Corvinus, is a much more significant factor in his life than his financial state. Tibullus mentions him frequently—Messalla enters over a third of the elegies—and he mentions him with obvious devotion. Messalla was a distinguished general, orator, and statesman, a man of sturdy but not troublesome republican instincts, and a beneficent supporter of letters. He not only gathered about himself a group of poets of whom, to judge from what we may read in the *corpus Tibullianum*, far and away the best was Tibullus, but he was a critic as well. 'Scrupulously careful about good Latinity', notes Seneca the Elder (*c.* 55 B.C.–*c.* A.D. 40),[30] and doubtless Messalla encouraged Tibullus in his resolve to write 'pure Latin'. The literary tastes of the two men must have been congenial.

Tibullus did not, then, belong to the imperial circle of Maecenas, of which Virgil, Horace, and the perhaps slightly uncomfortable Propertius, were members. This did not mean that Messalla's group was anti-governmental—Asinius Pollio would have been a better candidate for such a leadership than Messalla—but that the latter's circle remained aloof from the affairs of the régime. This may partly explain the absence of imperial references in Tibullus' poetry.

Now at last to Tibullus' women. To qualify in neo-classical terms as a Latin elegist, a poet had to publish a whole book of elegies, that is, of longish poems in elegiac verse, and only one woman could be celebrated in the book. Hence we understand why Catullus, though he had written three lengthy elegies (66, 67, and 68), was not included by the canonical Quintilian in his list of elegiac poets. The book, though devoted to one woman, might be dedicated to someone else. Both of Tibullus' are dedicated to his patron—quite naturally. But one woman must dominate. In Tibullus' first book, it is Delia; in his second, a low creature with the appropriate name of Nemesis.

Of the ten elegies of Book 1, five contain addresses to this Delia (1, 2, 3, 5, and 6). No. 7 treats the triumph of Messalla, and no. 10, a most revealing poem, inveighs against war, avarice, the breaking of one's word, and modern ways in general, and gives us the best statement we have of what Tibullus disliked and what he wanted, as man and as artist. The three other poems tell of a boy-favourite (4, 8, and 9), the first two of which call the *puer delicatus* Marathus.

About Delia herself, the poet is vague. Propertius revels in listing Cynthia's beauties and in sensuously enumerating her charms. But about Delia, we know no more than that she had soft arms and long golden hair—hardly distinctive features for a mistress! We are also told that at one time she had a *coniunx*— this is not a husband but the man who is currently keeping her— and that she was unfaithful to him by simply taking on a third lover. Obviously she was a typical, hard-working courtesan of considerable attraction, but indistinguishable from her sisters.

In no. 1 Tibullus imagines that Delia might be with him in his country world. Underneath, of course, he knows this to be impossible. Quite apart from her financial interests in Rome, Delia most surely would have been bored to death out on Tibullus' acres. But at least Tibullus can dream about the possibility. In no. 2 her *coniunx*, who has temporarily left Rome, has prudently had Delia put under watch, and Tibullus, the *exclusus amator*, is shut out. So far no one can definitely blame Delia herself. In no. 3 Tibullus lies sick at Corcyra—this is what comes of going to war with Messalla—and recalls that Delia had made vows for his safe return. If he dies now, let this epitaph be graven on his tombstone:

HIC IACET INMITI CONSVMPTVS MORTE TIBVLLVS,
MESSALLAM TERRA DVM SEQVITVRQVE MARI
(1.3.55 f.)

HERE LIES TIBULLUS, CONSUMED BY HEARTLESS DEATH
WHILE HE FOLLOWED MESSALLA ON LAND AND SEA.

We may smile, but, as we have observed, for Tibullus death had
a pathological fascination. He closes the elegy more hopefully:
'be chaste, Delia'. In no. 5 she has taken on a rich lover, she and
Tibullus have quarrelled, she has shut him out and, capable girl,
she has even acquired an additional lover besides the rich one.
But Tibullus, darting from point to point in his painful analysis,
still for a moment pictures Delia in *his* countryside—pure enjoyment of misery. In the last one, no. 6, the irony is masterful. The
situation remains the same, Now however he realizes that it is he,
Tibullus, who taught her how to deceive with art and stealth.
Now *he* has become the concierge before her door!

Two things should be recalled: that Tibullus never gives us a
clear picture of Delia, and that he himself arranged the order of
these ten elegies. The second fact tells us that he wanted his love-
affair to move from dreams and hope to final disillusionment.
Excellent elegiac artistry! The drama increases, and so do the
poet's reactions—the various ways in which he probes and
studies his own private anguish. Indeed, we might say that the
key word in Latin elegy is *miser,* and that the elegist's chief art
lies in analytically holding up this *miseria* to be viewed in all its
possible facets. The situation is old, the *dramatis personae* are
stock, the motives are conventional, but the specific handling is
personal and therefore new.

When all is said and done, Delia does not matter very much. It
is the poet's unsuccessful love and his wretchedness that are
important. Or rather, it is how he looks at his situation and describes his personal state that matters. Indeed, Delia may never
have existed as one woman at all.[31] She might be a composite of
two or three or countless women Tibullus had known. What did
exist, however, were his own experiences, upon which the un-
folding of his relations with a Delia are based. It is in these
experiences, not in Delia as he paints her, that reality lies.

Now perhaps, we may gain a better perspective on the affair
of the 'delicate lad'. It is not of moment whether he, too, ever
existed, or whether Tibullus had such boy-favourites. He probably did, but that is neither here nor there for our purposes. What
is noteworthy is the position of the Marathus-poems.

The first of these is no. 4, itself a kind of love-elegy in didactic guise. Priapus—who better?—tells the poet how to win the lad Marathus. In the preceding two poems Tibullus' suspicions and torments over Delia had been building up, clashing more insistently with his futile hopes. The *At tu casta precor maneas*: 'But you, I beg you, remain chaste', at the end of no. 3 (line 83) is cast in the form of a prayer or wish, but in actuality it is a statement of torturing disillusionment. The sudden shift now from Delia to Marathus at once sustains the theme of Tibullus' unsuccessful love, but at the same time it puts the poet and his reactions to unrequited love in a new, a more distant, focus. No. 4 is, in fine, a reflective pause after the fever of no. 3. That it is only a pause in the Delia-sequence is shown by the poet's immediate return in no. 5 to Delia:

Asper eram et bene discidium me ferre loquebar.

I was bitter, and kept saying that I could bear our separation well.

The position of the other two boy-poems is equally deliberate —no. 8 and no. 9. Then in no. 10 bursts out the full agony and disenchantment as the poet studies himself and life—what the relationship between the two ought to be and what it really is. The striking fact that he does not even mention Delia in this final elegy makes it abundantly clear that it is not she, but he himself, who really matters.

To glance at the people who appear in one or another of the six elegies of the second book, they are new faces save for Messalla, and no more important than the old ones. An unknown Cornutus has a birthday poem addressed to him (no. 2) and no. 3 again salutes him, though this poem in reality is concerned with quite another person, Nemesis. It is she who has supplanted or replaced Delia, and she appears in nos. 3–6.

Nemesis is well named—a harder and more flagrantly covetous courtesan than Delia. Like Delia, and perhaps even more so, she doubtless is merely a *pastiche*. But what she shows us is important. Tibullus' existence and the experiences out of which he compounded Nemesis have plainly become harder and bitterer. All through the second book the sharp, realistic 'undercutting' is much more frequent than in the first book. Even in its opening elegy, addressed to Messalla and describing a country festival and country life, the specific realistic touches have wiped away much of the idyllic dreaminess of the first book's Arcadia. In the tension which Tibullus felt between his ideal Golden-Age countryside and the corrosive features of Rome, it is the City now which is exerting the stronger pull. This becomes clear through his reactions to Nemesis, and the very first elegy about her, no. 3, analyses this tension.

Nemesis has been taken to the country by a rich lover. In the case of Delia, we recall, the poet had only dreamed that she might be in the country (1.5.21 ff.). But Nemesis is bodily there, and if only Tibullus might see her, that is, if only she would be in the country with *him*, he would toil as hard as Apollo for Admetus:

> Felices olim, Veneri cum fertur aperte
> servire aeternos non puduisse deos.
> Fabula nunc ille est: sed cui sua cura puella est,
> fabula sit mavolt quam sine amore deus. (2.3.29 ff.)

Happy the men of old who lived in a time when they say the deathless gods themselves were not ashamed OPENLY to be slaves of love. Now a man in love is the talk of the town. But a man who loves his girl would rather be the talk of the town than a god without any love at all.

The themes of the Golden Age and the slave of love appeared, of course, in the first book. But not with quite this sharp personal application. Then the mood of the poem shifts radically. It is only money that Nemesis wants, and then follows a sensuous passage:

> Heu heu divitibus video gaudere puellas:
> iam veniant praedae, si Venus optat opes,
> ut mea luxuria Nemesis fluat utque per urbem
> incedat donis conspicienda meis.
> Illa gerat vestes tenues, quas femina Coa
> texuit, auratas disposuitque vias;
> illi sint comites fusci, quos India torret,
> Solis et admotis inficit ignis equis;
> illi selectos certent praebere colores
> Africa puniceum purpureumque Tyros. (2.3.49 ff.)

Ah, I see that girls like only men who are rich. Then let money be offered, if it is wealth that makes Venus happy, so that my Nemesis may float in luxury and move across the City while all the men stare at her, gowned in my gifts. Let her wear the soft silk which some woman of Cos wove and then striped with paths of gold. Let her have pages, dark youths from out of burning India, youths whom the Sun's fire stains as he drives his steeds so close. Let the nations vie to give her their rarest hues, Africa her crimson and Tyre her purple.

I accept, he says, the situation. I must have her. Very well, she shall blaze through Rome, and I will pay. The interlocking word-order of *mea luxuria Nemesis* could not be improved upon. Even when he had known that Delia was unfaithful, he could still dream of fidelity and hope that somehow she would seek simplicity and fit into his bucolic dream of goodness. But with Nemesis, no dreams—only realistic surrender. 'This is what Rome is like, and I must live and move within Roman terms', he declares.

Then another abrupt shift. The countryside is now charged with having taken Nemesis away from the City, where she ought to be—because there Tibullus could perhaps have her:

> Haud inpune licet formosas tristibus agris
>   abdere. (2.3.65 f.)

No one can bury an attractive girl in the dull countryside without being punished for it.

So let there be no grain growing, if only there be no girls in the country. We could live in the old-fashioned way on acorns. 'The old-fashioned way'—this suggests quite another and familiar thought: the men of old lived on acorns but *openly* made love wherever they were.

> May the days of old return, if it be right so to ask:
>
> . . . si fas est, mos precor ille redi. (2.3.74)

So now for a moment we are back in the dream-world of the earlier elegies, with even the reverential *si fas est*: 'if it be right so to ask'. But the 'openly' summons back reality, and he 'undercuts' his momentary dream by the sharp reminder that when Nemesis is in the City she is under lock and key. Therefore, 'take me away to the country; I shall abjectly plough at my Nemesis' command'. The elegy ends with the poet's once more wishing to be in the fields, as Nemesis' slave:

> Ducite: ad imperium dominae sulcabimus agros,
>   non ego me vinclis verberibusque nego. (2.3.79 f.)

Take me away. I shall plough the furrows as my mistress orders. Chains and lashes, I do not deny myself to these.

Chains and lashes—these are what Nemesis is, and at the close of all these analytical shiftings the poet candidly and almost happily confesses his utterly helpless state. It is a wearying course he had followed in this elegy, and the course of a wearied man.

The other three poems continue the black realization of what is happening to himself in his affair with Nemesis.

> Nunc et amara dies et noctis amarior umbra est,
>> omnia nunc tristi tempora felle madent.
> Nec prosunt elegi nec carminis auctor Apollo:
>> illa cava pretium flagitat usque manu. (2.4.11 ff.)

Now the day is bitter and the shadows of night are bitterer; now every moment is drenched in sour gall. Poetry is no help, no, nor Apollo who inspires my verse. Constantly she stretches out her hollow palm for money.

Nemesis is unworthy and degrading; he himself is hurt and corrupted by this passion; he is hopelessly weak! All this he understands, and likes the understanding. In the middle of this outburst he can even sound the idyllic note, saying, and knowing it to be untrue, that it is the greed of the modern world and not Nemesis who is to blame. The tension between the real and the idealized begins again, until he reaches the sentimental verdict of the aged man who places a garland on her tomb—a bit of imaginary realism which may not have appealed very much to Nemesis:

> et 'bene' discedens dicet 'placideque quiescas,
>> terraque securae sit super ossa levis.' (2.4.49 f.)

And as he goes away he will say 'Sleep well and in peace, and may the earth be light upon your untroubled bones.'

Even in his last elegy, no. 6, out of his slavery arises hope:

> Spes facilem Nemesim spondet mihi, sed negat illa. (2.6.27)

Hope promises me that Nemesis will be good to me, but Nemesis herself says No.

This pull between fact and hope, between his realization of what is being done to him and his dream of what might be done for him, this is the stuff out of which his poetry is made, and he knows it. That he knows it, throughout all his tortured self-examination, is evidenced by the line just quoted. He may tell us that he is torn between hope and despair, and he may almost openly rejoice in his own emotional infirmity, but all the same a strong artistic control dictated the polished antithesis of this almost epigrammatic line. It is from this fascinating contrast between *what* Tibullus says about himself and *how* he says it, this contrast between emotional debility and sure artistic mastery, that much of his quiet appeal arises. He may never sweep one away in a passionate avalanche, but he will hardly ever bore the reader who has a cultivated respect for the artful manipulation of words themselves, an instinctive feel for the appropriate image, and a sensitive ear for pliable rhythms.

Up to now a good deal has been said about Tibullus, but he himself has hardly had a chance to get a word in. The extracts quoted have been scrappy and they were always cited for an immediate purpose. But if we are to have this poet fairly set before us, we need an entire elegy. At the very least, the full text, if read aloud, will reveal his easy-flowing and melodious versification— a subject almost impossible to discuss and yet easily comprehended by oral trial.[32] I propose, therefore, to close this essay with the text and a translation of an elegy already referred to several times, the fifth of the first book, and with a few comments which may pull together some of the points previously made.

1.5: *To Delia*

Asper eram et bene discidium me ferre loquebar,
    at mihi nunc longe gloria fortis abest.
Namque agor ut per plana citus sola verbere turben,
    quem celer adsueta versat ab arte puer.
5   Vre ferum et torque, libeat ne dicere quicquam
    magnificum post haec: horrida verba doma.
Parce tamen, per te furtivi foedera lecti,
    per venerem quaeso conpositumque caput.
Ille ego, cum tristi morbo defessa iaceres,
10   te dicor votis eripuisse meis,
ipseque te circum lustravi sulpure puro,
    carmine cum magico praecinuisset anus;
ipse procuravi, ne possent saeva nocere
    somnia, ter sancta deveneranda mola;
15   ipse ego velatus filo tunicisque solutis
    vota novem Triviae nocte silente dedi.

Omnia persolvi: fruitur nunc alter amore,
et precibus felix utitur ille meis.
At mihi felicem vitam, si salva fuisses,
20   fingebam demens et renuente deo.
Rura colam, frugumque aderit mea Delia custos,
area dum messes sole calente teret,
aut mihi servabit plenis in lintribus uvas
pressaque veloci candida musta pede;
25   consuescet numerare pecus, consuescet amantis
garrulus in dominae ludere verna sinu.
Illa deo sciet agricolae pro vitibus uvam,
pro segete spicas, pro grege ferre dapem.
Illa regat cunctos, illi sint omnia curae,
30   at iuvet in tota me nihil esse domo.
Huc veniet Messalla meus, cui dulcia poma
Delia selectis detrahat arboribus;
et tantum venerata virum, hunc sedula curet,
huic paret atque epulas ipsa ministra gerat.
35   Haec mihi fingebam, quae nunc Eurusque Notusque
iactat odoratos vota per Armenios.
Saepe ego temptavi curas depellere vino,
at dolor in lacrimas verterat omne merum.
Saepe aliam tenui, sed iam cum gaudia adirem,
40   admonuit dominae deseruitque Venus.
Tunc me discedens devotum femina dixit,
a pudet, et narrat scire nefanda meam.
Non facit hoc verbis, facie tenerisque lacertis
devovet et flavis nostra puella comis.
45   Talis ad Haemonium Nereis Pelea quondam
vecta est frenato caerula pisce Thetis.
Haec nocuere mihi, quod adest huic dives amator:
venit in exitium callida lena meum.
Sanguineas edat illa dapes atque ore cruento
50   tristia cum multo pocula felle bibat;
hanc volitent animae circum sua fata querentes
semper et e tectis strix violenta canat;
ipsa fame stimulante furens herbasque sepulcris
quaerat et a saevis ossa relicta lupis,
55   currat et inguinibus nudis ululetque per urbes,
post agat e triviis aspera turba canum.
Eveniet: dat signa deus; sunt numina amanti,
saevit et iniusta lege relicta Venus.
At tu quam primum sagae praecepta rapacis
60   desere, nam donis vincitur omnis amor.

96

Pauper erit praesto semper tibi, pauper adibit
    primus et in tenero fixus erit latere,
pauper in angusto fidus comes agmine turbae
    subicietque manus efficietque viam,
65   pauper ad occultos furtim deducet amicos
    vinclaque de niveo detrahet ipse pede.
Heu canimus frustra, nec verbis victa patescit
    ianua, sed plena est percutienda manu.
At tu, qui potior nunc es, mea fata timeto:
70   versatur celeri Fors levis orbe rotae.
Non frustra quidam iam nunc in limine perstat
    sedulus ac crebro prospicit ac refugit,
et simulat transire domum, mox deinde recurrit
    solus et ante ipsas excreat usque fores.
75   Nescio quid furtivus amor parat. Utere quaeso,
    dum licet: in liquida nat tibi linter aqua.

1 I was bitter, and kept saying that I could bear our separation well.
But such brave boasting is now far from my heart. For I am driven
like a top spinning swiftly along the even ground before the lash,
when a nimble lad who knows his business has once set it twirling.

5 Brand the wild man and torture him, that he may never wish again
to talk so mightily. Tame his rough speech.

7 Yet spare me, Delia, I beg you, by the compact of our secret
couch, by our love, by your head which has lain next to mine. I
am the man, all say, who snatched you by my vows from death
itself, when you lay faint and worn from grim fever. It was I who
paced all about you with purifying sulphur, when the old hag first
chaunted her magical spells. It was I who made holy atonement
for your cruel dreams, thrice averting them with sacred meal, that
they might do you no ill. It was I who wound the wool about my
head, loosed my tunic, and in the stillness of the night made nine
vows to the Goddess of the Moon.

17 I have paid those vows. Now another enjoys my love, and he is
the happy man who uses the prayers I made. But I used to dream
of a happy life for myself, if only you were spared. I was mad, and
God said No.

21 These were my dreams: 'I shall live in the country, and my Delia
shall guard the grain while the threshing-floor treads out the har-
vest in the glowing sun. Or she shall watch the grapes in the full
vats as the swift feet press down the white-shining new wine. She
shall learn to tell the herd; the chattering peasant child shall learn

to play on a loving mistress' lap. Delia will know the gift to bring for the farmer's god—a cluster of grapes for the vines, spikes of grain for the cornfield, an offering of food for the flock. Let her alone rule all the folk about; let everything be her mandate; and let my only joy be in my very nothingness throughout the entire house. Here my Messalla shall come, and Delia shall pluck sweet fruit for him from the choicest trees, and doing homage to the great man and devotedly tending him she shall make ready his repast and be his maidservant and bear it to him.'

35 These were my dreams, and now the East wind and the South wind toss them over all of perfumed Armenia.

37 Often I have tried to drive out my grief with wine, but the pain turned all the wine into tears. Often I have held another girl—but just when I was poised on pleasure, Venus made me think on my mistress and deserted me. Then the other girl, going away, pronounced me under a spell and—the disgrace—told all the world that my love was skilled in the black arts. But no, it is not by magical charms that my mistress does this. It is her beauty and soft arms and golden hair that bewitch me. Such was sea-blue Thetis, the Nereid, when in days of old she rode her bridled fish to Peleus of Haemonia.

47 This is what has done me ill: a rich lover waits about for her, and the artful bawd works my destruction. Bloody be the crone's food, gory be her lips, and rank gall be the bitter cup she drinks. May ghosts of the dead, bewailing their fates, fly ceaselessly around her, and may the vampire sing shrill from her rooftop. May starvation drive her mad, and goad her to search for weeds upon tombstones and for bones that the wild wolves have left. Let her loins be bare and let her race and wail through the towns, and let a savage pack of dogs from out the cross-roads hunt her on from behind.

57 Yes, this will come to pass. God gives the sign! A lover has secret powers to help him, and Venus rages when she has been unfairly deserted.

59 But, Delia, quickly quickly leave the teachings of the greedy witch. For there is no love on earth that is not defeated by gifts of money. The poor man will always be ready to serve you. The poor man will be the first to come to you and he will stay fast by his tender girl. The poor man will be your unswerving companion in the pressing crowd and he will offer you his arm and make you safe passage. The poor man will privately escort you to the secret dinners of his friends and he himself will take the sandals from off your snow-white feet.

67 Alas, I sing in vain. The door will not be won over, will not open to words. It is only a well-filled palm that should do the knocking.

69 But you, my rival, though you have won for now, yet fear for yourself my fate in the times ahead. Fortune spins along lightly on her fleetly whirling wheel. Not without design a man at this very moment, patiently watching, stalks about her threshold. Again and again he looks about for her, then darts back, then pretends that he was merely passing by the house, then soon runs back, always alone, and coughs loudly before her very doors. Furtive love is making secret plans. So enjoy your love, I invite you, while you may; your boat swims in clear waters.

Tibullus' elegies, unlike most of Propertius', are made up of a number of discrete sections. Each section furnishes the poet with an occasion for looking, directly or indirectly, at his reactions to his love-affair and for analysing these feelings. His mood shifts with his immediate subject, so that his focus on himself is now sharp and now blurred. At one moment he presents us with a 'close-up' and at another with a long-range or oblique view. In all cases the ultimate subject is the same: himself.

For critical convenience, I set down in humdrum fashion the various subjects and moods in the elegy just quoted and translated:

1. (lines 1–4)—'I cannot live without Delia.' The mood is one of utter helplessness: she spins the 'top' and Tibullus goes where she whirls him.

2. (lines 5–6)—'I will be her slave.' Mood is one of self-abnegation.

3. (lines 7–16)—'Yet spare me and save me, even as I saved you when you were near death.' Mood shifts in mild contrast. While the section enables him to show the depth of his love— like all men in love he no longer is completely rational—it also gives him a chance to let her know that he has momentarily regained some self-control and self-confidence.

4. (lines 17–20)—'All that I did for you (really for myself), I did unwittingly for another man. But I used to dream.' Mood is transitional, leading to the striking contrast between present reality and earlier dreams.

5. (lines 21–34)—'My earlier dreams.' Mood is idyllic.

6. (lines 35–36)—The old cliché of love-poets: 'The winds have swept all my dreams away.' The mood is transitional and presages the following 'undercutting'.

7. (lines 37–46)—'I tried to forget Delia through wine and women. Delia's innocence, and her charms.' The mood is rather complicated. Again, after the 'self-undermining', he returns to some degree of self-confidence, and with the skilful turn to Delia's physical charms, he now shifts radically and makes verbal love to her and is even hopeful.

8. (lines 47–56)—'Delia is not to blame. The bawd is responsible, and I curse the bawd.' The mood is one of extreme emotion. The intensity of his curses indicate the intensity of his love. He still hopes.

9. (lines 57–58)—'I shall win Delia back, with Heaven's help.' The mood is transitional, and reflects so much confidence in its staccato style that he even indirectly rebukes Delia for her faithlessness (*iniusta lege*).

10. (lines 59–66)—'Leave your rich lover and come with me. In our simple life together I shall take care of you.' The mood of idyllic dreams and of hope continues.

11. (lines 67–68)—'I only delude myself. It's money she wants.' The mood is one of 'undercutting' the dream.

12. (lines 69–76)—'You, too, my rival, will have a rival in turn, and he will succeed.' The mood is one of generalization. There is no mention of Delia—only of her lover.

It is clear that a Tibullan elegy is full of variation in its procession of changing themes and moods. While such *variatio*, if each section is well handled, makes for interesting reading—indeed, we are given no time in which to become bored with any single topic or attitude—it is Tibullus' remarkable achievement that he never lets an elegy degenerate into a mere collection, a hodgepodge, of separate subjects. Somehow the distinct parts make up a whole of which we are conscious. How is this 'unity amid variety' established in, say, our elegy (no. 1.5)?

To answer this question from the point of view of an elegy's structure, three explanations immediately suggest themselves: the feeling of continuity that arises from his quiet, smooth manner of writing; the facile transitions; and the deft repetition of certain words after an interval of some thirty or so lines.

We have already said enough about Tibullus' 'even' style of expression. As for his skill in manipulating his transitions, that is self-apparent from the text of our elegy and need not detain us long. Lines 17–20 or lines 35–36 illustrate his method: quickly conclude a previous subject and mood and then unobtrusively glide over to what will be presented in the next section. The celerity and smoothness with which he 'shifts gears'—no jolts and jerks—is a good example of how art may conceal art.

The strategically repeated words call for rather more examination here, since neither they themselves nor their subtle effect is especially noticeable on a first reading. Their iteration is managed entirely in the 'Tibullan way', quietly and without calling attention to themselves. Let me give examples.

In line 4, speaking of the nimble lad (i.e. Delia) spinning the top (i.e. himself), Tibullus uses the words *celer . . . versat*, '(the lad) swiftly spins (the top)'. At the close of the elegy, in line 70, now speaking of his rival, he echoes the earlier phrase and figure with his *versatur celeri*, '(Fortune) spins on swift (foot)', thus deliberately joining himself and his rival and the beginning and end of the poem. Or again, to continue with Tibullus and his rival, in line 18 the poet says that another lover now is making use (*utitur*) of the prayers that he, Tibullus, had made. In the poem's penultimate line, with confident arrogance Tibullus advises his rival to go ahead and use (*utere*) his good luck with Delia while he may. Or consider the twist given to *tristis*, always a somewhat difficult word to translate—it takes on a specific meaning from its immediate context, but in general connotes 'sad' or 'gloomy'. In line 9 Delia lies sick *tristi morbo*, 'with a grim fever'. But later on, in line 50, when he is 'whistling in the dark' by declaring that Delia herself is not to blame—the bawd is—he bitterly curses the old hag by prophesying for her *tristia pocula*, 'bitter potions'. In another instance, Tibullus' hopeful *fingebam* of line 20, 'I used to dream', is intentionally picked up in line 35 by the hopeless *Haec mihi fingebam*, 'These were the dreams I dreamt for myself'. To give one last example—the reader will find others—in lines 13–14 Tibullus recalls the holy rites he performed to prevent cruel nightmares from doing ill (*nocere*) to Delia. The verb is turned on himself in line 47, and now it is the rich lover who does ill to Tibullus (*nocuere*). Such repetitions, few but forceful, bind the various sections together and help create the unity of which we spoke.[33]

But there is something else which is much more responsible for this over-arching unity. This is the fact which we have stressed several times, that underneath the varied assortment of subjects and feelings lies one essential and ubiquitous subject: Tibullus' psychological reactions to his current love-affair. Let me show what I mean by examining two items or topics in our elegy. In lines 11–16 he describes the magical charms he used to try to avert Delia's sickness. Now any detailed description of holy rites and magic always makes good reading of and by itself. Tibullus, like many another poet, knows this universal truth and he frequently 'digresses' to recount such black and arcane ritual. So, too, with curses. If curses are pronounced with the dire bitterness and awfulness of Tibullus' on the bawd, lines 49–56, verses which quite refute the legendary image of Tibullus as incapable of vehemence and which in the comparative calculus of imprecations stand up well against James Stephens's superb

> May she marry a ghost and bear him a kitten, and may
> The High King of Glory permit her to get the mange,

then, of course, curses—I mean robust curses—entirely justify their presence in any context simply by the pure interest they arouse. But yet, behind the magic and behind the curses stands Tibullus as the ultimate subject.

The magic charms are described in connexion with Delia's sickness. That Tibullus tells us that he used such rites at that time enables him to show, first of all, how much he loved Delia by showing us how much he feared for her life. Then, too, these magic charms presage the charge of the other girl with whom he slept in his attempt to forget Delia, to wit, that Delia had bewitched Tibullus. This accusation in turn neatly allows him to exclaim that Delia indeed has charms, but they are physical and not magical. Suddenly we realistically pull ourselves up short and sceptically ask: 'Did people like Tibullus and his contemporary readers really believe in magic?' The answer is: 'Certainly not. Such naïve credence belonged to the lower classes in Rome.' Why, then, does magic keep coming into Latin elegiac poetry? Because in this way the poet can reveal to us that love has temporarily so swept him away—he has reached such a point of irrationality— that now he even trusts in such superstitious ritual.[34]

As for the splendid curses, in the end they give Tibullus a good opportunity for disclosing the fullness of his love for Delia —it is the bawd who perverts her—and for revealing the extent of his frustration and his desire for vengeance without suggesting that Delia be punished. In short, the curses, enjoyable as they are in themselves, serve his underlying purpose—to let us know just how he feels and suffers in his unsuccessful love.

It is by such means that the general, overall unity of an elegy is achieved. The individual sections may seem, superficially, to have little or no connexion with one another. But closer study will show that through a common style of writing, through smooth transitions and adroit repetitions of words and images, and above all through the fact that 'behind the scene' of every section is present the same figure, Tibullus being tortured in love —that through these devices the poet has ingeniously succeeded in knitting all the diverse parts of his elegy together into a firm oneness.

Each elegy, accordingly, is made out of one fabric. But we must not mislead ourselves. The fabric may be one—it may be a whole piece. Yet this single piece may have strong strains and stresses within it. I revert to my previous proposals.

Earlier we noted two elements or sources of tension in Tibullus' poetry. One is the conflict which the reader frequently feels between Tibullus' idyllic dreams and his subsequent deliberate 'undercutting' of such dreams. The other was even more pervasive—the striking contrast between the clarity of his manner of writing and the obscurity of what he really wanted for himself, where he thought his life should lie, and what indeed he thought that he should do with himself in relation to the Augustan world. It was suggested at that time that, in fact, he had never resolved these private problems. Hence his poems are personal documents, and hence the pull, the tug, that we feel within the fabric of his verse. Basic unity—yes—but a unity that, to change the figure, is only a kind of mute background; the foreground is Tibullus' articulate struggle. It is such a fairly dramatic if latent opposition between the unity of form and subject on the one hand and the disparate and constantly shifting emotional attitudes on the other that makes him an appealing and attractive poet. In the final analysis, we realize that we have been listening to someone who could not 'keep pace' with his companions—thank heaven for such men—and who knew this fact and felt torment therefrom. In fine, we have been listening to an Augustan who heard the distant call of Thoreau's 'different drummer'.

NOTES

[1] L. Trilling, *Emma* (Riverside Press, Cambridge, Mass., 1957), p. v.

[2] Schuster in *Tibull-Studien* does not, however, subscribe to the usual opinion. His work is epochal in the history of the literary appreciation of Tibullus.

[3] J. W. Duff—A. M. Duff, *A Literary History of Rome*—Golden Age (3rd ed., London, 1953), 409.

[4] Not, of course, in his 'Pindaric' odes, e.g. 1.12; 3.4; 4.4; or 4.14.

[5] If, as seems likely, Propertius be the 'Callimachus' of *Epist.* 2.2.100.

[6] *Indignos* is difficult to translate. 'Undeserving locks' is fairly meaningless. The general sense is: 'Elegy did not deserve to suffer the fate of Tibullus' death.'

[7] M. Platnauer, *Fifty Years of Classical Scholarship* (Oxford), p. 324.

[8] It is usually assumed that Books 1 and 2 of the *corpus Tibullianum* were written by Tibullus, and that Book 3 (sometimes divided into Books 3 and 4) came from other members of Messalla's circle. No. 3.19 (4.13) declares, however, that its author is Tibullus, and perhaps he is.

[9] Save for those by Sulpicia, 3.13–18 (4.7–12), whose direct sincerity goes a long way toward compensating for her lack of elegance.

[10] An exception may be No. 2.5. This is certainly a poem of national interest, and contains definite references to the Julian line.

[11] 'The project of writing a national epic on some subject connected with Augustus' achievements seems to have been brought to the notice of every poet of any ability.' H. J. Rose, *A Handbook of Latin Literature* (2nd ed., London, 1949), p. 247 and n. 52.

[12] G. Luck's *The Latin Love-Elegy*, pp. 76–92, 'Alexandrian Themes in Tibullus', is most instructive.

[13] Though Propertius can advise a friend (2.34.32) to imitate 'the dreams of disciplined Callimachus' (*non inflati somnia Callimachi*).

[14] 1.4.61 ff. also tell us something about Tibullus' views on poetry.

[15] For what follows here on diction, I am indebted to a work which seems to me to have been insufficiently appreciated, B. Axelson, *Unpoetische Wörter* (Lund, 1945), 18 ff. and *passim*.

[16] Catullus, to be sure, doubtless had made similar stylistic efforts in No. 68, but it is far from clear just how he himself viewed this strange poem. I agree with Luck (op. cit., p. 58) that it is such an experimental blend of personal and traditional motives that it is dangerous to give it too prominent a position in the development of the Latin personal love-elegy.

[17] While this is markedly true of the longer poems in the elegiac metre, 66–68, it is also true to a lesser extent of the epigrams (though certainly these contain diminutives, e.g. 69.4; 80.7; 99.2; 99.14 and, as we should expect, some of them are entirely built around 'colloquial' themes, e.g. 69 or 71). See J. Svennung, *Catulls Bildersprache* I (Uppsala Universitets Årsskrift, 1945: 3, Uppsala), pp. 20–34.

[18] Many of which, of course, are as old in literature as Plautus.

[19] In 1.5.32 Delia is deprived of even the *mea*, since Messalla had received that distinction in the previous line: *Messalla meus*.

[20] In contrast, Tibullus' *Forma nihil magicis utitur auxiliis* (1.8.24) is more epigrammatic than functional.

[21] Whether or not Tibullus had in mind Catullus 64, surely the description in that poem, lines 382 ff., of the 'olden days' and their purity must have strongly appealed to Tibullus when writing, say, 1.3.35 ff., or 1.10.19 ff., or 2.1.37 ff.

[22] Trilling (op. cit. xx–xxiv) makes some very acute observations on the idyll in general (and on Jane Austen's particular version).

[23] The same *florida serta*, 'flowery garlands', which here are laid on a tree-trunk or on an old stone, are as easily laid upon Delia's doorposts in the next elegy (line 14).

[24] One way in which the poet establishes the mood of the idyllic simplicity of the 'olden days' is by repeating key epithets. Thus in this first elegy *tener*, 'soft'; *iners*, 'inactive'; *parvus*, 'little'; *exiguus*, 'small'; *pauper*, 'poor'; *securus*, 'free from care'; *antiquus*, 'olden'; and *desertus*, 'lonely'.

[25] I mean, of course, a stern moral satirist of society's vices, or even an 'Horatian' satirist of society's shortcomings. In this respect Virgil and Tibullus are exceptional. On the other hand, Tibullus is capable of literary satire, e.g. 1.8.

[26] See F. O. Copley, *Exclusus Amator. A Study in Latin Love Poetry* (Mongr. Amer. Philol. Assoc. XVII, 1956), who deals with Tibullus, pp. 91–112.

[27] Horace, too, must have had rather similar reactions to the City. For example, in *Od.* 3.29 he urges Maecenas to leave Rome's luxuries and palaces for the simple life of the countryside: *omitte mirari beatae/fumum et opes strepitumque Romae* (11–12), 'cease to marvel at the smoke, the wealth, and the noisy bustle of rich Rome'.

[28] Sentimentalism in Tibullus may appear naïve, but it is always calculated to serve his self-centered purposes. In 1.6.57 ff. he prays that Delia may be spared, not for her own sake but for that of her old mother. In 2.6.39—an extreme case—he begs Nemesis to be merciful to him by the bones of her sister who died young, having fallen out of a high window and having landed bloodstained (*sanguinolenta*) in the world below. In each instance Tibullus hopes to move the girl by such memories, and specifically to move her to be good to him.

[29] A. W. Allen, 'Elegy and the Classical Attitude toward Love: Propertius I, 1', *Yale Class. Stud.* 11 (1950), 257 f.

[30] *Contr.*, 2.4(12).8; cf. Quint., 10.1.113.

[31] Despite Apuleius, *Apol.*, 10.

[32] The best presentation I know of the subject is that of M. Platnauer, *Latin Elegiac Verse* (Cambridge, 1951).

[33] By any chance could the *linter* of the last line take on a disparaging colour from the *lintribus* of line 23?

[34] Magical references in the elegiac poets are collected by Copley, op. cit., p. 164, n. 16. But magic is not used by these poets, as Copley there suggests, for pure 'embellishment' but, as Allen (op. cit., pp. 272 ff.) maintains, 'to reveal still further the disturbance of the lover's mind'.

SUNT QUI PROPERTIUM MALINT

Archibald W. Allen

QUINTILIAN's critical estimate of the four Roman elegists is well known: *Elegia quoque Graecos provocamus, cuius mihi tersus atque elegans maxime videtur auctor Tibullus. Sunt qui Propertium malint. Ovidius utroque lascivior, sicut durior Gallus.* (In elegy, too, we rival the Greeks. Tibullus seems to me the most polished and elegant of the elegists. There are those who prefer Propertius. Ovid is more playful than either, just as Gallus is harsher: Quint. X. 1.93.) Today the number of those *qui Propertium malint* has probably increased at the expense of Tibullus; Propertius has on his side judges so different as Housman and Pound. Quintilian's judgement of Gallus has been ratified by an unkind fate which has left us only one line of his work. The most marked agreement of modern critics with Quintilian, however, is the preference for both Tibullus and Propertius over Ovid. Postgate's opinion, written in the height of the Victorian period, represents the still prevailing attitude toward Ovid: 'His calm surface is most rarely disturbed by genuine feeling. With Tibullus and Propertius love was at any rate a passion. With Ovid it was *une affaire de coeur.*'[1] It is interesting to note the apparent agreement between the ancient critic and the modern, but it is more important to observe that the criteria by which they reached their judgements are significantly different. Postgate and most moderns have preferred Propertius (or Tibullus) because they find a 'sincerity' which they miss in Ovid. Classical criticism approached the matter differently.

The terms *tersus, elegans, lascivus,* and *durus* (polished, elegant, playful, harsh), which Quintilian used in describing the elegists, are all technical terms of stylistic criticism. The qualities that he found most admirable in Tibullus were his formal perfection and his sureness of taste. These are qualities that we should expect to be admired by Quintilian, who said of the rhetorical style that most persuasively reveals the character of the speaker: *proprie, iucunde, credibiliter dicere sat est.* (It is enough to speak precisely, pleasantly, and convincingly: VI. 2.19) It is evident that in such a style it is not the peculiar character of a unique individual that is revealed, but rather a general type of character to which the speaker conforms or seems to conform. If we look beyond Quintilian we find that these are not simply the criteria adopted by a teacher of rhetoric. Poets also used such terms of stylistic identification when they wished to characterize in a single word the essential quality of another poet. So Propertius, in urging his friend Lynceus to turn from epic to elegiac verse, wrote:

> incipe iam angusto uersus includere torno,
> inque tuos ignis, dure poeta, ueni.
>
> (II. 34.43–44)

Begin now to confine your verses on a narrow wheel, and come, harsh poet, to your own fires.

The writing of elegy can, as here, be described both as writing in a limited, polished style (the image of the potter's or turner's wheel is one of many used to contrast less expansive poetic forms with epic) and as writing of one's own love. As an epic poet Lynceus was *durus*, but if he would turn to elegy and the theme of love he would become a *tener poeta*—not simply because he would write as a lover, but because he would write in a style that is *tener* (graceful) in contrast to the *durus* style of epic. From this point of view the personality of the poet himself, in so far as he is a poet, is determined by the style in which he writes.

While Quintilian was concerned with the style of the elegists and not with their personality as it might exist apart from their style, Postgate was concerned with the style as it reveals the personality of the poet. He found in Tibullus and Propertius proof of the sincerity and genuine passion which he evidently regarded as a prime requisite of poetry. They, rather than Ovid, awakened in him the impression that a passionate feeling inspired their verse. Finding them superior to Ovid in the quality of their feeling, he considered them superior also as poets. The ethical standard for him was prior and determined literary judgement.

This point of view is no longer so widely held in literary criticism as was the case a few years ago, but it has had a very considerable influence in classical scholarship. In criticism of the Roman elegists, so much of whose work is of a personal and ostensibly confessional nature, the question of the relation between poetry and the personality of the poet has assumed particular importance. We must, therefore, consider the difference between the ancient and modern views of the nature of poetic sincerity, and seek to avoid the danger of applying misleading standards of judgement to the Roman elegists. The interest in individual personality which is characteristic of modern thought has led to the development of a concept of artistic sincerity which is basically different from that which the contemporaries of the elegists considered relevant. Instead of being regarded as a function of style, sincerity has come to be regarded as a function of personality. Before judging a Roman poet by modern standards we must be careful to understand him by the standards of which he was himself conscious, and take care that other preconceptions do not cause us to misunderstand him.

In classical literary criticism this problem did not receive the amount of attention that it has in modern criticism, but it was not ignored. Since the theory of rhetoric was more carefully considered and fully developed than a corresponding theory of poetic, it is in the rhetoricians that we find the matter most systematically treated. Rhetorical theory recognized that the orator faces the practical requirement that he must get people to believe what he says; therefore he must not only convince an audience by his argumentation, but also persuade them of his sincerity. *Fides* is the word which in Latin comes nearest to expressing the idea contained in our word 'sincerity', but there is an important difference. *Fides* contains simultaneously the ideas of 'sincerity' and 'persuasiveness'. Heinze's study of its precise meaning showed that it contains an essential notion of a relationship existing between an individual and others who assume a particular attitude toward him. *Fides* therefore includes both a subjective element and an objective element; in its former aspect the closest English equivalent is sincerity, while in the latter it is persuasiveness. The *fides* of an orator depends on the conviction which he arouses that he possesses the qualities which he claims. *Fides* involves a relationship between the speaker and his audience; it means both good faith on the part of a speaker and the acceptance by an audience of his pretension to speak in good faith. If the speaker is to create a belief in his sincerity he must, Quintilian says, himself either possess or seem to possess the good qualities which he praises in others: a bad speech is one which fails properly to present the character of the speaker. The proper solution for the orator is simply that he should speak in such a manner as will present his character in the light he desires, and the style of his discourse is the means by which he presents his character to the audience. An excess of adornment destroys belief in the sincerity of the speaker's emotion, but on the other hand charm of manner is in itself a means of persuasion. The successful orator is one who understands the art of charming his listeners, without falling into excess and affection, and so can convince them of the soundness of his character and the justice of his case. His *fides*, the impression of sincerity resulting from persuasiveness, is, according to this doctrine, a product of style. Sincerity, then, as we find it in ancient criticism, involves a relation between the artist and the public; it is established by the style of the work of art. The personality of the artist, except as it appears to the public in the work of art, is irrelevant to the question of sincerity.

In modern critical theory, on the other hand, the real personality of the artist is an essential factor in the concept of sincerity, which is regarded as lying in the relation between the artist and the product of his art. The difference between the ancient and modern ideas of sincerity arises from our interest in individual psychology; ancient criticism tended to regard the finished work of art as the complete subject of critical concern, while modern criticism tends to regard the work of art genetically, as a creative process. In the one case the work of art is a final and sufficient object of study; in the other the work of art is only a partial expression of the artist's experience, and the nature of this original experience becomes an object of interest to criticism. In their study of the basic principles of modern literary theory, Wellek and Warren define sincerity in poetry as 'a sincere expression of the poem, i.e. the linguistic construct shaping in the author's mind as he writes'. Since the terms of this definition are 'the linguistic construct' and 'the author's mind', it is evidently in the relation between these that they look for sincerity, rather than in the relation between the finished work of art and the readers or audience.[2] The objective element in the classical *fides* has disappeared.

When there has been established for the judgement of poetry a standard so subjective as the relation between the artist and the product of his art, it is not surprising that critics have often looked for proof of sincerity not chiefly in the artistic illusion created by the poem itself but rather in the relation existing between the poem and the external facts of the poet's life. Indeed, some critics have gone further, and from a forceful impression of sincerity have inferred a necessary existence of the external facts. The current judgement concerning Propertius and Ovid illustrates this habit of mind. Since the poetry of Ovid is deliberately 'conventional', many critics deny him sincerity, and as a corollary assume that his poetry is pure fancy supported neither by true feeling nor by real experience. This is the judgement of the standard history of Latin literature on the *Amores*:

> [Corinna] existierte aber nur in dem Geiste des Dichters, um seine Phantasiestücke individuell zu beleben. So muss Corinna die Figur für eine Reihe erdichteter Situationen abgeben. . . . Keines dieser Lieder verrät eine tiefere Empfindung, es sind leichte Spiele der Phantasie. . . . Ein Band zwischen Leben und Dichtung besteht nicht.[3]

It is easy to see the method of reasoning: we do not receive from the elegies of Ovid an impression of sincerity; we may therefore conclude that there exists in them no connexion between life and poetry. For Propertius the situation is simply reversed; we are convinced of the reality of his passion:

> Tiefe und starke Gemütsbewegung und eine überwältigende Leidenschaft, lebhafte Phantasie eines erregten Herzens machen sich in leuchtenden Gemälden der Freude und des Leides Luft; Glut der Empfindung lodert überall.[4]

And it follows, for these critics, that Cynthia has a role in the biography of Propertius which is denied to Corinna in that of Ovid. Butler and Barber, in the introduction to their edition of Propertius, likewise find in the quality of Propertius' poetry a guarantee of its biographical truth:

> It is with Cynthia we must begin. The story of their love is in outline simple enough. . . . There is no need to be unduly sceptical

about the poet's story of his love. Many of the poems, it is true, seem to follow conventional forms; the details may often be fictitious; but underlying all there is such fire and vehemence that we can scarcely doubt the general truth of the story that emerges as we read.[5]

The propriety of testing the sincerity of a Roman elegist by relating his poems to the external facts of his life is fortunately subject to some measure of objective verification. We can both examine 'the story that emerges' from his elegies to determine whether it is coherent and convincing; and we can consider whether the statements of the Latin poets themselves justify such a method of interpreting their work. If we find this method invalid, it will remain to investigate whether sincerity, regarded simply as a function of style, offers a more useful criterion.

Many critics have thought that in the elegies of Propertius they can trace the story of his romance with Cynthia. Since the first necessity in preparing an adequate biography is the establishment of a chronology, it will be convenient to gather the passages which have been used as historical data in constructing an account of Propertius' relations with Cynthia. There are seven which are sufficiently precise to seem useful:[6]

> et mihi iam toto furor hic non deficit anno,
> cum tamen aduersos cogor habere deos.   (I. 1.7–8)

And now this madness has not left me for a whole year, even though I am forced to endure the gods' hostility.

> 'uix unum potes, infelix, requiescere mensem,
> et turpis de te iam liber alter erit.'   (II. 3.3–4)

'You can hardly keep quiet a single month, poor fellow, and now we shall have another disgraceful book about you.'

> ergo iam multos nimium temerarius annos,
> improba, qui tulerim teque tuamque domum?
> (II. 8.13–14)

So I have been too trusting for so many years, shameless woman, I who put up with you and your household?

> septima iam plenae deducitur orbita lunae,
> cum de me et de te compita nulla tacent.   (II. 20.21–22)

Now the seventh full moon has completed its round: for so long no street corner has been silent about you and me.

Sic ego non ullos iam norim in amore tumultus,
   nec ueniat sine te nox uigilanda mihi:
ut mihi praetexti pudor est elatus amictus
   et data libertas noscere amoris iter,
illa rudis animos per noctes conscia primas
   imbuit, heu nullis capta Lycinna datis!
tertius (haud multo minus est) cum ducitur annus,
   uix memini nobis uerba coisse decem.
cuncta tuus sepeliuit amor, nec femina post te
   ulla dedit collo dulcia uincla meo.   (III. 15.1–10)

As I pray that I may know no troubles in my love, and that no
night may come that I must pass in wakefulness without you: when
the inhibition of the boy's cloak was taken from me and freedom was
given to know the path of love, it was Lycinna—oh, not won by any
gifts—who initiated my inexperience, a companion in those first
nights. Now it is the third year (almost) since then, and I can hardly
remember that we have exchanged ten words. Your love has buried
everything, and no woman since you has put her sweet bonds around
my neck.

     peccaram semel, et totum sum pulsus in annum. (III. 16.9)

I had once offended her and was exiled for a whole year.

     quinque tibi potui seruire fideliter annos.   (III. 25.3)

I was able to serve you faithfully for five years.

In the first of these passages, which occurs in the elegy that
introduces Book I, Propertius says that the madness of love has
possessed him for a whole year. II. 3.3–4 are probably to be understood as the words of a friend, addressed to the poet shortly after
the publication of Book I. II. 8.13–14 are from an elegy complain-
ing of his mistress's infidelity. II. 20.21–22 presumably refer to the
period which has passed since publication of Book I. III.15 is
the only elegy in which Lycinna appears. In III. 16.9 memory of
a year of banishment occurs to the poet when he is debating
whether to obey a midnight summons of his mistress: her order
is dangerous to obey, but more dangerous to disobey. III. 25, in
which Propertius claims to have served Cynthia faithfully for five
years, is the concluding poem of the book and an epilogue to his
love poetry.

The first effort to apply historical method to the interpretation
of these passages was made in the latter part of the eighteenth

century by F. G. Barth, who arranged according to the years of the poet's life the events of his affairs with Cynthia and her predecessor Lycinna.[7] Relying on the statement in III. 15, he assumed that the first love-affair of Propertius was with Lycinna, and that it began shortly after he put on the *toga virilis*. About two years later he fell in love with Cynthia, and his love for her lasted for five years (III. 25.3). Since the usual age for assuming the *toga virilis* was sixteen, Barth supposed that the love-affair began when the poet was about seventeen years old. By assigning two years to the affair with Lycinna and five years to the affair with Cynthia, he found that the events which form the subject of the first three books of Propertius extended over a period of seven years, from his seventeenth to his twenty-fourth years. This chronology was adopted by Lachmann, but with one important modification.[8] He drew attention to the year of separation which Propertius mentions in III. 16.9 and identified this year with the *toto anno* of I. 1.7. He felt that Propertius could not have included this year of separation—the *annus discidii* as it has generally been called since Lachmann—among the *quinque annos* of faithful service. He therefore reckoned the five years of III. 25.3 as having begun only with the resumption of relations after the *annus discidii*. He further suggested that the elegy in which Lycinna appears (III. 15) was written immediately before the separation. A period of two years has already elapsed since love for Cynthia has erased all thought of Lycinna from his mind. Lachmann therefore arranged the chronology of the love-affairs as follows: one year for Lycinna, two for the earlier period of relations with Cynthia, one for the separation, and five for the second period of relations with Cynthia. Thus the seven years in the chronology of Barth became nine in that of Lachmann.

Despite the apparent precision of Barth's conclusions, as modified by Lachmann, they have since shown themselves open to attack at every point. The identification of the year of I. 1.7 with that of III. 16.9—which Lachmann believed to be the most important contribution of his chronological system to the interpretation of Propertius and which he made the keystone of his system—is extremely doubtful, since it requires the assumption that I. 1 was written at the end of the *annus discidii*, and therefore three years after Propertius' relations with Cynthia began. This assumption led Lachmann to regard I. 1 as a farewell to love, a complete misconception of the elegy. Further, the composition of III. 15 was assigned to a period before the publication of Book I. The reckoning of years is also much less certain than Lachmann indicated. The year assigned to Lycinna is a mere guess, and there is no satisfactory means of determining whether the five years mentioned in III. 25 do or do not include the year of separation and the previous period of relations between Propertius and Cynthia. These difficulties are further complicated by the differences between the short periods of time mentioned in II. 3.3 and II. 20.21 and the *multos annos* of II. 8.13. The result of the numerous flaws which have been found in Lachmann's theory is that many efforts have since been made to reconcile the chronology of Propertius' romance with the chronology of his poems. The methods followed by Birt[9] and by Butler and Barber are typical.

The solution offered by Birt is the more radical. He believed that expressions of time have in general only a subjective meaning for the poet: they signify only that a given period of time has seemed long or short. Birt found it possible to argue that when Propertius says three years (III. 15.7) he really means exactly the same length of time as when he says five years (III. 25.3). He could also argue, on the same basis, that when Propertius says a year he really means a month, and when he says a month he really means a year:

Schreibt nun also Properz III. 16, 9: *Peccaram semel et totum sum pulsus in annum,* so genügt es, da Properz sich möglichst stark ausdrücken will, nicht ein Jahr, sondern einen Monat der Trennung zu verstehen; schreibt er dagegen II. 3, 3: *vix unum potes, infelix, requiescere mensem, et turpis de te iam liber alter erit,* so ist das in diesem Fall eine ganz offenbare Uebertreibung in das Minus, und wir dürfen wiederum ruhig als Abstand zwischen der Monobiblos des Properz und dem Beginn seines sog. zweiten Buches den Zeitraum eines vollen Jahres ansetzen.

All things are, in fact, possible under this method, even Birt's conclusion that Propertius really loved Cynthia for only three years, and then spent seventeen years in writing poetry about her. But since such conjectures are no more susceptible of disproof than of proof, they are entirely beyond critical control.

The method of Butler and Barber seems more circumspect. They deny chronological importance to II. 3.3, to II. 8.13, and to

II. 20.21, reject the *annus discidii* from their reckoning, and take the *toto anno* of I. 1.7 simply as indicating the period of composition of Book I. They are then left with only two passages from which to determine the chronology of Propertius' love story; but each of these offers particular difficulties. The first of these passages is that in which Lycinna is mentioned (III. 15.1–10). It was she, Propertius says, who initiated him into the experience of love, but his later love for Cynthia has made him forget her, and in almost two years they have scarcely exchanged ten words. Butler and Barber, who date the beginning of Propertius' love for Cynthia in 29 B.C. and the composition of Book III in the years 25 to 22 B.C., are troubled by the poet's statement that it is only two years since he left Lycinna for Cynthia. They therefore follow Lachmann in suggesting that these lines actually were composed earlier than the rest of the book:

> III. xv, though its date is uncertain, cannot well be later than 27 B.C. It is, that is to say, as far as 1–10 at least are concerned, an early poem which would naturally have found a place in Book II. It is possible that 1–10 represent an early fragment, which was later made use of to introduce the story of Dirce and Antiope, which like the story of Hylas in I. xx, is in reality the main theme of the poem.

This is not absolutely impossible, of course. It is possible that an occasional elegy was rejected by Propertius in publishing an earlier book and included in a later; but it would be a malign coincidence that caused the elegy that contains the most precise chronological statement of all to appear so far out of its proper chronological order. The technique of III. 15 is, moreover, that of Book III rather than Book I.

A similar difficulty is raised by the *quinque annos* of III. 25.3. These five years cannot be counted from the publication of the book, for they would then carry us back only to 27 or 28 B.C., when the first book had already appeared. Butler and Barber therefore offer the following explanation:

> If the liaison was broken at the end of 25 B.C. or early in 24 B.C., and Bk. III was published in 22 B.C. (and it cannot at most have been more than a few months earlier), at least two years must be assumed to have elapsed between the composition of the Cynthia poems in this book and their publication. In this there is nothing impossible. Ell. xxiv and xxv may well have been composed and sent to Cynthia at

the time of the rupture. Propertius kept them by him and when the time came for publishing saw that they would give an artistic conclusion to the volume.

The upshot of this is that the evidence for the chronology of the romance has been reduced to two passages, each of which, it is admitted, cannot mean what it seems to mean. It is sheer caprice that chooses to explain III. 15.7 and III. 25.3 as literally true, while regarding the *multos annos* of II. 8.13 as 'no doubt exaggerated', and leaving uncertain the meanings of II. 3.3 ('It is unlikely to indicate with any precision the interval between the publication of Bk. I and the commencement of Bk. II') and of II. 20.21 ('Perhaps the seventh month from the publication of Book I. But there can be no certainty').

The analysis of the chronological evidence on which the biographical critics of Propertius have built their story of his romance compels two conclusions. The first is that no hypothetical reconstruction of the story can ever be convincing, since it must rest upon conjectures which are not capable of verification. Propertius simply does not give us the facts we need. The second conclusion, which necessarily follows from the first, is that Propertius did not intend that his elegies should be read as a story. It is an essential quality of a story that it present a sequence of events; without progression in time a story cannot exist. And there is no progression in time in the elegies. The opening elegy is an introduction to love, and the last elegy of the third book is a valediction to love. Between these two are elegies which treat all the aspects of love, fruition and loneliness, renunciation and renewal, hope and despair, jealousy and penitence. But there is no plot which unites them and determines the order in which they shall appear. Propertius is not concerned to tell a story, but rather to impart the quality of an experience. Explicit statements of time, place, person, and circumstance have meaning not as references to a private sphere of the poet's own experience, into which the reader is only occasionally and, as it were, by chance allowed an entrance; they have meaning rather as details which serve to enforce perception of the essential and typical aspects of experience in love.

The effort to transfer the elegiac treatment of love from the poetry in which it was written into the form of an historical biography has failed; it was inevitable that no two scholars who attempted to retell the story of the romance should reach quite the same conclusions, since they can never quite agree on their data. Biography is a branch of historical study, and history demands facts, which Propertius does not give us. The particular events of his own life were not for him a given framework to whose imperious rigidity he must adapt his poetry. He created, changed, or ignored particular facts as best served his purpose. Cynthia was his first love (I. 1.1) and the only woman he ever cared for (IV. 1.139–46); but if his poetic intention required a personal occasion for telling the story of Dirce and Antiope, Lycinna could appear for the moment (III. 15) and then disappear from his verse. He could claim to have served Cynthia faithfully for five years (III. 25.3) and yet meanwhile have called upon his own experience to prove the advantage of having two mistresses at one time (II. 22), or have declared that he was resorting to girls of the street (II. 23 and 24). He could even regard Cynthia in his elegies sometimes as a courtesan and sometimes as a woman of social position. Such contradictions cannot be resolved; they must be recognized, and the method of our interpretation must be adapted to the kind of poetry we are reading.

We set out to determine whether the quality of Propertius' poetry can be regarded as proof of its biographical truth. It is now apparent that the theory fails to pass the first test: there is no coherent story which emerges from the elegies. All the circumstantial accounts that have been written about the relations of Propertius with Cynthia are based on dubious interpretations of a few passages whose relation to biographical fact we have no means of determining.

There remains the second test, the statements of the poets themselves. Propertius had urged his friend Lynceus not only to write in the polished style, but also to write of his own love (*ignes*). Concerning Propertius himself, Ovid wrote:

> saepe suos solitus recitare Propertius ignes. (*Tristia* IV. 10.45)

It was Propertius' habit often to read aloud his fiery passions.

Such statements have sometimes been thought to support a belief that his poetry is autobiographical. The alternative is to regard these statements as referring to poetry written in a personal form without implication as to its factual accuracy. Roman writers from Catullus to Ausonius do actually contend that the poet's life and his work must be kept separate.

Catullus, in lines which were often quoted or imitated by later writers, declared that there must be a complete distinction between the poet and his poetry:

> castum esse decet pium poetam
> ipsum, uersiculos nihil necessest;
> qui tum denique habent salem ac leporem,
> si sunt molliculi ac parum pudici.　　(xvi. 5–8)

The true poet should be chaste himself; his verses need not be. They have wit and charm only if they are relaxed and uninhibited.

The essential quality of such verses as Catullus is writing is that they should be *molliculi ac parum pudici*; only so will they properly accord with their literary type. A similar contrast appears in Ovid:

> crede mihi, distant mores a carmine nostro:
> uita uerecunda est, Musa iocosa mea. (*Tristia* II. 353–4)

My conduct, believe me, is different from my poetry: my life is decent, but my Muse has fun.

Again we find in Martial:

> lasciua est nobis pagina, uita proba.　　(I. 4.8)
> My page is racy, but my life is pure.

Martial also, in another epigram, insisted that he was bound by the law governing the kind of poetry he wrote:

> lex haec carminibus data est iocosis,
> ne possint, nisi pruriant, iuuare.　　(I. 35.10–11)

This law has been laid down for playful verses, that they can't give delight if they're not dirty.

Catullus' verses were appealed to by the Younger Pliny, surely one of the most virtuous figures in Latin literature. It is evident that he was hurt by moralistic criticism of poems he had written: two of his letters (IV. 14 and V. 3) defended his poetry. In the first he declared that his actual fault was that, through timidity, he had abstained from the really outspoken language that Catullus had proclaimed as proper to such verse. In the other he defended himself against the specific criticism that such poetry ought not to be written by a man in his position. He placed the writing of light and sometimes amorous verse on a level with attending mimes and comedies, and with reading lyric poetry. His own writing he justified by the authority of the good and illustrious men who had done the same. Asserting that men whose purity of character (*sanctitas morum*) is unquestionable do not abstain from racy subject-matter (*lascivia rerum*) in their verse, he gave his answer to the question whether poetry need have a basis in real experience. Apuleius also had occasion to quote the verses of Catullus, in his *Apology* (*Apol.* 11), when he found it necessary to defend himself against the charge that his erotic epigrams were an indication of his own immorality. He preserved for us a line of the Emperor Hadrian, for inscription on the tomb of the poet Voconius:

> lasciuus uersu, mente pudicus eras.

Racy in your poetry, you were chaste in mind.

Hadrian would never have written thus, Apuleius reminded his accusers, if witty poems were to be regarded as proof of immorality (*si forent lepidiora carmina argumentum impudicitiae habenda*). Ausonius, recalling this passage of Apuleius, neatly summarized the distinction between poetry and poet: Apuleius was in his life a philosopher, in his epigrams a lover (*Apuleium in vita philosophum, in epigrammatis amatorem: Cento Nuptialis*).

This doctrine has been constantly repeated: erotic poetry, though its form may be personal, cannot be taken as an indication of the conduct of the writer. This does not mean that erotic poets were never in love, but it does mean that classical literary doctrine did not assume any specific and normal connexion between personal poetry and the actual experience of the poet. The doctrine insisted upon the independence of the poet and his right freely to choose fitting material wherever he might wish, provided only that it accorded with the kind of poetry he was writing. Doubtless there were always hunters of gossip who pretended that they could judge the deeds of a poet from his verse, but the poets themselves explicitly rejected such interpretation. When we are tempted to take the statements of a poet as indicating the facts of his life, ignoring the warnings of Catullus and those who followed him throughout the whole course of Roman literature, we have fair warning in Apuleius' judgement of his accusers:

'They have read so crudely and naïvely that they make you hate them' (*tam dure et rustice legere ut odium moverent*).

Interpretation of the Roman elegists in terms of the modern standard of sincerity has proved futile, and the opinion of competent Roman critics has shown that such poetry must not be interpreted as autobiographical. As an alternative, the classical conception of *fides* suggests that we restrict our attention to the elegists as poets and concern ourselves with sincerity as a function of style. The sincerity that we can look for in them is the kind of sincerity which lies in a consistency between the style of their poetry and the emotional condition their elegy depicts. The question we should ask is not 'Did the elegist really feel this?' but rather 'Is it reasonable that the lover whose character appears in the elegies should speak in this manner?'

This question is, in fact, raised in Prop. II. 24a 1–2:

> 'Tu loqueris, cum sis iam noto fabula libro
> et tua sit toto Cynthia lecta foro?'

'Do *you* say this, when you are already a legend because of your famous book and your "Cynthia" is read everywhere in the forum?'

In the previous elegy Propertius had assumed the role of a moralist in the tradition of the popular philosophers, and had sententiously declared that the man who is to be free must not yield to love. Elegies II. 23 and 24a form a contrasting pair. In 23 Propertius steps out of character as the distraught lover, but in 24a he is recalled to his usual role. The two poems differ as markedly in style as they do in the point of view expressed, and an analysis of them will clarify the rhetorical doctrine that style should reveal the speaker's character.

This is the text of II. 23:

> Cui fugienda fuit indocti semita uulgi,
>   ipsa petita lacu nunc mihi dulcis aqua est.
> ingenuus quisquam alterius dat munera seruo,
>   ut promissa suae uerba ferat dominae?
> et quaerit totiens 'Quaenam nunc porticus illam   5
>   integit?' et 'Campo quo mouet illa pedes?',
> deinde, ubi pertuleris, quos dicit fama labores
>   Herculis, ut scribat 'Muneris ecquid habes?',
> cernereue ut possis uultum custodis amari,
>   captus et immunda saepe latere casa?   10

quam care semel in toto nox uertitur anno!
    a pereant, si quos ianua clausa iuuat!
contra, reiecto quae libera uadit amictu,
    custodum et nullo saepta timore, placet.
cui saepe immundo Sacra conteritur Via socco,   15
    nec sinit esse moram, si quis adire uelit;
differet haec numquam, nec poscet garrula, quod te
    astrictus ploret saepe dedisse pater,
nec dicet 'Timeo, propera iam surgere, quaeso:
    infelix, hodie uir mihi rure uenit.'   20
et quas Euphrates et quas mihi misit Orontes,
    me iuerint: nolim furta pudica tori;
libertas quoniam nulli iam restat amanti,
    nullus liber erit, si quis amare uolet.

I was determined to avoid the path of the ignorant mob, but now even water drawn from a public pool seems sweet to me. Can any free-born man give presents to another man's slave, so that he will carry a promised message to his mistress? Can he ask again and again 'What portico shades her now?' and 'In what field does she walk?' Then, when you have borne the legendary labors of Hercules—so that she may write 'Have you got a present?' or so that you may see the face of her sour protector and often hide yourself in a dirty shed—at what a price your night comes round once in a whole year! I've no use for men whom a closed door delights! My choice is a girl who throws back her cloak and walks free, not fenced about by any fear of her protectors; the Sacred Way is often tramped by her dirty sandals, and she makes no delay if a man wants to come to her; she will never put you off or demand with many words a present your hard-pressed father will often lament that you have given, and she will not say 'I am frightened; hurry and get up now, please; poor dear, my husband is coming home from the country today.' Let girls the Euphrates and girls the Orontes have sent me be my delight: I want no decent adultery; since no lover keeps his liberty, no one who chooses to be a lover will be free.

In this poem Propertius is adopting the conventional moral attitude of his time. To have relations with prostitutes was not considered reprehensible; instead it was regarded as reasonable conduct, a sensible means of avoiding both the disturbance of reason caused by passionate love and the crimes of adultery or the follies of extravagance to which passion leads. Relations with common prostitutes were a lesser evil than entanglement with a married woman or a fashionable courtesan. The classical moralists constantly bring against the latter type of affair the objection that it costs the lover his liberty, his wealth, and his reputation. Lucretius, for example, in his arraignment of love, makes these three charges in lines that succeed each other like clauses in a judicial indictment:

> Adde quod alterius sub nutu degitur aetas;
> labitur interea res et Babylonica fiunt;
> languent officia atque aegrotat fama uacillans.
>
> (Lucr. IV. 1122–4)

Consider further that their life is passed subject to another's will; wealth meanwhile slips away, exchanged for Babylonian luxuries; duty's call is weak and shattered reputation pines away.

The classical moralists do not urge continence as an alternative. Their attitude is rather the one typified by the story Horace tells about the elder Cato in *Satires* I. 2.31–35:

> quidam notus homo cum exiret fornice, 'macte
> uirtute esto' inquit sententia dia Catonis;
> 'nam simul ac uenas inflavit taetra libido,
> huc iuuenes aequum est descendere, non alienas
> permolere uxores.'

When a man he knew was coming out of a whore house Cato's splendid judgement was: 'Nobly done! For as soon as ugly lust has swollen the veins it is proper for young men to come down here, and not bother other men's wives.'

Later in the same satire Horace warns against the dangers and the delays that occur in affairs with married women, and gives his own advice:

> tument tibi cum inguina, num, si
> ancilla aut uerna est praesto puer, impetus in quem
> continuo fiat, malis tentigine rumpi?
> non ego; namque parabilem amo uenerem facilemque.
>
> (*Sat.* I. 2.116–19)

When you are swelling with lust, if a maid or slave-boy is handy, whom you can attack without delay, would you rather burst with desire? Not I! For I like an easy and available love.

Horace emphasizes the loss of wealth and reputation in *Sat.* I. 2, and in *Sat.* II. 7 he ridicules the slavery of the lover. In elegies II. 23 and 24a Propertius presents these dangers as they threaten a man who allows himself to fall in love with a courtesan (or perhaps a married woman) rather than satisfy himself with 'an easy and available love'. In 23 the danger to be avoided is loss of liberty, in 24a it is loss of reputation, and in both the waste of money plays a role. An attractive case can be made for the suggestion that Propertius is deliberately imitating Horace. (Book I of the *Satires* appeared about ten years before Propertius' second book.) But there are no certain verbal reminiscences of the satire in the elegy, and there is nothing common to the two poems that cannot be paralleled elsewhere. The similarity between the two poets is adequately explained as resulting from their writing within a common social tradition and drawing upon a common store of literary material, each adapting this material to his own kind of poetry.

In II. 23 Propertius expresses ideas entirely in accord with those of Horace and Lucretius, and the conventional material of the elegy appears in an ordered, indeed a schematic form. It is presented as an ordered analysis of common experience, formally enclosed in a frame of personal statement (lines 1–2, 21–22), followed by a final sententious distich stating the conclusion drawn (23–24). The central discussion itself falls into two parallel sections, presenting first the disadvantages of serving a mistress and then the advantages of patronizing girls of the street. Each of these sections contains ten lines, which balance each other distich for distich: a mistress is surrounded by servants who must be flattered and bribed, while the approach to a prostitute is direct and unimpeded (3–4, 13–14); a mistress must be sought for, a prostitute is always at hand (5–6, 15–16); a mistress first demands every sacrifice and then her greed is insatiable, but a prostitute comes at call and her price is low (7–8, 17–18); the unpleasantness and danger involved in serving a mistress are absent from relations with a prostitute (9–10, 19–20). The first section closes with a rejection of the mistress (11–12), the second with a welcome to the prostitute (21–22). The final distich is a logical conclusion, answering the question whether a freeborn man can act as a lover does.[10] Rhetorical development has demonstrated that true freedom is incompatible with love.

This ordered balance of arrangement and this subordination of immediate personal feeling to the clear rhetorical development of a conventional theme are not characteristic of Propertius, just as the attitude of superiority to passion is unusual in him. His usual presentation of love insists upon its irrationality and its rejection of philosophy, morality, and logic. Moderation—the Horatian ideal—has no place in his love:

> errat, qui finem uesani quaerit amoris:
> uerus amor nullum nouit habere modum.
>
> (II.15. 29–30)

He is wrong who seeks the limit of mad love: true love cannot know a mean.

He urges Lynceus to forget philosophy if he is to become a lover:

> Lynceus ipse meus seros insanit amores!
> solum te nostros laetor adire deos.
> quid tua Socraticis tibi nunc sapientia libris
> proderit? (II. 34.25–28)

My friend Lynceus himself is growing mad with late-blooming love! I am glad that you above all others are turning to my gods. How will the wisdom gained from books of the Socratics help you now?

So he prepares for the advice that Lynceus turn to Propertius' own kind of poetry and to the subject of love. The irreconcilable separation between reason and love is asserted firmly in the elegy just preceding II. 23:

> quaeris, Demophoon, cur sim tam mollis in omnis?
> quod quaeris, 'quare' non habet ullus amor.
> cur aliquis sacris laniat sua bracchia cultris
> et Phrygis insanos caeditur ad numeros?
> uni cuique dedit uitium natura creato:
> mi fortuna aliquid semper amare dedit. (II. 22.13–18)

You ask, Demophoon, why I am so susceptible to every woman. In answer to your question—there is no 'why' in love. Why should a man lacerate his arms with sacred knives and why slash himself to the maddening measures of the Phrygian piper? To everything at birth nature has given its own vice: to me fortune has given this, forever to be in love.

Love as a violent, irrational passion, hated but welcomed, is the usual subject of Propertius' poetry. Who was he, his reader might ask, that he should preach such doctrine as II. 23 presents? All Rome knew of his passion for Cynthia; by undertaking to express the precepts of accepted morality he made himself ridiculous. II. 24a presents his sudden realization of the effect love has had on his reputation:

'Tu loqueris, cum sis iam noto fabula libro
  et tua sit toto Cynthia lecta foro?'
cui non his uerbis aspergat tempora sudor?
  aut pudor ingenuus aut reticendus amor!
quod si tam facilis spiraret Cynthia nobis,   5
  non ego nequitiae dicerer esse caput,
nec sic per totam infamis traducerer urbem,
  urerer et quamuis, nomine uerba darem.
quare ne tibi sit mirum me quaerere uilis:
  parcius infamant: num tibi causa leuis?   10
et modo pauonis caudae flabella superbae
  et manibus dura frigus habere pila,
et cupit iratum talos me poscere eburnos,
  quaeque nitent Sacra uilia dona Via.
a peream, si me ista mouent dispendia, sed me   15
  fallaci dominae iam pudet esse iocum!

'*You* say this, when you are already a legend because of your famous book, and your "Cynthia" is read everywhere in the forum?' Whose temples would not be moist with sweat at these words? Either a free man's self-restraint or a love-affair on the quiet! But if Cynthia breathed so softly on me I would not be called a model of folly; I would not be shamed with ridicule in the whole city, and even though on fire I would fool the world with my good name. So do not be surprised that I am chasing cheap women: they cost one's reputation less; can you think that reason unimportant? Now it is a fan from a peacock's proud tail that she wants, and the coolness of a hard crystal ball to hold in her hands, and she wants me (angry though she makes me) to buy ivory dice and all the cheap gifts that shine in the Sacred Way. But oh! it is not the money that troubles me; now I am ashamed that my deceitful mistress laughs at me.

This elegy is a difficult one because the sequence of ideas is subject to shifts of feeling, rather than controlled by a reasoned progression of argument as in elegy 23. It reflects the sudden disturbance of the poet's mind caused by the realization that his character as the slave of love is firmly established in men's eyes. The initial question is presented as spoken by a reader of the previous elegy, who scoffs at such sentiments from Propertius. This criticism he immediately recognizes as justified; sweat breaks out on his forehead, revealing the shame with which he realizes his situation. His fault is that he has followed neither of two permissible courses of action, 'either a free man's self-restraint or a love-affair on the quiet'. The phrase 'a free man's self-restraint' (*pudor ingenuus*) contains an echo of the third line of elegy 23. There the poet asked whether any free man (*ingenuus*) can act as a lover does, and showed that it is impossible. Here self-restraint, which does not rule out relations with common prostitutes and which is the characteristic of free men, is again contrasted with love, but now love is not something that must be rejected. The poet is too far enslaved to hope for that. He can only long for a love which can be kept quiet. Shame, however, quickly yields to a desire for self-justification, and he puts the blame on Cynthia. It is not a noble defence, but we should not look to an elegist for noble sentiments. If Cynthia were more kind he would not be called the perfect example of folly, nor be an object of shameful ridicule to the whole city. Though he burned with passion he would deceive men under cover of a good reputation. Therefore he has turned to the cheap girls of the streets; they are a means of escape from his present disgrace. The form of his statement that cheap women are relatively harmless to one's reputation shifts his thought to another fault of Cynthia. *Parcius infamant* normally means 'they bring disgrace in less degree', with a faded meaning of *parcius*; but the original meaning of *parcius* is 'at less expense'. This aspect of the word's meaning is caught up in the next lines. Cynthia is expensive; she is always demanding gifts. For a moment he dwells on this fault in her. But then, recognizing that these are trivialities, he brushes away such complaints in the closing lines. The real cause of his unhappiness is the shame his faithless mistress causes him when she makes open sport of him. Thus the end of the elegy returns to the beginning, to the shame which love for Cynthia has brought upon him. Shame is now mingled with jealousy, since Cynthia is *fallax*, and it is doubtless before his successful rival that she holds Propertius up to ridicule. The situation of the poem is treated as a purely personal one. The maxim which Propertius states in line 4 appears as a rule based simply on his own experience, rather than on such general reflections as justified the maxim that concluded elegy 23. The complaints about Cynthia's extravagance in lines 11–14 are entirely personal and specific, in contrast to the generalized *muneris ecquid habes?* of 23.8. The lack of formal connexion between line 10 and line 11 has led some editors to assume a lacuna in the text at this point. It is possible that they may be right, but such sudden transitions reveal the distraught state of the lover's mind. Although more clearly marked grammatically, the emotional transitions at lines 5 and 15 are even more violent.

In this elegy, unlike the preceding one, the conventional elements are entirely subordinated to personal feeling. The elegy is not concerned with the faults of the typical mistress, but of Cynthia, a figure to whom Propertius has already given vivid life and being. The central point of both elegy 23 and elegy 24a is a general statement, but there is a difference: in one case the general statement is presented as a conclusion reached by ordered argument and a reasoned balancing of facts drawn from common experience, while in the other it is offered as a course of personal conduct, the propriety of which has been learned by the poet from the facts of his own immediate situation. In contrast with 23, 24a seems spontaneous and directly inspired by personal feeling and experience, although it is actually no less conventional in the ideas it contains and no less influenced by the traditional material of erotic commonplace. A dramatic vividness results both from the introduction of another speaker in the opening lines and from the successive changes in the mood of the poet as his defence proceeds. The arguments seem to arise immediately from the situation rather than to follow a predetermined course. In 23 reason is in control, and the style is clear and evidently disciplined to present reasoned argument, while in 24a the poet has surrendered to his situation and reveals his distracted condition of mind. In each of these elegies, if considered in isolation, *fides* is maintained, since the style is proper to the sentiments expressed. But, because of its departure from the usual character of the Propertian lover, 23 seems insincere, as the scoffing questioner of 24a devastatingly reveals. In both poems traditional themes are adapted by Propertius to elegiac treatment, but the manner in which he treats the conventional elements and the degree to which he gives personal form and intensity to traditional material vary widely in the two poems. In each case the style accords with the attitude assumed by the poet.

In Ovid's *Amores*, which are so frequently accused of insincerity, we find a style similar to that of Propertius II. 23. It is both more lucid and less passionate than the usual style of Propertius. Greater clarity of language, more orderly progression of ideas, and smoother verse structure combine to suggest a lover who is more in control of his emotion than Propertius. Ovid seems less concerned to present the impact of love upon an individual than to reveal its typical working; he treats conventional elements in such a way that their general truth will be established. The lover who appears in the elegies of Ovid differs from the normal Propertian lover primarily in that he is more in control of his own attitude toward love. The attitude that we find in Propertius is actually more conventional and more firmly established in literary tradition than that of Ovid. Propertius writes entirely within the psychological theory that love is the most ungovernable of passions, a state of the soul in which it is completely impervious to reason. Professor Hermann Fränkel has shown how much more complex than this is Ovid's presentation of the nature of love, and describes Ovid as 'proposing that it was love which gave man a feeling soul in addition to his body, and that it was sexual love which taught him to know and understand and like his fellow human beings, so that he would build up a society'.[11] Love itself, if it is to be this civilizing force, must be subject to control: so we find in the *Amores* the constant suggestion that passion, although it can and should not be denied, must in some manner be mastered and placed under restraint by the lover. This may require that he deceive himself or beg his mistress to hide from him her infidelities, but it is a deliberate and necessary kind of deceit. This is a complex and new interpretation of love, for which the style of Propertius would be altogether unsuitable, but which finds effective form in the sure and controlled style of Ovid. In it convention can be presented so nakedly because the attitude expressed is so unconventional.

The particular function of Roman love elegy was to give personal form to typical experience, as both Propertius and Ovid themselves declared. The normal manner of Propertius in his love elegies is highly personal and is distinguished from that of Ovid by the fact that the conventional element in his work is disguised by the personal form. There is, however, one characteristic feature of his style in which convention seems to be sought for its own sake. This is his constant introduction of examples from mythology.

Criticism has tended to see in the examples simply an element which embellishes a poem and serves to ennoble a present character or situation by lifting it into a world of ideal grandeur and beauty, a world which was very present to the Roman reader because his literature was so filled with myth and because its plastic and pictorial representations were constantly before his eyes. Such a view of the function of mythology can hardly fail to lead to the further conclusion that on the whole his examples are unsuccessful; for in so large number they would end by wearying rather than pleasing the reader, and more often chill with their learning than excite with their vividness. The examples may therefore seem, by interposing external and impersonal subjects into the expression of the poet's feeling and emotion, to retard and check the flow of his passion.[12] This criticism is not a superficial one, but comes very close to the heart of Propertius' poetry: a judgement of his work and of the position which should be assigned him among Latin poets must be affected by the decision whether such strictures are justified. The question which requires consideration is this: Is mythology simply a decorative and ennobling element or is it an essential part of his poetry?

In primitive societies it is a function of myth to provide authoritative sanction for custom and belief. In an advanced society it may remain as a body of universally respected truth, establishing the validity of the fundamental assumptions upon which the ordering of society is based. When Cicero, in his defence of Sestius, claimed immortality of fame as the reward of the good man who has served his country well, it was in the example of Hercules that he found that this belief received consecration. Since Propertius, like Cicero, regarded myth as symbolically true, as providing known and accepted examplification of known and accepted principles, he found in myth a means of expressing universal and absolute truth, a standard of validity more real than any single and isolated experience. The Classical world was profoundly sceptical of the individual phenomenon: only by reference to its accepted category did the individual thing acquire reliability and truth. Myth served to raise experience from an individual to a universal level.

A clear example of such use of mythology occurs in the third elegy of Propertius' first book, which is one of the best known and most generally admired of the love elegies:

Qualis Thesea iacuit cedente carina
  languida desertis Cnosia litoribus;
qualis et accubuit primo Cepheia somno
  libera iam duris cotibus Andromede;
nec minus assiduis Edonis fessa choreis   5
  qualis in herboso concidit Apidano:
talis uisa mihi mollem spirare quietem
  Cynthia non certis nixa caput manibus,
ebria cum multo traherem uestigia Baccho,
  et quaterent sera nocte facem pueri.   10
hanc ego, nondum etiam sensus deperditus omnis,
  molliter impresso conor adire toro;
et quamuis duplici correptum ardore iuberent
  hac Amor hac Liber, durus uterque deus,
subiecto leuiter positam temptare lacerto   15
  osculaque admota sumere et arma manu,
non tamen ausus eram dominae turbare quietem,
  expertae metuens iurgia saeuitiae;
sed sic intentis haerebam fixus ocellis
  Argus ut ignotis cornibus Inachidos.   20
et modo soluebam nostra de fronte corollas
  ponebamque tuis, Cynthia, temporibus;
et modo gaudebam lapsos formare capillos;
  nunc furtiua cauis poma dabam manibus;
omniaque ingrato largibar munera somno,   25
  munera de prono saepe uoluta sinu;
et quotiens raro duxti suspiria motu,
  obstupui uano credulus auspicio,
ne qua tibi insolitos portarent uisa timores,
  neue quis inuitam cogeret esse suam: 30
donec diuersas praecurrens luna fenestras,
  luna moraturis sedula luminibus,
compositos leuibus radiis patefecit ocellos.
  sic ait in molli fixa toro cubitum:
'tandem te nostro referens iniuria lecto   35
  alterius clausis expulit e foribus?
namque ubi longa meae consumpsti tempora noctis,
  languidus exactis, ei mihi, sideribus?
o utinam talis perducas, improbe, noctes,
  me miseram qualis semper habere iubes!   40
nam modo purpureo fallebam stamine somnum,
  rursus et Orpheae carmine, fessa, lyrae;
interdum leuiter mecum deserta querebar
  externo longas saepe in amore moras:

131

dum me iucundis lapsam sopor impulit alis.   45
illa fuit lacrimis ultima cura meis.'

As Cretan Ariadne lay on the deserted shore, relaxed in sleep, while
Theseus' ship sailed away; and as Cepheus' daughter Andromeda
reclined in her first sleep, free now from the hard rocks; and as, no
less wearied by her long dancing, the Thracian bacchant has fallen
faint on the grassy bank of the Apidanus: so Cynthia appeared to me
to breathe soft sleep, resting her head on her unsteady hands, when I
came staggering in with drunken steps and my slaves were waving
their torches late at night. Not quite wholly senseless, I tried to go to
her, so soft a burden for her couch; and though both Love and Wine,
each a hard god, commanded me, filled with twin fires, to make trial
of her, slipping my arm gently beneath her as she lay, and to take kisses
and weapons in hand, still I did not dare disturb my mistress's peace,
fearing the reproaches of an anger I have experienced; but I lingered
unmoving, like Argus seeing the strange horns of Inachus' daughter.
And now I was taking the wreathes from my forehead, Cynthia, and
placing them on your brow; and now I was finding delight in shaping
your disordered hair; again to your cupped hands I was offering
stealthy gifts of fruits; and all my gifts I bestowed on thankless sleep,
gifts that often rolled away from your sloping lap; and each time you
sighed with a rare movement, I was terrified, believing the empty
omen, that some dream might bring you strange fears, or that someone
might be forcing you to be his against your will: until the moon,
running past the windows facing us—the busy moon with lingering
light—with gentle rays opened her shut eyes. Thus she spoke, resting
her elbow on the soft couch: 'Has another woman's harshness driven
you back at last to my bed and forced you from her closed doors?
Where have you spent the long hours of *my* night, slack now, when
the stars, alas, are setting? I pray that you may live through such nights
as, unkind, you always bid me pass in sorrow. For now I held off
sleep by spinning with purple thread, and again, though weary, by
the music of Orpheus' lyre; sometimes, alone and to myself, I softly
spoke my complaint at your long and frequent lingering with another
love: until I sank down and sleep touched me with his welcome wings.
That was my tears' last concern.'

The mythological comparisons open the poem with unhurried
dignity. They also present the images of the heroines with parti-
cularity of detail. When Ovid imitated this passage (as he did in
Amores I. 10), he sketched the stories of the heroines with a few
brief strokes, presenting the beauty of the heroines by stating the
effect that it had on the course of events in the myths in which

they appear. Propertius, instead, particularizes by isolating a single moment in each myth and presenting it as a visual image. Upon this scene of calm and of mythic beauty the poet breaks in, stumbling with drunken footsteps. His blurred senses, guided by drunkenness and desire, carry him to the verge of rape. (Various devices of interpretation and 'emendation' have been attempted in order to bowdlerize this part of the poem. Professor Enk in his edition sensibly remarks that the passage is more drastic than nice-minded scholars try to persuade us.)[13] There is a brutal realism in the lover's entrance which could not be in sharper contrast with the calm loveliness of the girl. This contrast suddenly forces itself even upon his dulled senses. He stops and gazes upon her like Argus at the strange vision of Io's metamorphosis. The rest of his acts are tributes to her: he takes the wreath from his forehead and places it on hers, puts in order the locks of her hair, presents gifts to her thankless sleep. So he falls entirely under her spell, until he becomes so far subordinated as to identify his feelings with hers. When she stirs in sleep and sighs, he is fearful for her, fearful that she may be troubled by dreams, that perhaps in a dream someone may be attempting to violate her against her will. So the act of violence which he had been on the verge of committing has not only been averted by the effect she produces on him, but the poet himself—the intruding lover— has passed from the plane of present reality and has become a figure in a dream, an unsubstantial shadow. (If lines 13–16 are not taken to imply a drunken urge to make a sexual attack on the sleeping girl, the splendid irony of line 30 is quite lost.) The realistic character who burst in upon the sleeping girl has faded away when confronted with the quality of mythic beauty incorporated in her. The end of the elegy returns to the situation of its beginning. The light of the passing moon awakens Cynthia; she reproaches her lover for having left her to watch alone the fading of the stars while he looked elsewhere for amusement. This desertion was her last thought before she fell asleep. The elegy ends, as it began, with sleep. Cynthia's words revive the opening images of the sleeping heroines. She thus returns, in the reader's consciousness, to a realm of timeless being and permanent reality, which she shares with the heroines. The two figures in the poem are presented in very different ways: the lover in a completely realistic manner, the girl idealized in her likeness to the mythological heroines. But the realistic character of the lover fades into the unreality of dream, while Cynthia remains in a world beyond time.

In this elegy the mythological examples have been used to establish a contrast between two elements in a situation—between the temporary impulses of the poet and the overriding factors which determine his conduct. Realism provides terms for describing what is temporary, mythology for describing what is permanent. In using myth as a symbol of what has more than merely temporary validity, Propertius is exploiting the central artistic value which mythology presented to the poet writing of personal experience.

Propertius very frequently presents an example as parallel to his own situation, and thus shows that his private experience is consonant with or justified by universal human experience. This is a technique that he follows in another elegy in which he has in a wild rage threatened to kill both himself and Cynthia (II. 8). Such an act, he admits, would be dishonourable; yet Achilles, too, acted dishonourably, Propertius goes on, when he passively watched the Greeks routed by Hector and saw Patroclus killed; but he did this because of his love for Briseis. So, Propertius asks,

mirum, si de me iure triumphat Amor? (II. 8.40)

Is it strange if love rightly triumphs over me?

Love *rightly* triumphs; the standard here followed is not a moral one, but rather a purely pragmatic one; it is a law of human experience which Achilles' example establishes and to which Propertius' conduct conforms. In another elegy the example of Nestor proves that a man can live too long (II. 13); or again, Paris' conduct toward Menelaus proves that Love can override the laws of friendship and hospitality (II. 34); or Protesilaus' return, when he came back from the lower world to revisit his wife, proves that love can survive the grave (I. 19). The example in each case vouches for the general idea and is itself a specific embodiment of it.

In the opening elegy of Propertius' first book this use of myth to establish norms of experience and conduct is illustrated the more sharply because here mythological example is adduced to prove, by contrast, the uniqueness of the poet's experience.[14] The poem expresses the despair of a lover whose hopes have been disappointed and who is in deep emotional distress caused by the unreason and injustice under which he feels himself to be suffering. The spiritual conflict caused by unwillingness to accept disappointment is reflected in the paradoxical tone of the poem. The opening lines confess the poet's total subjection to Love. But confession has brought no relief, for Cynthia and the gods are unkind. Indeed, it is only hate that Love has taught him:

> Amor me docuit castas odisse puellas. (I. 1.5)

Love has taught me to hate chaste girls.

Since the 'castae puellae' are girls who, like Cynthia, reject a lover, the paradox of the situation is that Love has taught him to love and to hate the same object. The poem is an intensely personal complaint; there is no attempt to present the individual as a typical example. It is rather the uniqueness of his experience upon which the poet lays stress. The poem is one of self-pity and personal revolt against an unacceptable yet unescapable reality. In order to prove that all the laws which properly govern experience have in his case been violated, he offers the example of Milanion:

> Milanion nullos fugiendo, Tulle, labores
> saeuitiam durae contudit Iasidos.
> nam modo Partheniis amens errabat in antris,
> ibat et hirsutas ille uidere feras;
> ille etiam Hylaei percussus uulnere rami
> saucius Arcadiis rupibus ingemuit.
> ergo uelocem potuit domuisse puellam:
> tantum in amore preces et bene facta ualent. (I. 1.9–16)

By avoiding no sufferings, Tullus, Milanion broke Atalanta's cruelty; for now he wandered insane amid the caves of Mt. Parthenium, and he went to face shaggy beasts; struck, too, by the blow of Hylas' club, he groaned, wounded, among the Arcadian rocks. Therefore he was able to tame the swift girl; so much do prayers and services avail in love.

Inclusion of the dedicatory address to Tullus within the example is an indication of the central importance of the example. It extends through eight lines. They do not relate the story of Milanion; the reader is expected to know it. The lines consist rather of allusive details. We are told that Milanion wandered distractedly in the forest, but not why; that he was wounded by the centaur, Hylas, but nothing of the battle or its cause. The reason for this is clear: to relate the whole story would not advance Propertius' purpose, since it is only in the suffering of the hero for the sake of love and in his subsequent happiness that the legend is significant. The point of the example is made explicit in the last line, which states directly, in the form of a maxim, the meaning of the myth: the service of a lover has power to win his beloved.

Milanion is here presented not as a single individual of the past with whom the poet compares himself, but as the type of the suffering lover, whose obedient service to love brings an eventual reward: in him a principle is established which is a law of human experience. Consequently, when Propertius returns from the example to his own experience it is with clear emphasis on its unique and personal character:

> in me tardus Amor non ullas cogitat artis,
>   nec meminit notas, ut prius, ire uias.   (I. 1.17–18)

In my case sluggish Love invents no stratagems and has forgotten how to travel his familiar ways.

When the principle which is established by Milanion's example is violated, the basis for the natural and orderly conduct of life is destroyed. The gods have changed; and in this change lies the explanation of the paradox that Love has taught him to hate.

The elegy closes with a general address to the readers, expressing the hope that they may never find themselves in the poet's unhappy position. In the course of this address Propertius again contrasts his own with general experience, and there is the same emphasis on its personal character:

> uos remanete, quibus facili deus annuit aure,
>   sitis et in tuto semper amore pares.
> in me nostra Venus noctes exercet amaras,
>   et nullo uacuus tempore defit Amor.
> hoc, moneo, uitate malum: sua quemque moretur
>   cura, neque assueto mutet amore locum.
> quod si quis monitis tardas aduerterit auris,
>   heu referet quanto uerba dolore mea!   (I. 1.31–38)

Remain steadfast, you whose prayers the god has heard with listening ear, and may you always be joined in untroubled love. In my case our goddess Venus punishes me with bitter nights, and Love is never absent. Avoid this evil, I warn you. Let each man's affection hold him, and let it not change its place when love has grown familiar. If anyone turns sluggish ears to my warnings, with what pain, alas, will he recall my words!

The situation of other, normally happy, lovers is used, like the example, to show that norm of experience with which the poet's own experience is at variance. The mythological example, the maxim, and the direct address have a parallel artistic purpose: the introduction of standards of an external and objective character.

It is notorious that Propertius makes great demands on his readers for sympathetic and intelligent attention. His words are made to bear so heavy a weight of meaning that without this careful attention he often seems altogether obscure. The examples show this same close and densely ordered style. The reader has to perceive in the example not only the particular fact but also the general idea which is implicitly contained in it, and further he has to realize the application of this general idea to the case before him. Since the example relates to a situation which, like any human situation, is complex in character, the example may be used to establish and join two different principles, and so a transition may be made without any explicit statement of the relation between two different ideas.

Such a structurally complex use of an example is to be found in II. 8. This is the elegy in which Achilles' role in the *Iliad* is seen as shameful conduct, but conduct perfectly explicable because of Achilles' love for the girl who was taken from him. (We may be startled by this reading of Homer, but such startling reinterpretation of conventional values is a way by which Propertius gives insight into the mad logic of love.) The elegy had begun with Cynthia lost to a rival. Jealous despair seems to reach a climax of masochistic joy in the thought of dying while Cynthia cruelly triumphs over him:

> sic igitur prima moriere aetate, Properti?
> sed morere; interitu gaudeat illa tuo!
> exagitet nostros Manis, sectetur et umbras,
> insultetque rogis, calcet et ossa mea!   (II. 8.17–20)

Will you then die like this in your first youth, Propertius? But die! Let her rejoice in your destruction. Let her torment my spirit, pursue my shade, insult my pyre, and trample on my bones!

Then follows an example which Housman and others have found hopelessly irrelevant to the context:

> quid? non Antigonae tumulo Boeotius Haemon
> corruit ipse suo saucius ense latus,
> et sua cum miserae permiscuit ossa puellae,
> qua sine Thebanam noluit ire domum?   (21–24)

Did not Boeotian Haemon fall at Antigone's tomb, his side pierced by his own sword? And did he not mingle his bones with the bones of the unhappy girl? Without her he was not willing to return to his Theban home.

A reasonable, common-sense world may find it hard to see Cynthia in Antigone, Propertius in Haemon. But Cynthia's distracted lover seeking a pattern for his own tragic condition finds a natural parallel in the pathos of Haemon's noble death for love's sake. But as he writes the incongruity comes obliquely to the lover's mind. The *ossa puellae* of line 23 recalls the *ossa mea* three lines before: Haemon chose that in death his bones should be mingled with those of his mistress; Propertius' mistress will trample on his bones. Awareness of the incongruity leads to a sudden change of mood and a fresh decision:

> sed non effugies: mecum moriaris oportet;
> hoc eodem ferro stillet uterque cruor.
> quamuis ista mihi mors est inhonesta futura:
> mors inhonesta quidem, tu moriere tamen.   (25–28)

But you will not escape: you must die with me; let the blood of both of us drip from this same blade; though that death will be inglorious for me, inglorious though the death, you still will die.

As Antigone was already dead when Haemon killed himself, so Cynthia's death must precede her lover's suicide. The momentary dream of glory suggested by thought of Haemon has to be renounced, but the pattern of the myth must be realized. So the poem passes from the theme of suicide to that of murder, and the necessary link binding the parts of the elegy is contained implicitly in the myth. The example has been used as an essential part of the poem to make a transition between two different ideas, as the seeming climax of threatened suicide leads to the full climax of murder.

Free as Propertius was in his use of examples from mythology, he rarely used examples from nature. Evidently he found a value in myth that he did not find in nature. A look at I. 2, which contains two series of examples, shows why mythology was more meaningful for him.

Quid iuuat ornato procedere, uita, capillo
    et tenuis Coa ueste mouere sinus,
aut quid Orontea crinis perfundere murra
    teque peregrinis uendere muneribus,
naturaeque decus mercato perdere cultu,   5
    nec sinere in propriis membra nitere bonis?
crede mihi, non ulla tuae est medicina figurae:
    nudus Amor formae non amat artificem.
aspice quos summittat humus formosa colores,
    ut ueniant hederae sponte sua melius,   10
surgat et in solis formosius arbutus antris,
    et sciat indocilis currere lympha uias.
litora natiuis persuadent picta lapillis,
    et uolucres nulla dulcius arte canunt.
non sic Leucippis succendit Castora Phoebe,   15
    Pollucem cultu non Hilaira soror;
non, Idae et cupido quondam discordia Phoebo,
    Eueni patriis filia litoribus:
nec Phrygium falso traxit candore maritum
    auecta externis Hippodamia rotis: 20
sed facies aderat nullis obnoxia gemmis,
    qualis Apelleis est color in tabulis.
non illis studium uulgo conquirere amantis:
    illis ampla satis forma pudicitia.
non ego nunc uereor ne sim tibi uilior istis: 25
    uni si qua placet, culta puella sat est;
cum tibi praesertim Phoebus sua carmina donet
    Aoniamque libens Calliopea lyram,
unica nec desit iucundis gratia uerbis,
    omnia quaeque Venus, quaeque Minerua probat.   30
his tu semper eris nostrae gratissima uitae,
    taedia dum miserae sint tibi luxuriae.   (I. 2)

Why does it give you pleasure, my dear, to go out with your hair done so darefully, and to move diaphanous folds of Coan silk? Or to drench your hair with myrrh from the Orontes, and try to add to your worth with foreign tribute? Why spoil nature's charm with adornment you buy, and why not let your body shine with its own virtues?

Believe me, there is no way to improve your appearance: naked Love does not love artificial beauty. See what colours the beautiful earth sends forth, how ivy grows better of its own accord, and the arbutus springs more beautifully in lonely glens, and waters know how to run in untaught paths; the shores of the sea charm, dappled with their native pebbles, and by no art do birds sing more sweetly. It was not thus that Leucippus' daughter Phoebe fired the heart of Castor, nor did her sister Hilaira rouse Pollux by adornment; not so was Evenus' daughter once a cause of strife between Idas and eager Phoebus on her father's shores; Hippodamia, carried away on foreign chariot wheels, did not draw her Phrygian husband by a counterfeit brilliance: but their beauty, a colour like that of Apelles' paintings, owed nothing to jewels. They had no desire to seek lovers everywhere; for them chastity was beauty enough. I have no fear now that I may be of less account in your eyes than those others: if a girl please one man she is adorned enough; especially since Phoebus presents you his gift of poetry, and a willing Calliope her Aonian lyre, and no single attraction is wanting in your charming words, and you have all that Venus and all that Minerva admire. With these gifts you will always be the greatest delight of my life, if only you grow tired of these dreary luxuries.

The central part of the elegy contains the two series of examples. They fill sixteen lines and form precisely half the elegy, since they are enclosed by an introduction and a conclusion each consisting of eight verses. This general symmetry of structure suggests that, within the central part, each of the series might be expected to equal the other in length. However, this is not the case. In six lines examples from nature illustrate how little need Cynthia's beauty has for the aid of art (9–14); in the next six lines the same point is illustrated by the experience of the heroines (15–20). If the function of the two series were the same we might now expect a return from the illustrations to the thing illustrated; but what actually occurs is further development of the mythological examples. Lines 21–22 amplify the references to myth by stating positively what has been implied by a series of negations. In the next distich an entirely new theme appears when beauty, for the heroines, is identified with chastity (23–24). The subject of the poem is no longer simply the superiority of beauty that is natural and unadorned to beauty overladen with artificial and meretricious decoration; natural beauty now becomes an outward sign of a moral characteristic: for a woman who is chaste, her chastity is sufficient adornment.

This shift of theme within the examples gives a new direction to the poem, as did the Haemon-Antigone example in II. 8. When Propertius, after establishing within the frame of the examples a connexion between simple beauty and chastity, returns from general reflection to the particular relations of Cynthia and himself, he is able to apply to her the principle which he has discovered in the myths: 'If a girl please one man she is adorned enough.' This verse is a maxim stating as a general proposition the rule inferred from the examples. He can confidently assert that Cynthia values his love more than that of all his rivals; like the heroines she is not concerned to win a multitude of lovers. This is the premise which makes possible application to her of the lesson taught by the examples. The poet does not have to insist explicitly upon the conclusion that is necessarily implied: if Cynthia now refuses to forgo the artifices of fashion she will prove that she is not satisfied *uni placere*. If a girl pleases one man, if she is satisfied to be faithful to one lover—for this is the meaning of a woman's *pudicitia* in the world of the elegiac convention—then, like the heroines, she will have no use for artificial adornment. Otherwise, she will belong not to the category of the heroines, the great lovers of antiquity for whom chastity is itself beauty, but rather to the class of women who are merely promiscuous. The particular charm of the elegy lies in the indirectness with which the poet has indicated censure of his mistress. Directly he has only asked her not to spoil her native charm with unnecessary adornment; but as he recalls that Hippodamia and the others did not desire 'to seek lovers everywhere', Cynthia is warned that, if she would be true to her own character as it is exemplified in the heroines, she must not only be ready to forgo the artifices of fashion, but also be satisfied *uni placere*. This indirectness is a neat example of the lover's *blanditia* to which Propertius lays claim. Here it permits him to pass easily from implied censure to the graceful compliments with which the elegy closes.

The two series of examples have worked in the poem in different ways. The examples from nature, however beautiful in themselves, are no more than an embellishment of the poem: they all illustrate one theme and all have the same level of validity; they illustrate by analogy. Those from mythology, on the other hand, provide an inevitable part of the thought of the poem, and without them there would be no poem, or a different poem.

Within their framework the poem advances and develops; the whole character and experience of the heroines is the complex symbol with which the poet is operating, and within this complex symbol the theme of chastity is linked with the theme of beauty. Propertius has no feeling of an identity between human and non-human nature; there are only single points of outward resemblance, where the one may be used as an analogy to the other. The analogy is not pressed beyond its immediate application and has validity only as an illustration, not as a proof, compelling assent. But the figures of mythology are the prototypes and models of humanity, and their character and conduct provide the norms for the character and conduct of contemporary men; what is true in myth is also true and significant in the immediate present.

Between Propertius' attitude and a modern romantic attitude there is a great difference. The eighteenth and nineteenth centuries largely reversed these values of mythology and nature. The gods and heroes faded; instead of a living and permanent reality they became only a stock source of poetic ornamentation. Romantic feeling meanwhile found a kinship of man with nature. Those standards for testing the truth of individual experience that poets once sought in their own creation, the conventional stories of mythology, they now more readily seek in nature. We are therefore constantly in danger of reading and judging anachronistically, as Sellar[15] did when he wrote of the examples in I. 2: 'The charm of I. 2, which grows in intensity till line 14 by all the illustrations of the unadorned beauty of natural things, seems to fade away in the irrelevant learning of lines 15–20.' There is actually nothing in Propertius of the romantic attitude toward nature. It is true that he has brief descriptive passages of great beauty; but such passages are rare, and while they embellish a poem they do not suggest any deeper significance than appears on their surface. There is in them no suggestion of a concept of communion and sympathy between man and nature. In I. 17, in which Propertius, having gone on a voyage away from Cynthia, has been forced by a storm to land at night on an inhospitable shore, his feeling is not awe before nature's majesty, but simple and normal fear. Besides fear it is anger that he feels in regarding the raging sea—anger at the greed and folly of men who are so mad as to court their own destruction.

The following elegy, I. 18, is one in which the poet imagines himself as driven by Cynthia's cruelty into a lonely wilderness. Rothstein (whose edition nevertheless provides what is still the best commentary on Propertius) said in his introduction to this elegy:

Eine beinahe modernes, unsere Romantik verwandtes Empfinden herrscht in dieser Elegie. . . . Eine felsige Waldlandschaft, deren stimmungswirkung hier mit ungewöhnlichem Interesse geschildert wird, sucht der Dichter auf um sein Liebesleid zu klagen, nicht nur aus Furcht vor Cynthia, die von seinen Klagen nichts wissen darf, sondern auch seinem eigenen Gefühl folgend, das ihn auch früher schon dazu getrieben hat im Waldesschatten den Namen seiner Geliebten ertönen zu lassen oder ihn in die Rinder der Bäume einzuschneiden.[16]

It is true that such a wild and lonely place is one to which 'his own feeling' might well drive a romantic poet who wished to find that communion with nature which would compensate him for the failure he felt in his human relations, or in the wildness and vastness of which he could discover the counterpart of his own wild and uncontrollable passion. Rothstein would have it that the poet has been led here not only by the need to be alone but also by his own positive desire. But there is no suggestion of such desire in the poem. The single feature of the landscape in which Propertius is interested, the one on which he dwells with the heavy emphasis of frequent repetition, is its loneliness. Even the mention of chattering birds serves to heighten the impression of loneliness, for the chattering of the birds is utterly untouched by the poet's troubles. The natural habitat of man is among men—this is the feeling which lies behind the poem—and that the poet should so isolate himself is a sign of the strong compulsion which has driven him hither. This poem, both in theme and setting, is very like the one which precedes it; and in that poem it is his own folly in separating himself from his mistress and undergoing the dangers of the sea and an unknown land for which he reproaches himself. The loneliness and danger wherein he finds himself are the penalty he pays for leaving Cynthia. In neither poem is there a word which suggests that the scene has been chosen for its own sake or that there is in it anything congenial or sympathetic to the poet's feeling. The scenes are presented simply as lonely, bare of human life, unfit for human habitation.

In each of these poems, however, there is one break in the harsh unsympathy of nature, a break which in one case suggests that present hardship may yet be lightened, and in the other softens the poet's own unhappiness by the reflection that his sorrow is not unique:

> at uos, aequoreae formosa Doride natae,
> candida felici soluite uela choro;
> si quando uestras labens Amor attigit undas,
> mansuetis socio parcite litoribus.   (I. 17.25–29)

But you sea-daughters of lovely Doris, unfurl my white sails as you dance propitiously; if ever Love gliding down has touched your waves, spare a fellow-lover and make gentle your shores.

> uos eritis testes, si quos habet arbor amores,
> fagus et Arcadio pinus amica deo.   (I. 18.19–20)

You will be my witnesses, if ever a tree has loved—beech, and pine loved by the Arcadian god.

But in both of these passages the language is that of mythology, not of nature. Only in this way is a bridge fashioned between nature and man. Mythology can serve to humanize nature and give it significance for man—a procedure which Ovid found so congenial—but nature in itself is irrational, unfeeling, and without meaning beyond its surface, whether that be wild and dangerous or soft and beautiful.

This is why nature is so rarely the source of examples for Propertius. A surface resemblance, a single point of analogy, may be used to embellish a poem but cannot be vested with a broader meaning capable of new turns and development. The example from nature is always a retarding element in his poems, a simple illustration of a single point; the mythological example, vividly setting forth the general truth of which the individual experience is a particular manifestation, may be an essential motive in the design of the poem. Development of thought need not stop; we need not simply linger over a single point. Since what is true of the general type is true also of the individual, the poem may advance from idea to idea within the frame of the example. It is possible to regard the example from nature as simply a decorative element within the poem. But no such restricted definition is acceptable for the mythological example; it was essential to the kind of poetry Propertius wrote. The experience of the individual gained, through the relation to myth, a significance that for the Roman reader it did not have in its own right. The merely personal, sporadic, unrelated had neither importance nor serious interest. Only when measured by the rule of the norm could the individual and discrete experience be evaluated and understood. Propertius was undertaking to establish a respected place in serious literature for the love elegy, that is, for poetry dealing in a personal way with private emotion. By relating private emotion to general standards he gave importance to private emotion.

The elegists write of their experience in love, but they also present an anatomy of love. The poet wishes that in his experience every lover may recognize the pattern of his own love:

> me legat assidue post haec neglectus amator,
>   et prosint illi cognita nostra mala. . . .
> tum me non humilem mirabere saepe poetam,
>   tunc ego Romanis praeferar ingeniis;
> nec poterunt iuuenes nostro reticere sepulcro
>   'Ardoris nostri magne poeta, iaces.'   (I. 7.13–14, 21–24)

May I be carefully read by the neglected lover hereafter, and may the knowledge of my misfortunes aid him. . . . Then you will often admire me as no minor poet; then I shall be preferred to all Roman geniuses; and young men cannot but say at my tomb: 'You lie here, our passion's great poet.'

> me legat in sponsi facie non frigida virgo
>   et rudis ignoto tactus amore puer;
> atque aliquis iuuenum, quo nunc ego, saucius arcu
>   agnoscat flammae conscia signa suae,
> miratusque diu 'Quo' dicat 'ab indice doctus
>   composuit casus iste poeta meas?'
>   (Ovid, *Amores*, II. 1.5–10)

May I be read, with her new husband, by the girl whose heart is not cold, and by the inexperienced boy, when he is touched by the strangeness of love; and may a youth wounded by that bow which now wounds me recognize the signs of the fire we share. And in long admiration let him say: 'How could he know? How could that poet write what has happened to me?'

It is true that Roman love elegy is 'subjective'; in it the poet writes as one declaring what he himself has felt and thought and done. But of the peculiar circumstances and the facts of purely private significance he tells us almost nothing. He writes only of what he knows will be interesting to others because it is part of common experience. To modern taste the individual style of Propertius appeals as giving proof of sincere and genuine feeling. The modern reader has been trained to find in the particular, in the individual and the unique, an intrinsic importance and value. He seeks in the work of a poet those features of the poet's experience which are his unique and personal possession. The presence of conventional and generalizing elements appears as a sign of insincerity, a flaw which may sometimes be excused, but can scarcely ever be admired. It seems to him a paradox that all the Roman elegiac poets had the same experiences, though each wrote of his own experience. Yet the ancient reader expected this conformity of individual with general experience. When the elegist took for his material traditional commonplaces of erotic literature, he did so because those commonplaces were the repository of a practised attitude toward love and because through them the poet established a community of experience with his readers.

The excellence which we are accustomed to find in Propertius lies in his lively personal realization of convention. The characteristic effect of his poetry is one of personal immediacy. The violence of language which results from the density of particular detail in his verse and the abruptness of the transitions which accompany the swift changes in his mood are the means by which he achieved this effect. (They are also sources of his difficulty, which therefore arises from the same source as his excellence.) They create an impression of passionate feeling, but we should not forget that this impression is a product of Propertius' style and that, as we have seen, he could also write in a different style. If sincerity is considered a function of style, both Propertius and Ovid, writing in their characteristic manners, are sincere, because each employs a style which accords with the character his elegies portray. When we regard the elegists in this way we have a more firm approach to understanding them than when we attempt to find in the elegies a reflection of the real character and experience of their authors. We may still prefer Tibullus or Propertius to Ovid, as Quintilian did, but we shall be able to do so in terms pertinent to poetic

style rather than in terms of uncertain inferences drawn from
style.

NOTES

[1] J. P. Postgate, *Select Elegies of Propertius* (London, 1881, and frequently
reprinted), p. lxxix.

[2] R. Wellek and A. Warren, *Theory of Literature*, New York, 1949, p. 215.
Wellek and Warren themselves doubt the value of sincerity, thus defined, as a criterion of literature, and state further that 'the frequently
adduced criterion of "sincerity" is thoroughly false if it judges literature
in terms of biographical truthfulness, correspondence to the author's
experience or feelings as they are attested by outside evidence' (op. cit.,
p. 74).

[3] Schanz-Hosius, *Geschichte der Römischen Literatur* II[4] (Munich, 1935), pp.
212–13.

[4] Ibid., p. 201.

[5] H. E. Butler and E. A. Barber, *The Elegies of Propertius* (Oxford, 1933),
p. xi.

[6] Quotations of Propertius are from the text of E. A. Barber (2nd ed.,
Oxford, 1960), with these exceptions: in I. 2.13, I. 3.16, and II. 24.4
the readings of the MSS. are followed; after II. 34.10 no lacuna is
marked; in III. 15.3 Guyet's emendation *elatus* is accepted; in II. 23.9
cernereue ut is read for *cernere uti* as proposed in *Classical Philology* XLV
(1950), p. 160, n. 48; in I. 2.9 I doubt that *formosa* is right, though I have
not quite courage enough to substitute *non culta*, which I suggested in
the same issue of *Classical Philology*, pp. 36–37.

[7] *Sex. Aurel. Propertius Varietate Lectionis et Perpetua Adnotatione Illustratus*
(Leipzig, 1777), pp. lxxviii–lxxxviii.

[8] K. Lachmann, *Sex. Aurelii Propertii Carmina* (Leipzig, 1816), pp. xxiii–
xxvii.

[9] T. Birt, 'Die Fünfzahl und die Properzchronologie', *Rheinisches Museum*
LXX (1915), pp. 253–314.

[10] A nice legal distinction is also made between possession of *libertas* and the
condition of being *liber*, as pointed out by D. R. Shackleton Bailey,
Propertiana (Cambridge, 1946), p. 109.

[11] Hermann Fränkel, *Ovid: A Poet Between Two Worlds* (Berkeley and Los
Angeles, 1945), p. 62.

[12] So, for example, Schanz-Hosius, op. cit., p. 202: 'Mythologische . . .
Einzelheiten, sparsam zugemessen ein Schmuck und Mittel der Ideali-
sierung, erdrücken durch ihren Uebermass, und die Menge von Göt-
tinnen und Heroinen . . . lassen weniger die Schönheit Cynthias in
hellerem Lichte erstrahlen, als dass sie den Leser ermüden.'

[13] P. J. Enk, *Sex. Propertii Elegiarum Liber I* (Leiden, 1946), *Pars Altera*,
p. 37: 'Locus lascivior quam pudici philologi nobis persuadere conan-
tur' (on line 15). In his note on line 16 he says: 'Qui oscula sumit puellae
admota manu, eo ipso pruriginis arma sumit ad bellum Venereum
gerendum.'

[14] This elegy has provoked many discussions, including my article 'Elegy and the Classical Attitude Toward Love', in *Yale Classical Studies*, VII (New Haven, 1950), pp. 255–77, in which I discussed the Milanion example more fully.

[15] W. Y. Sellar, *The Roman Poets of the Augustan Age: Horace and the Elegiac Poets* (2nd ed., Oxford, 1899), p. 306.

[16] Max Rothstein, *Propertius* (2nd ed., Berlin, 1920), pp. 175–6.

TENERORVM LVSOR AMORVM

A. G. Lee

ONE'S immediate impression, after reading the first elegy of each, is that Tibullus, Propertius, and Ovid have nothing in common except metre and general subject. Ovid's *Arma gravi numero*, an imaginary scene between a poet who professes epic leanings and a god whose arrow points the way to elegy; Tibullus' *Divitias alius*, a pastoral rondo drifting into the theme of love and death; Propertius' *Cynthia prima*, the *cri de coeur* of a seeming neurotic—these three poems are apparently the product of totally different minds. But as one reads more (and grinds through the commentaries), the difference becomes blurred and a similarity begins to assert itself. One sees that *Divitias alius* has points of contact with Propertius 1.6; *Cynthia prima* with Tibullus 2.4; and *Arma gravi numero* with Propertius 2.29a and 3.3. It becomes plain that the three poets are working within a common tradition—a tradition that can be said (at the risk of oversimplification) to go back through Catullus and the Neoterics to Greek poetry of the Hellenistic age. And for a time a general confusion supervenes on the first clarity of one's impressions. Quote the following fragments to a connoisseur who has not read the elegists for some time, and he will find it difficult to place them correctly:

> talis ad Haemonium Nereis Pelea quondam
> vecta est frenato caerula pisce Thetis.

So to Thessalian Peleus the Nereid, sea-blue Thetis, was once carried on a bridled fish.

> illic assidue tauros spectabis arantis,
> et vitem docta ponere falce comas;

149

A. G. LEE

> atque ibi rara feres inculto tura sacello,
> haedus ubi agrestis corruet ante focos.

There you shall watch the oxen constantly ploughing, and the vine shedding its hair under expert pruning-hook; and there you shall offer rare incense at some primitive shrine, when the kid falls dead before the rustic brazier.

> si tibi forte comas vexaverit, utilis ira:
> postmodo mercata pace premendus erit.
> denique ubi amplexu Venerem promiseris empto,
> fac simules puros Isidis esse dies.

If he happens to have disarranged your hair, anger is useful: before long he must be burdened by the price of reconciliation. Then, when your embrace has been bought and you have promised him Love, be sure to pretend that the days are days of abstinence in honour of Isis.

The first might be Propertius or Ovid, the second looks like Tibullus and the third strongly suggests Ovid. In fact, Tibullus wrote the first; Propertius the second and third.[1] The similarities here point to some of the many procedures and themes that are accepted without question by all three poets. They imply a common attitude towards the poet's art and a common attitude towards love. Both these attitudes are complex and sophisticated. They are also interconnected. What is more, each is made up of conventional and personal elements, in such a way that it is often difficult and sometimes impossible to decide whether what is said is genuinely felt or autobiographically true. To take the elegiac attitude to poetry—each poet says his inspiration is a woman:

> usque cano Nemesim, sine qua versus mihi nullus
> verba potest iustos aut reperire pedes. (Tib. 2. 5.111–12)

Always I sing Nemesis, without whom no verse of mine can find proper words or metre.

> non haec Calliope, non haec mihi cantat Apollo:
> ingenium nobis ipsa puella facit.   (Prop. 2. 1.3–4)

It is not Calliope, it is not Apollo who sings me these songs: the girl herself creates my inspiration.

> nec nisi tu nostris cantabitur ulla libellis;
> ingenio causas tu dabis una meo.
> (Ov. *Am.* 2. 17.33–34)

Nor shall any woman but you be celebrated in my books of verse; you alone shall provide themes for my wit.

But sometimes she does not figure at all, and when she does it is often merely as an excuse for a poem of a particular sort: to that extent the elegiac *femme fatale* is a convention. Again, the elegist says he writes poetry either to touch the hard heart of his mistress or to be of help to other and less experienced sufferers:

> ad dominam faciles aditus per carmina quaero:
> ite procul, Musae, si nihil ista valent. (Tib. 2. 4.19–20)

Through poems I look for easy approach to my mistress: Muses, get you gone, if those achieve nothing.

> me legat assidue post haec neglectus amator
> et prosint illi cognita nostra mala. (Prop. 1. 7.13–14)

Hereafter let the neglected lover read me carefully and may knowledge of my misfortunes help him.

> me legat in sponsi facie non frigida virgo
> et rudis ignoto tactus amore puer. (Ov. *Am.* 2. 1.5–6)

Let the uninhibited virgin read me in front of her fiancé, and the gauche boy touched by unknown love.

But such professions are clearly designed to fit particular poems whose aim is purely aesthetic. Here again we are dealing with a convention, based on the belief that poetry should have a practical purpose and ultimately derived from the old idea of the poet as a teacher. Similarly with the elegiac attitude to love. This love has nothing to do with marriage. Marriages are respectably arranged, but *Amor* is beyond human control, irrational, anti-social, invading the personality and compelling his victim to act, feel and think like a madman, but at the same time giving his life its full meaning. Love is a religion whose seers and prophets are the poets and whose complicated code of observances ensures for the faithful a final reward:

> o me felicem, o nox mihi candida, et o tu
> lectule deliciis facte beate meis.
> quam multa apposita narramus verba lucerna
> quantaque sublato lumine rixa fuit.

nam modo nudatis mecum est luctata papillis,
   interdum tunica duxit operta moram.
illa meos somno lapsos patefecit ocellos
   ore suo et dixit 'sicine, lente, iaces?'
quam vario amplexu mutamus bracchia, quantum
   oscula sunt labris nostra morata tuis.   (Prop. 2. 15.1–10)

O lucky me! O my white darkness! And O you little bed made happy by my delight! How many words we babbled while the lamp was by, and what a brawl there was when the light was removed! For now she wrestled with me, her breasts naked, now covered by her tunic she interposed delay. She opened my sleep-fallen eyelids with her lips and said 'You slacker, how can you lie like that?' With what various embracing we changed arms! How my kisses lingered on your lips!

at Venus inveniet puero concumbere furtim
   dum timet et teneros conserit usque sinus,
et dare anhelanti pugnantibus umida linguis
   oscula et in collo figere dente notas.   (Tib. 1. 8.35–38)

But love will find a way to lie together with a boy secretly while he's afraid and keeps hugging your tender bosom, and to give him, as his breathing quickens, moist kisses with fighting tongues and print tooth-marks on his neck.

deripui tunicam, nec multum rara nocebat,
   pugnabat tunica sed tamen illa tegi.
quae cum ita pugnaret tamquam quae vincere nollet,
   victa est non aegre proditione sua.
ut stetit ante oculos posito velamine nostros,
   in toto nusquam corpore menda fuit.
quos umeros, quales vidi tetigique lacertos.
   forma papillarum quam fuit apta premi.
quam castigato planus sub pectore venter.
   quantum et quale latus. quam iuvenale femur.
                              (Ov. Am. I. 5.13–22)

I tore off her tunic. Being fine-woven it was not much in the way, but yet she fought to be protected by the tunic. But since she fought as though not wanting to win, she was beaten easily by her own betrayal. When she stood before my eyes without her dress, nowhere on all her body was there a blemish. What shoulders, what arms I saw and touched! The shape of her nipples, how it invited pressure! How flat the stomach beneath her finely-moulded breasts! How long and well-made her figure! What youthful thighs!

But of course the elegists were rationally irrational and socially anti-social. They did not fully subscribe to their daemonic and anarchical creed. They used it for artistic purposes, sometimes sincerely, sometimes ironically, but always fully aware that personal poetry demands a *persona*, a mask. The poems they wrote, like most poems at any time, were an amalgam of fact and fiction, convention and invention.

One basic fact, common to them all, is the sensuality exploited in these last three examples—a sensuality that must have been as shocking to prudish convention then as it is now. More pervasive, though, are the qualities of sensibility and wit that Ovid implies in his self-description *tenerorum lusor amorum*—a phrase that from the ancient point of view would apply with equal propriety to Tibullus and Propertius, too. In the three passages above one is conscious of a similar sensibility; and wit, too, is present in all of them, though not dominantly. In Propertius there is the combination of apparent contraries in the phrase *nox candida*, and the meaning of *iaces* is given a special twist by *lapsos* in the previous line. In Tibullus one feels the suggestiveness of *teneros conserit usque sinus*: it suggests *conserere manus*, a phrase used of hand-to-hand fighting, and prepares for the explicit metaphor in *pugnantibus*. In Ovid, most obviously of the three, there is the characteristic epigram *victa est non aegre proditione sua* (where it is worth noting that *non aegre* suggests both *facile* and *libenter*), and it would appear from the *Thesaurus Linguae Latinae* that he is using *castigato* in an original way, though the evidence makes it difficult for us to sense the precise implications of the word.[2]

There is, then, much in common between the three Roman elegists and one's first impression needs to be adjusted to this fact. At the same time that first impression proves to have been soundly based. Each of the three elegists can be shown to have his own dominant note. The musical analogy, though rough, may help to clarify the relationship and is worth pushing a little further. Let us suppose that Ovid's favourite key is that of D Major. Propertius will then be represented by the key of B Minor, though he moves at times into its relative Major, Ovid's range. And Tibullus will be represented by a pentatonic scale that starts from D, a more limited range, reminiscent sometimes of B Minor, sometimes of D Major, but still strongly individual. Ovid's contribution to Roman elegy can then be put like this: before his

time the plangent Minor scale was that most often used; he saw
no possibility of further development there and chose, for artistic
reasons and because it suited his temperament, to develop the
brighter tone colour of the relative Major.

Paradoxically the difference between Ovid and Propertius is
sometimes most marked where the resemblance is closest, as in the
following:

> qualis Thesea iacuit cedente carina
> languida desertis Cnosia litoribus;
> qualis et accubuit primo Cepheia somno
> libera iam duris cotibus Andromede;
> nec minus assiduis Edonis fessa choreis
> qualis in herboso concidit Apidano;
> talis visa mihi mollem spirare quietem
> Cynthia non certis nixa caput manibus,
> ebria cum multo traherem vestigia Baccho
> et quaterent sera nocte facem pueri. (Prop. 1. 3.1–10)

As Ariadne lay limp on the deserted beach, while Theseus' ship
sailed away; and as Cephean Andromeda reclined in first sleep, free
now from the hard rocks; and as the Thracian Maenad, no less weary
from continual dancing, sank down by grassy Apidanus: so Cynthia
seemed to me to breathe soft rest, leaning her head on relaxed hands,
when I dragged my feet along, drunk with much wine, and the boys
shook their torches in the small hours.

> qualis ab Eurota Phrygiis avecta carinis
> coniugibus belli causa duobus erat,
> qualis erat Lede quam plumis abditus albis
> callidus in falsa lusit adulter ave,
> qualis Amymone siccis erravit in Argis
> cum premeret summi verticis urna comas,
> talis eras; aquilamque in te taurumque timebam
> et quidquid magno de Iove fecit amor.
> nunc timor omnis abest animique resanuit error
> nec facies oculos iam capit ista meos.
> (Ov. *Am.* 1. 10.1–10)

As was she who caused war between two husbands, when carried
off from the Eurotas in Trojan ships; as Leda was, whom the crafty
adulterer, hidden by white feathers, deceived in the false shape of a
bird; as Amymone went astray in waterless Argos when a pitcher
pressed the hair of her topmost head: such were you; and for you I was

afraid of eagle and bull and whatever love made of great Jupiter. Now all fear is gone and my delusion cured, nor does that beauty of yours any longer arrest my eyes.

In Propertius each of the mythological examples bears directly on the present figure of Cynthia asleep, and there is a languor in the movement of the verse that reinforces the explicit statement of *languida* and *mollem spirare quietem*.[3] In Ovid, who undoubtedly has this passage of Propertius in mind, the mythology is there to illustrate the general idea of *facies* in an appropriately decorative way. Ovidian wit appears in the unexpected turn *aquilamque in te taurumque timebam* (shown by the pentameter to be semi-serious hyperbole), and in the added surprise of *timor* meaning in this context *amor*. The rhythm in the *qualis* hexameters, though more spondaic perhaps than Ovid's usual, has no specific purpose as in Propertius but provides a general impressiveness which the purely dactylic fifth couplet is intended to explode. The decorative opening then turns out to have been intentionally misleading and the poem develops in a direction that one could not have guessed.

Such calculated use of surprise tactics is distinctively Ovidian and makes as good a starting-point as any for the attempt to disengage other Ovidian procedures and characteristics in the *Amores*. To say anything new about Ovid in the twentieth century is pretty well impossible; one must be careful about reading modern preoccupations and presuppositions into ancient poetry. At the same time it ought to be possible to do more than parrot stock judgements whose edge has been worn away by repeated use. It ought to be possible to revivify the traditional points at issue and throw fresh light by the close examination of particular poems. I have chosen to discuss the *Amores*, mainly because they tend to be undervalued in comparison with the *Ars Amatoria*, but also because it is more illuminating to deal with short poems, complete in themselves, than with parts of a long work. Let the first exhibits be *Am.* 2.7 and 8.

> Ergo sufficiam reus in nova crimina semper?
>   ut vincam, totiens dimicuisse piget.
> sive ego marmorei respexi summa theatri,
>   eligis e multis unde dolere velis;
> candida seu tacito vidit me femina vultu,   5
>   in vultu tacitas arguis esse notas;

si quam laudavi, miseros petis ungue capillos;
   si culpo, crimen dissimulare putas;
sive bonus color est, in te quoque frigidus esse,
   seu malus, alterius dicor amore mori.   10

Atque ego peccati vellem mihi conscius essem;
   aequo animo poenam qui meruere ferunt.
nunc temere insimulas, credendoque omnia frustra
   ipsa vetas iram pondus habere tuam.
aspice ut auritus miserandae sortis asellus   15
   assiduo domitus verbere lentus eat.

Ecce novum crimen: sollers ornare Cypassis
   obicitur dominae contemerasse torum.
di melius quam me, si sit peccasse libido,
   sordida contemptae sortis amica iuvet.   20
quis veneris famulae conubia liber inire
   tergaque conplecti verbere secta velit?
adde quod ornandis illa est operata capillis
   et tibi per doctas grata ministra manus.
scilicet ancillam quae tam tibi fida rogarem?   25
   quid nisi ut indicio iuncta repulsa foret?
per Venerem iuro puerique volatilis arcus
   me non admissi criminis esse reum.   (2. 7)

Then am I to be available as defendant on fresh charges always?
Though I win, it's tedious to fight my case so often. If I look round
at the highest rows of the marble theatre, you choose one out of many
women as object of your resentment. Or if a beautiful woman glances
at me with silent expression, you try to prove there are silent meanings
in the expression. If I praise a woman, you attack my unfortunate hair
with your nails. If I criticize her, you think I'm covering up my guilt.
If my colour is good, I'm also said to be indifferent towards you; if
bad, to be dying of love for another.

Indeed I could wish I *were* guilty of unfaithfulness; those who have
deserved punishment bear it with equanimity. As it is you slander me
indiscriminately, and by foolishly believing everything you automatically prevent your anger from carrying weight. See how slowly the
wretched long-eared donkey moves along, in spite of constant beating.

Here's a fresh charge: Cypassis, trained to do your hair, is alleged
to have dishonoured her mistress's couch. God forbid that, if I felt
like being unfaithful, a cheap tart of that contemptible sort should
take my fancy! What free man would want to have intercourse with
a slave and to embrace backs cut by the lash? Besides she is committed

to doing hair and thanks to her skilful hands is a favourite servant of
yours. As if I would ask a maid so loyal to you! Why, except to make
sure that rejection would be combined with disclosure? I swear by
Venus and Cupid's bow that I am accused of a crime I have not committed.

Ponendis in mille modos perfecta capillis,
  comere sed solas digna, Cypassi, deas,
et mihi iucundo non rustica cognita furto,
  apta quidem dominae, sed magis apta mihi,
quis fuit inter nos sociati corporis index?   5
  sensit concubitus unde Corinna tuos?
num tamen erubui? num verbo lapsus in ullo
  furtivae veneris conscia signa dedi?

Quid quod in ancilla si quis delinquere possit
  illum contendi mente carere bona?   10
Thessalus ancillae facie Briseidos arsit,
  serva Mycenaeo Phoebas amata duci.
nec sum ego Tantalide maior, nec maior Achille;
  quod decuit reges, cur mihi turpe putem?

Vt tamen iratos in te defixit ocellos,   15
  vidi te totis erubuisse genis.
at quanto, si forte refers, praesentior ipse
  per Veneris feci numina magna fidem.—
tu, dea, tu iubeas animi periuria puri
  Carpathium tepidos per mare ferre Notos.—   20
pro quibus officiis pretium mihi dulce repende
  concubitus hodie, fusca Cypassi, tuos.

Quid renuis fingisque novos ingrata timores?
  unum est e dominis emeruisse satis.
quod si stulta negas, index anteacta fatebor   25
  et veniam culpae proditor ipse meae,
quoque loco tecum fuerim quotiensque, Cypassi,
  narrabo dominae, quotque quibusque modis.

Expert at arranging hair in a thousand styles, but deserving,
Cypassis, to comb only goddesses, and known to me as sophisticated
from our pleasant intrigue, a treasure to your mistress but more so to
me, who was the informant of our bodily union? Whence did Corinna
learn you slept with me? But did I blush? Did I by any verbal lapse
give guilty signs of illicit love?

What if I *did* insist that anyone who can commit an offence with a maid is not of sound mind? Achilles caught fire at the beauty of the maid Briseis; Cassandra the slave-girl was loved by Agamemnon. I am not greater than the descendant of Tantalus, nor greater than Achilles. What was good enough for kings, why should I think bad for me?

Yet when she fixed angry eyes on you, I saw you blush all over your cheeks. But if by chance you remember, with how much greater presence of mind did I myself produce conviction by the great divinity of Venus?—Goddess, bid the warm south winds to carry the perjuries of a guiltless mind over the Aegean sea.—And for these services, dark Cypassis, pay me the sweet price of sleeping with me today. Why shake your head and ungratefully imagine fresh dangers? To serve one of your masters is enough. Well, if you stupidly refuse, as informer I shall confess past acts and appear as betrayer of my own offence and report to our mistress where I was with you, and how often, and in how many, and what, ways.

These poems are well contrived as a contrasting pair and the dramatic technique in both is cleverly managed. The first proves to be a logical development of its indignant opening couplet. The second comes as a surprise and develops with equal logic; its piquancy is increased when we find that Cypassis is a coloured girl (22 *fusca*). The style, in general, is presumably that of idealized conversation, mostly economical, always crisp, but supple. It makes the business of handling a very demanding form look thoroughly easy, but lines like *ergo sufficiam reus in nova crimina semper?* and *si culpo, crimen dissimulare putas* do not occur to poetasters. One detects the occasional stop-gap, e.g. *marmorei* (7.3), an epithet that seems obtrusively ornate in this context; and the same device is used twice in Poem 7—line 15 *miserandae sortis* and line 20 *contemptae sortis*. But otherwise the conventional elements are pulling their weight: to trot out heroic *exempla* in Poem 8 lines 11–13 adds to the entertainment and leads into the neat double antithesis in line 14; and though lines 19–20 in that poem are detachable one would be sorry to lose the cheek of the phrase *animi periuria puri*. The last couplet in Poem 8 is one of Ovid's best, particularly for its internal timing—the gradual climax of the indirect questions. The two poems together give us the essential features of the *persona* that Ovid adopts in the *Amores* and enlarges in the *Ars Amatoria*—jaunty, raffish and shrewd, but thoroughly civilized.

The use of dramatic argument directed at another person, real
or imaginary, in order to build up a poem can be seen at its most
concentrated in *Amores* 3.4 and 2.19; like the two poems just
quoted these also are written from contrary points of view: the
first argues against a man who keeps his mistress under guard,
the second against a man who does *not* do so. Here are samples of
each:

> Dure vir, inposito tenerae custode puellae
>   nil agis: ingenio est quaeque tuenda suo.
> siqua metu dempto casta est, ea denique casta est;
>   quae quia non liceat non facit, illa facit.
> ut iam servaris bene corpus, adultera mens est,
>   nec custodiri ne velit illa potest.
> nec corpus servare potes, licet omnia claudas;
>   omnibus occlusis intus adulter erit.
> cui peccare licet peccat minus: ipsa potestas
>   semina nequitiae languidiora facit.
> desine, crede mihi, vitia inritare vetando;
>   obsequio vinces aptius illa tuo   (*Am.* 3. 4.1–12)

Hard man, by putting a guard on a tender girl you achieve nothing:
each one must be protected by her own nature. If any is chaste when
fear has been removed, she is indeed chaste; she who refuses because
it is forbidden, consents. Even though you watch the body well, the
mind is adulterous, and cannot be guarded from wishing. Nor can you
watch the body, though you shut everything; when everything's shut
up, inside will be the adulterer. One free to sin sins less: the very
power makes the seeds of wantonness less active. Believe me and stop
encouraging vice by veto; you will overcome it more effectively by
giving in.

> Iamque ego praemoneo: nisi tu servare puellam
>   incipis, incipiet desinere esse mea.
> multa diuque tuli. speravi saepe futurum,
>   cum bene servasses, ut bene verba darem.
> lentus es, et pateris nulli patienda marito;
>   at mihi concessa finis amoris erit.
> scilicet infelix numquam prohibebor adire?
>   nox mihi sub nullo vindice semper erit?
> nil metuam? per nulla traham suspiria somnos?
>   nil facies cur te iure perisse velim?
> quid mihi cum facili, quid cum lenone marito?
>   corrumpit vitio gaudia nostra suo.
> quin alium quem tanta iuvet patientia quaeris?
>   me tibi rivalem si iuvat esse, veta.   (*Am.* 2. 19.47–60)

And now I give due notice: unless you begin to watch the girl, she will begin to cease being mine. Much and for long have I endured. I often hoped it would happen that when you had watched well I should cheat well. You are insensitive, and suffer what no husband *should* suffer. But if she is not denied to me there will be an end of love. Honestly, shall I, the unfortunate, never be forbidden to come near? Will night, for me, be always without the threat of revenge? Am I to fear nothing? Am I to heave no sighs in my sleep? (*or* Shall I prolong sleep for lack of sighing?) Will you give me no just cause for wishing you dead? What have I to do with an easy, with a pimping, husband? He spoils our enjoyment by his fault. Why don't you find someone else whom such long-suffering can please? If it pleases you to have me as your rival, forbid me to be so.

In the first the incisive, gnomic manner and the skilful concatenation of the argument need no comment, nor does one need to expatiate on the ludicrous effect of the second. It would be hard to find better examples of Ovidian wit and humour respectively. Obviously the poet is not developing his personal views here or disclosing his personal feelings. He is not writing out of a real situation. It is not his intention to do any of these things—only to appear to be doing so. Both poems are constructions in which the 'I' is a useful convention for the sake of immediacy—constructions to exercise the reader's intelligence in a paradoxical way and to entertain him by the unexpected combination of ideas. The poet confesses as much in *Tristia* 2.353–6:

> crede mihi, distant mores a carmine nostro;
>   vita verecunda est, Musa iocosa mea.
> magnaque pars mendax operum est et ficta meorum;
>   plus sibi permisit compositore suo.

Believe me, my character differs from my poetry; my life is respectable, my Muse gay; and a large part of my work is fictitious and imaginary; it allowed itself more latitude than its author.

In one of his most ambitious attempts, *Amores* 3.11a, the argument is more internal than external, more the poet arguing with himself than with the woman who is addressed directly in certain lines but referred to in the third person in lines 25–26. This is a technique derived from Catullus Poem 8 *Miser Catulle, desinas ineptire*, 'Poor Catullus, stop making a fool of yourself'. In Catullus the pull of the conflict can be felt, though it is not directly

stated, most clearly in lines 11, 14 and 19, but more subtly elsewhere, too: Catullus remembers the golden days of his affair and
in the very act of doing so implies a criticism of them (*cum venti-
tabas quo puella ducebat*, 'When you used to go wherever the girl led',
depicts him as a puppet) and hints that the relationship was not
as ideal as it seemed (*quae tu volebas nec puella nolebat*, 'Which *you*
wanted and the girl did not refuse', gives me the feeling that
Lesbia, though willing, was a shade less so than Catullus).
Similarly, we are not told directly what Lesbia has done, though
clearly she has cooled off (*nunc iam illa non vult*, 'Now she is no
longer willing'). But the implication of *perditum* (in its double
meaning), *scelesta, quae vita*, 'what sort of life . . .?' suggests that
in Catullus' eyes she is now little better than a common tart.
From this point of view lines 16–18 are at once a nostalgic
memory of their past love-making and a bitter forecast of her
promiscuity in future. It is useless to look for this subtle sensibility in Ovid's poem. Everything there is explicit and generalized.
The list of grievances, built up logically enough, communicates
to the reader a vigorous but indiscriminate feeling of indignation.
Despite the apparently ambitious opening humour creeps in:

> dicta erat aegra mihi. praeceps amensque cucurri.
> veni, et rivali non erat aegra meo   (*Am.* 3. 11.25–26)

I was told she was ill. Headlong and distraught I ran. I arrived and
she was not ill for my rival,

and we realize we are listening to a lover on stage in a comedy of
manners whose author is Ovid. The actor's *persona* is typical, but
his lines are unmistakably Ovidian, and to that extent he is
individual—for example, the elegance of lines 29–30:

> iam mea votiva puppis redimita corona
> lenta tumescentes aequoris audit aquas

Now my ship, wreathed with a votive garland, hears unmoved the
swelling waters of the sea,

where one can feel Ovid's brand of subtlety in the choice of the
suggestive adjectives *lenta* and *tumescentes*.

In 11a the poet persuades himself that he has shaken off his
love; in 11b, developing the theme *odi et amo* (suggested probably
by Catullus 76 and 85) he depicts the reverse process and ends up

in love again. It is possible that he intends the two halves to form a single poem. Certainly the MSS. show no division and the slightly intrusive couplet (lines 7–8)

> perfer et obdura. dolor hic tibi proderit olim.
> saepe tulit lassis sucus amarus opem

Endure and be firm. This pain will help you later. Often bitter medicine has brought strength to the weak,

with its suggestion of a painful conflict, may be meant to pave the way for 11b. But if this is Ovid's intention he fails to achieve it: one can feel no intrinsic connexion between the two halves; they fall apart and are best taken as separate and contrasting pieces. The technique of the second is different. It proceeds not so much by argument as by a kind of analysis:

> Luctantur pectusque leve in contraria tendunt
>   hac amor hac odium—sed puto vincit amor.
> odero si potero: si non, invitus amabo.
>   nec iuga taurus amat, quae tamen odit habet.
> nequitiam fugio, fugientem forma reducit;   5
>   aversor morum crimina, corpus amo:
> sic ego nec sine te nec tecum vivere possum
>   et videor voti nescius esse mei.
> aut formosa fores minus aut minus inproba vellem;
>   non facit ad mores tam bona forma malos.   10
> facta merent odium, facies exorat amorem;
>   me miserum, vitiis plus valet illa suis.
> parce per o lecti socialia iura, per omnis
>   qui dant fallendos se tibi saepe deos,
> perque tuam faciem, magni mihi numinis instar,   15
>   perque tuos oculos, qui rapuere meos.
> quidquid eris, mea semper eris. tu selige tantum
>   me quoque velle velis anne coactus amem.
> lintea dem potius ventisque ferentibus utar,
>   ut, quam, si nolim, cogar amare, velim.   20

Love on this side, hate on this, are struggling, and pulling my light heart in opposite directions—but I think love is winning. I shall hate if I can: if not, I shall love unwillingly. Neither does the ox love the yoke, yet what he hates he has. I fly your promiscuity, your beauty brings me flying back; I shun your moral failings, your body I love: thus I can neither live with you nor without you and I seem not to know what I want. I could wish you were either less beautiful or less immoral; such good looks do not suit such bad character. Your misdemeanours deserve hate, your demeanour demands love. Alas, it outweighs its own sins. O be merciful, by the mutual rights of our bed, by all the gods who allow themselves to be deceived by you so often, and by your face which for me is a powerful divinity, and by your eyes which have ravished mine. Whatever you are, you will always be mine. Only choose whether you want me to want you freely or to love you against my will. I would rather spread my sails and enjoy following winds, so as to want to love one whom I should be compelled to love even if I did not want to.

The effect here depends on the direct and objective statement of emotion, as it does in Catullus Poem 85:

> odi et amo. quare id faciam fortasse requiris?
> nescio, sed fieri sentio et excrucior

I hate and love. Perhaps you ask why I do that? I do not know, but I feel it being done to me and am tortured,

though there the contrast between voluntary and involuntary implied in *faciam* and *fieri*, and between intellect and emotion in *nescio* and *sentio*, is the main point. But whereas Catullus claims not to know why he loves and hates simultaneously, Ovid gives the impression of knowing precisely, and the point of his poem lies in analysis of the fact, not in the fact itself. This analysis is not subtle; it develops by opposed generalities cast into epigrammatic form—*nequitia . . . forma, morum crimina . . . corpus, formosa . . . inproba*, etc. But the concision and ordering of the epigrams is effective and gives the illusion of subtle penetration; so, too, does the syntactical complexity of the last two pentameters and the word-play in *facta . . . facies* and in *facies exorat* (the derivation of *orare* being from *os* 'mouth', according to Varro). To represent the internal conflict by this succession of balanced antitheses is to stress the intellectual in a situation that is fundamentally emotional. Admittedly in lines 12–16 a gesture is made towards the emotional, but it is too expansive, and the insistent dactylic rhythm deprives it of real weight and power, reducing this poem, too, to the level of light verse. One has only to quote Catullus in scazon or hexameter to appreciate the contrast:

> sed obstinata mente perfer, obdura   (8.11)
>
> But stubbornly endure, be hard.

una salus haec est, hoc est tibi pervincendum (76.15)

This is your one salvation, this you must achieve.

At this point in the examination one is tempted to make the obvious judgement and say that Ovid's poem fails in comparison with Catullus Poem 8 or 76 because of the disparity between its verse, its intellectual *élan*, and the ostensibly anguished emotional theme. But surely this is to miss Ovid's intention. He is not competing with Catullus; this is verse at a much lower level of intensity; the ostensible theme is simply an excuse for intellectual entertainment. When Ovid says *sed puto vincit amor* he does not go on to make one feel the pull of love as Catullus does, but he gives one the intellectual pleasure of recognizing, by the way, an allusion to Virgil's famous line (*Buc.* 10.69) *omnia vincit amor*; *et nos cedamus amori*, 'Love conquers all; we too must yield to love' (which in its turn may possibly be quoted by Virgil from Gallus, the recognised founder of Roman love elegy). If this definition of Ovid's intention is accepted, the poem as a whole succeeds. The only question is whether he gets away with the logical irrelevance of line 4

nec iuga taurus amat, quae tamen odit habet.

So far most of the emphasis has been on the argumentative backbone, the tougher constructional element in Ovid's work, the reason being that this element tends either to be overlooked (you will find nothing about it in Mackail or Sellar, for example) or to be obscured under the blanket term 'rhetoric'—a term whose vagueness and pejorative implication have done Ovid a great deal of harm in the past. The next exhibit (and the longest) is meant to show his more explicitly lyrical side, though this too is partially argumentative:

Prima malas docuit mirantibus aequoris undis
  Peliaco pinus vertice caesa vias,
quae concurrentis inter temeraria cautes
  conspicuam fulvo vellere vexit ovem.
o utinam ne quis remo freta longa moveret, 5
  Argo funestas pressa bibisset aquas.
ecce fugit notumque torum sociosque Penates
  fallacisque vias ire Corinna parat.

Quid tibi, me miserum, Zephyros Eurosque timebo
  et gelidum Borean egelidumque Notum?   10
non illic urbes, non tu mirabere silvas:
  una est iniusti caerula forma maris.
nec medius tenuis conchas pictosque lapillos
  pontus habet: bibuli litoris illa mora est.

Litora marmoreis pedibus signate, puellae,   15
  (hactenus est tutum, cetera caeca via est)
et vobis alii ventorum proelia narrent,
  quas Scylla infestet quasve Charybdis aquas,
et quibus emineant violenta Ceraunia saxis,
  quo lateant Syrtes magna minorque sinu.   20
haec alii referant: at vos quod quisque loquetur
  credite; credenti nulla procella nocet.

Sero respicitur tellus ubi fune soluto
  currit in immensum panda carina salum,
navita sollicitus cum ventos horret iniquos   25
  et prope tam letum quam prope cernit aquam.
quod si concussas Triton exasperet undas,
  quam tibi sit toto nullus in ore color.
tum generosa voces fecundae sidera Ledae
  et 'felix' dicas 'quem sua terra tenet.'   30
tutius est fovisse torum, legisse libellos,
  Threiciam digitis increpuisse lyram.

At si vana ferunt volucres mea dicta procellae,
  aequa tamen puppi sit Galatea tuae.
vestrum crimen erit talis iactura puellae,   35
  Nereidesque deae Nereidumque pater.
vade memor nostri, vento reditura secundo:
  inpleat illa tuos fortior aura sinus.
tum mare in haec magnus proclinet litora Nereus,
  huc venti spectent, huc agat aestus aquas.   40
ipsa roges Zephyri veniant in lintea soli,
  ipsa tua moveas turgida vela manu.
primus ego aspiciam notam de litore puppim
  et dicam 'nostros advehit illa deos.'
excipiamque umeris et multa sine ordine carpam   45
  oscula; pro reditu victima vota cadet,
inque tori formam molles sternentur harenae
  et tumulus mensae quilibet instar erit.

illic adposito narrabis multa Lyaeo,
    paene sit ut mediis obruta navis aquis   50
dumque ad me properas nec iniquae tempora noctis
    nec te praecipites extimuisse Notos.
omnia pro veris credam, sint ficta licebit:
    cur ego non votis blandiar ipse meis?
haec mihi quam primum caelo nitidissimus alto   55
    Lucifer admisso tempora portet equo.   (*Am.* 2. 11)

The pine felled on Pelion's summit was the first to teach wicked voyages, while the waves of the sea marvelled—the pine which recklessly carried the sheep famous for its golden fleece between the Clashing Rocks. O would that no one disturbed the long straits with the oar, that Argo had drunk the fatal waters and foundered. Look, Corinna deserts the familiar couch and the home we share and prepares to go a dangerous voyage.

Why, alas, am I to fear for you West and East winds and chill North and non-chill South? You will marvel at no cities there, no forests: the surface of the cruel sea is unrelieved blue. Nor does mid-ocean have delicate shells and coloured pebbles: those are attractions of the thirsty beach.

Print the beaches with your marble-white feet, maidens (thus far is safe, for the rest the way is blind) and let others tell you of the battles of the winds, of the waters which Scylla or which Charybdis infests, and of the rocks on which the stormy Ceraunians tower, of the gulf where lurk the Syrtes, great and lesser. Let others tell of these: but you are to believe what each one says; no gale harms a believer.

Too late is the land looked back on, when, with cable cast off, the curving keel runs into the immeasurable brine, when the anxious sailor dreads contrary winds and sees death as near to him as the water. But if Triton should roughen the tossing waves, how there would be no colour in all your face! Then you would call to the noble stars of fruitful Leda and say 'Happy the man whom his native earth protects!' It is safer to keep a couch warm, to read books, to strike a Thracian lyre with the fingers.

But if the swift gales carry my words away empty, yet may Galatea be kind to your ship. The loss of such a girl will be a crime on your part, Nereid goddesses and father of the Nereids. Go, remembering me, to return with a following wind: may that, a stronger breeze, fill your sails. Then let great Nereus slope the sea towards these shores; hither let the winds face, hither let the tide drive its waters. You yourself are to ask that only Zephyrs come into the canvas, you yourself are to trim to swelling sails with your own hand. I shall be the first to sight the familiar ship from the shore and shall say 'She brings my gods.' And I shall carry you ashore on my shoulders and wildly snatch many kisses; the victim promised for your return shall fall, and the soft sand shall be spread to form a couch and any dune will serve as a table. There with the wine beside you you will have many stories to tell—how the ship almost sank in mid-sea, and how you were not afraid of the dangerous night-time or the squally South winds as you hurried back to me. I shall take it all for true, though it be fiction: why should I not flatter my personal wishes? May the Morning Star, brilliant in high heaven, bring me these times on his galloping steed as soon as may be.

This poem is one of the same family as Propertius 1. 8, of which there is an intentional echo in line 34, reworking the Propertian pentameter *sit Galatea tuae non aliena viae*. In Ovid the occasion is left completely vague—Corinna is simply going away on a voyage and we are not told where or why. Propertius' Cynthia is off to Illyria with the poet's rival, so that *Ceraunia* in that poem has specific point, whereas in Ovid it appears with other conventional marine scenery depicting the hazards of sea-faring. The poem's effect, as usual, has nothing to do with a particular personal situation; it is generalized and works through Ovid's decorative and cantabile manner—his *melopoeia*, in Ezra Pound's sense of the word and not Aristotle's. This quality can hardly be missed in lines like

> litora marmoreis pedibus signate, puellae,

> vestrum crimen erit talis iactura puellae,
> Nereidesque deae Nereidumque pater

> vade memor nostri, vento reditura secundo.

All the same this is not poetry 'aspiring to the condition of music', nor is its purpose merely to please the ear. Anyone who takes the trouble to examine the epithets used will find that they are all doing work and can be justified on grounds of appropriateness (definable in various ways) and, once or twice, of wit—as in *egelidumque Notum*.[4] I find a solitary exception to this in *fecundae* in line 29 and see that Marlowe omits it in his translation of the poem. This question of appropriateness arises interestingly at the start. It may well be asked why the poem does not begin at line 7. Have the first three couplets any artistic purpose? In fact, they presuppose a literary background on the part of the reader, or rather of the audience, for the *Amores* (need it be said?) are designed to be read to an audience. The audience is expected to know the famous opening of Euripides' *Medea* and its Latin translation by Ennius: roughly 'Would that the pine-tree had not been felled . . . , then Medea would not have left her home . . .' The formula from high tragedy is applied to Corinna's intended departure by a kind of parody and this initial dash of irony sets the tone for the rest of the poem. It is not that the first six lines parody the high style—they *are* the high style, and genuinely impressive (the strong alliteration in line 4 conveying the effort of the heroes; the word *pressa* meaning 'sunk', but also glancing at the Argo's danger from the Clashing Rocks). It is rather by contrast at the join, lines 7–8, where Corinna replaces Medea, that the effect is achieved. Finally, two hexameters in this poem demonstrate that the use of conventional divine machinery can coexist with original invention:

> quod si concussas Triton exasperet undas . . .
> tum mare in haec magnus proclinet litora Nereus.

In the first one can feel the waves colliding; in the second the effect is of a swell with no breakers. The reader who agrees with this can easily find a plausible technical explanation. On consulting the *Thesaurus Linguae Latinae* I find that Ovid is alone in using *concussas* of waves, and Lewis and Short show that *proclinare* applied to the sea is his own idea, too (the *Thesaurus* has not yet reached the letter 'p'). But it must be admitted that the poem as a whole does not come off. There are weak spots—chiefly, I think, lines 11, 13 and 14, whose puerility does little credit to Corinna's intelligence, though in themselves they are svelte and musical.

Ovid's critics, whatever else they may dispute, will always grant that he can tell a story. The brief imaginary narrative at the end of *Amores* 2. 11 gives some hint of his fluency, but in the *Amores* as a whole he does not often appear in the role of story-teller. He was to develop it fully in later works. The longish, rather unimpressive example in 3. 6.49–82 compares unfavourably with the ornate incantatory manner of Propertius in 1. 20. Ovid is simpler and faster-moving, but he has not yet acquired the necessary economy, and the general effect there is too mechanical:

> 'quid fles et madidos lacrimis corrumpis ocellos
> pectoraque insana plangis aperta manu?

ille habet et silices et vivum in pectore ferrum
    qui tenero lacrimas lentus in ore videt . . .'
dixerat. illa oculos in humum deiecta modestos
    spargebat tepido flebilis imbre sinus . . . (*Am.* 3. 6.57 ff.)

'Why do you weep and spoil your wet eyes with tears, and beat your naked breasts with mad hand? That man has both flints and living iron in his breast who sees tears on a tender face without pity . . .' He spoke. Fixing modest eyes on the ground, she tearfully bathed her bosom with warm rain . . .

Quite the best piece of narrative in the *Amores* is to be found in 3. 1, though the major part of it consists of two speeches put into the mouths of the imaginary figures Tragedy and Elegy. The point throughout depends on the simple device of treating these two personifications as human beings and at the same time as poetic *genres.*[5] This particular fusion of reality and fantasy is an Ovidian invention and makes possible some attractive strokes:

venit odoratos Elegia nexa capillos
    et puto pes illi longior alter erat.
forma decens, vestis tenuissima, vultus amantis,
    et pedibus vitium causa decoris erat.   (3. 1.7–10)

Elegy came with her perfumed hair bound up, and I think one foot was longer than the other. Her form was becoming, her dress fine-spun, her face a lover's, and defect gave elegance to her feet.

The description as a whole works on two levels at once, but the effect is most perceptible in the double meaning of *forma, pedibus,* and *tenuissima* (*tenuis* being a stylistic technical term). Similarly in Elegy's speech:

altera, si memini, limis subrisit ocellis
    (fallor an in dextra myrtea virga fuit?):
'quid gravibus verbis, animosa Tragoedia,' dixit
    'me premis? an numquam non gravis esse potes?
imparibus tamen es numeris dignata moveri;
    in me pugnasti versibus usa meis.
non ego contulerim sublimia carmina nostris;
    obruit exiguas regia vestra fores.
sum levis et mecum levis est mea cura Cupido;
    non sum materia fortior ipsa mea . . .'   (33 ff.)

The other, if I remember, smiled with sidelong eyes (am I wrong or was there a myrtle wand in her right hand?): 'Why with grave words, passionate Tragedy,' she said, 'do you disparage me? Or can you never be non-grave? Yet you have deigned to move in unequal numbers; you have fought against me using *my* verses. I should not compare sublime poems with mine; your palace overwhelms my narrow door. I am light and my fond care Cupid is light like me; I am not stronger than my own subject-matter . . .'

Here *gravis* is both 'weighty' (of the style of the *genre*) and 'offensive' (of the words used by the imaginary figure); *regia* refers to the regular scenic background of a tragedy, *exiguas fores* to the connexion of elegy with the house-door (where the lover stood serenading his mistress or appealing to the doorkeeper to let him in) and to its restricted scope and stylistic level (cf. Horace *Ars Poetica* 77 *exiguos elegos*); *materia* means 'subject-matter' and 'nature'. Also worth noting is the pseudo-casual insertion of *si memini* and *fallor an . . .?*, another Ovidian contrivance, effectively seeming to give an air of reality to fantasy.[6]

To disengage various characteristics of Ovid's work and exemplify them by quotation is relatively easy. But to convey the effect of their combined operation when these parts have been put together as a whole is very difficult. It is a question of sensibility and cannot be isolated or pinned down. It is, of course, impossible to know what Ovid's poetry felt like to a contemporary Roman reader or shall we say to the reader he had in mind when he wrote. But it should be possible to convey what his poetry feels like to a twentieth-century Englishman with a fair knowledge of classical Latin. Clearly it is no use for such an Englishman to quote Ovid's Latin in order to make his feeling explicit. The total effect of that Latin is precisely the 'x' whose value has to be indicated in other terms. The only answer is for the Englishman to quote English poems that have for him an Ovidian feeling about them. The feeling of other Englishmen, presented with these particular English poems, is likely to be similar. In this way the idea that the man who quotes them has about 'x' will be expressed as clearly as it reasonably can be. I should add that translations are not suitable for this purpose. They are second-hand poems, or, if alive, have more of the translator than the original in them. Besides, the best translations of Ovid were done in the heroic couplet. Admittedly the heroic couplet seems to be the nearest equivalent in English to the Latin elegiac couplet. But the difference is as marked as the likeness. In particular the heroic couplet seldom achieves the lyrical quality that is native to Latin elegiacs.[7] Here then follows an interlude in which Ovidian tones can be heard in original English verse.

I

Come live with me, and be my love,
And we will some new pleasures prove
Of golden sands and crystal brooks,
With silken lines and silver hooks.

There will the river whispering run
Warm'd by thy eyes more than the sun;
And there the enamour'd fish will stay,
Begging themselves they may betray.

When thou wilt swim in that live bath,
Each fish which every channel hath
Will amorously to thee swim,
Gladder to catch thee than thou him.

II

Beneath a Myrtle shade
Which Love for none but happy Lovers made,
I slept, and straight my Love before me brought
Phillis, the object of my waking thought;
Undres'd she came my flames to meet,
While Love strow'd flowers beneath her feet;
Flow'rs, which so press'd by her, became more sweet.

From the bright Visions Head
A careless vail of Lawn was loosely spread:
From her white temples fell her shaded hair,
Like cloudy sunshine not too brown nor fair:
Her hands, her lips did love inspire;
Her ev'ry grace my heart did fire:
But most her eyes which languish'd with desire.

Ah, Charming fair, said I,
How long can you my bliss and yours deny?
By Nature and by love this lonely shade
Was for revenge of suffring Lovers made:
Silence and shades with love agree:
Both shelter you and favour me;
You cannot blush because I cannot see.

No, let me dye, she said,
Rather than loose the spotless name of Maid:
Faintly methought she spoke, for all the while
She bid me not believe her, with a smile.
Then dye, said I, she still deny'd:
And is it thus, thus, thus she cry'd
You use a harmless Maid, and so she dy'd!

I wak'd, and straight I knew
I lov'd so well it made my dream prove true:
Fancy, the kinder Mistress of the two,
Fancy had done what *Phillis* wou'd not do!
Ah, Cruel Nymph, cease your disdain,
While I can dream you scorn in vain;
Asleep or waking you must ease my pain.

III

Down, wanton, down! Have you no shame
That at the whisper of Love's name,
Or Beauty's, presto! up you raise
Your angry head and stand at gaze?

Poor bombard-captain, sworn to reach
The ravelin and effect a breach—
Indifferent what you storm or why,
So be that in the breach you die!

Love may be blind, but Love at least
Knows what is man and what mere beast;
Or Beauty wayward, but requires
More delicacy from her squires.

Tell me, my witless, whose one boast
Could be your staunchness at the post,
When were you made a man of parts
To think fine and profess the arts?

Will many-gifted Beauty come
Bowing to your bald rule of thumb,
Or Love swear loyalty to your crown?
Be gone, have done! Down, wanton, down!

Donne's *The Bait* (only the first three stanzas are given above)
is not characteristic of him. In *The Compleat Angler* Walton makes
Venator say that Donne wrote it 'to shew the world that he could

make soft and smooth Verses when he thought smoothness worth his labour'. The first line quotes the beginning of Marlowe's *The Passionate Shepherd to his Love*; the second unexpectedly twists Marlowe (cf. the beginning of *Amores* 2. 11). The epithets in lines 3 and 4 are not in themselves original, but in this context and combination have the clear-cut freshness of Ovid. Ovidian, too, is line 5, avoiding conventionality by a hair's-breadth (reverse the positions of noun and adjective to test that). The conceit in line 6 is of the same class as *Am*. 2. 16.11–12:

> at meus ignis abest—verbo peccavimus uno:
> quae movet ardores est procul, ardor adest.

But my flame is absent—I am wrong in one word: she who causes the burning is far away, the burning is present.

'The enamour'd fish' are potentially Ovidian and to be compared with the last couplet of *Am*. 2. 16. The compressed syntax in lines 8 and 12 is like Ovid, too. The omitted stanzas are too hyperbolical for him.[8]

The dramatic character of Dryden's *Song of the Zambra Dance*, its narrative setting and logical structure, the descriptive writing in stanza 2 (cf. *Am*. 1. 14.5–12), the conventional but elegant *galanterie*, the play on the word *dye*, the use of antithesis, and the pervasive melody, all combine to give this excellent poem a flavour distinctively Ovidian. Dryden's *Song* from *Cleomenes* beginning *No, no, poor suffr'ing Heart, no Change endeavour* is also exactly Ovidian and well worth reading.

For the idea of Graves's poem *Down, wanton, down!* compare *Am*. 3. 7.69–70:

> quin istic pudibunda iaces, pars pessima nostri?
> sic sum pollicitis captus et ante tuis.

Why do you not lie down decently, worst part of me? I have been deceived like this by your promises in the past also.

Then there is its argumentative-cum-lyrical construction and the use throughout of double meanings. Ovid does not share Graves's ambivalent attitude to sex, but might have argued the case this way round for fun.

The *Amores* spring from the play of a bright and sensitive intelligence with a limited number of themes, most of them conventional by Ovid's time to love elegy. It is Ovid's intelligence that is individual, not his sensibility (if one can separate the two). His sensibility deals in stock and generalized emotions of no great depth or strength, but his intelligent invention manipulates them and the themes related to them in a strongly individual way. The manipulation exercises the reader's mind and, up to a point, his feelings, and thereby provides him with enjoyment, and sometimes (though for the twentieth-century reader this is pretty rare) with a genuine insight into the human heart. It would appear that the germinal idea of most of the poems was intellectual and not emotional. This is suggested in *Am*. 3. 1.6 *quod mea quaerebam Musa moveret opus*, 'I was looking for a subject for my Muse to develop', and clearly that poem arose in this way. And since it ties up with the last poem in Book III, where Ovid says good-bye to elegy and turns to tragedy, the two may well have been conceived at the same time. To stress the intellectual genesis of Ovid's verse is not, of course, to pass an adverse criticism, but merely another way of saying that he is in the classical tradition.

What he says about composition in *Ex Ponto* 3. 9.21–22 probably applies to the *Amores* as well:

> scribentem iuvat ipse labor . . .
> cumque suo crescens pectore fervet opus.

While I am writing the actual labour is enjoyable . . . and as it takes shape the work glows, together with the feeling proper to it.

The pleasure of composition (cf. *Tristia* 5. 12.3 *carmina laetum sunt opus*, 'Poems are enjoyable work'), his enjoyment in creative labour as ideas flashed into consciousness, finds its reflection in the mobility and verve of the verse in the *Amores*, even when the subject, as in 3. 11b purports to be anguished. The discrepancy that can be clearly felt in this particular instance between the movement of the verse and the ostensible content argues, some would say, a lack of sensibility and of imaginative self-criticism. I do not entirely agree, for the reason given earlier. This is light verse (like the three English poems quoted above) and criticism should judge it by its own standards. In a good many of the poems, though, I should say that Ovid has enjoyed himself too much in the process of composition and that this enjoyment has prevented him from bringing effective self-criticism to bear in order to prune away redundancy. On these occasions he fails as an artist. In this sense there is nothing wrong with his *ingenium*, but his *ars* is at fault—a reversal of the usual verdict. To point to examples: in Book 2, which has more successful poems in it than 1 and 3, we find seventeen out of the twenty-four couplets of Poem 4 listing with reasons the types of girl he finds attractive. Had he cut out the weaker specimens the poem would have been stronger; Donne does the same thing much better in *The Indifferent*. In Poem 5 we get too many expansions such as:

> o utinam arguerem sic ut non vincere possem.
> me miserum, quare tam bona causa mea est?
> felix qui quod amat defendere fortiter audet,
> cui sua 'non feci' dicere amica potest.
> ferreus est nimiumque suo favet ille dolori
> cui petitur victa palma cruenta rea   (7–12)

O would that I could accuse without being able to win! Alas, why is my case so good? Happy the man who ventures boldly to defend what he loves, to whom his own mistress can say 'I did not do it'. Hard-hearted and too fond of his own suffering is the man who seeks a blood-stained prize by proving his beloved guilty.

> and   at illi
> conscia purpureus venit in ora pudor,
> quale coloratum Tithoni coniuge caelum
> subrubet aut sponso visa puella novo,
> quale rosae fulgent inter sua lilia mixtae,
> aut ubi cantatis Luna laborat equis,
> aut quod ne longis flavescere posset ab annis
> Maeonis Assyrium femina tinxit ebur.   (33–40)

But as for her, crimson shame came into her guilty face, as the sky, coloured by Dawn, the wife of Tithonus, blushes, or a girl when looked at by the man she has just become engaged to, as roses shine when mixed with the lilies that set them off, or the moon when her steeds are bewitched and she labours, or Assyrian ivory which a Maeonian woman tinted that it might not turn yellow from length of years.

Though each couplet is well made, the effect of their combination is diminishing and it would have been better to cut, even though the decision was painful. Similar redundancies occur in Poem 14 between lines 11 and 22. One could wish that Ovid had carried further the process of excision that reduced the first edition of the *Amores* from five books to the three we now have.[9]

This overexpansiveness, the making of a similar point over-many times in different ways, is his main fault (though there are times, as in 3. 11b, when he just gets away with it). This is the point of the standard ancient criticisms of Ovid—*nescit quod bene cessit relinquere*: 'He does not know how to let alone what has turned out well', and *nimium amator ingenii sui*: 'Too much in love with his own wit'.[10] Partly it is due to sheer pleasure in creation, partly to the fondness for lists and catalogues found in Hellenistic poetry. It was his artistic misfortune that a natural tendency of his own found such convenient support in Hellenistic literary theory and practice. Propertius is not immune and has other weaknesses on the constructive side (if his MSS. can be trusted); Tibullus, too, is notoriously ramshackle in construction. Ovid sticks to the point, but too tenaciously, though he constructs well. Horace provides a good contrast, with his insistence on *limae labor*. This 'labour of the file' was equally a part of Hellenistic theory and Ovid is aware of it, aware that every word must be brought under judgement (see *Ex Ponto* 1. 5.19–20 *lima mordacius uti* and *sub iudicium singula verba vocem*). But he applies it only to the unit of the couplet; each couplet is judged, polished, and 'exact', but it sometimes forms part of too long a chain. The next stage, applying *limae labor* to the poem as a whole, tends to be neglected. This is the point at which Horace shows his originality, his freedom from a prevailing literary fashion of the time—in a subtler appreciation of a poem's unity, a dislike of expansion and too obvious connexion. Partly, perhaps, he owes this to the fact that by nature he found composition a grind (see the opening of *Satires* 2. 3—paradoxically the longest, and not the best, of the satires in that book).

This stricture made and applied, there remains none the less a large enough handful of poems in the *Amores* on which to base the claim put forward in 3. 15 (itself one of the handful). This is the most serious poem in the whole collection (not forgetting the elegy on the death of Tibullus, written when Ovid was twenty-four).

> Quaere novum vatem, tenerorum mater Amorum:
>   raditur hic elegis ultima meta meis,
> quos ego composui, Paeligni ruris alumnus
>   (nec me deliciae dedecuere meae),
> si quid id est, usque a proavis vetus ordinis heres,
>   non modo militiae turbine factus eques.

Mantua Vergilio gaudet, Verona Catullo;
　Paelignae dicar gloria gentis ego,
quam sua libertas ad honesta coegerat arma
　cum timuit socias anxia Roma manus.
atque aliquis spectans hospes Sulmonis aquosi
　moenia, quae campi iugera pauca tenent,
'Quae tantum' dicet 'potuistis ferre poetam,
　quantulacumque estis, vos ego magna voco.'

Culte puer puerique parens Amathusia culti,
　aurea de campo vellite signa meo.
corniger increpuit thyrso graviore Lyaeus:
　pulsanda est magnis area maior equis.
inbelles elegi, genialis Musa, valete,
　post mea mansurum fata superstes opus.

　　Look for a new poet, mother of the tender Loves: here my elegies
shave the last turning-post—the elegies which I, a native of the
Paelignian countryside, have composed (nor has my hedonism dis-
graced me), if it counts for anything, heir to my ancient rank through
a line of ancestors and not recently made a knight by the whirlwind of
war. Mantua rejoices in Virgil, Verona in Catullus; I shall be called
the pride of the Paelignian race, whom a proper independence had
driven to honourable arms when troubled Rome feared her allies'
power. And so any stranger, looking at the walls of well-watered
Sulmo which enclose only a few acres of land, will say 'Walls which
could produce such a poet, insignificant though you are, I call you
great.' Cupid and Cupid's mother, the Amathusian, remove your
golden standards from my field. Horned Bacchus has urged me on
with the graver thyrsus: a larger course must be trodden by large
horses. Unwarlike elegies, sensual Muse, farewell—a work that will
live on after my death.

This poem has shape and balance and is well adapted to its purpose
and position. There is nothing otiose about it, except perhaps the
tautology of *quos ego composui* after *meis*. At first reading *deliciae* in
line 4 may appear to contrast a little uneasily with *honesta arma* in
line 9, but on consideration one sees that *sua libertas* unifies the
two ideas: *libertas* can mean both 'independence' and 'out-
spokenness'; it is thus the quality common to the light verse and
the fighting spirit of Paelignia, and it does them both honour
Ovid is making a point, as an Italian, against the narrow and
repressive Roman tradition that was later to wreck his life. The

poem ends, as it begins, in his lyric vein—with dactylic melopoeia.
The Latin language had never *sung* quite like this before.

NOTES

[1] Tib. 1. 5.45–46; Prop. 2. 19.11–14 and 4. 5.31–34.

[2] This raises a formidable problem: how far can we get inside poetry in a foreign language and, what is more, a dead one whose spoken rhythms are entirely unknown to us, whose spoken vocabulary is only patchily known, and whose poets have survived in exiguous proportion and sometimes by pure chance?

[3] I am thinking particularly of the four-syllable endings to the first three pentameters. Judging by what Quintilian says in 9. 4.64–65, we can call these metrical equivalents of the regular two-word ending in Ovid *praemollia* 'limp' or 'languid'.

[4] For more about that particular pentameter and about the poem's literary antecedents see L. P. Wilkinson, *Ovid Recalled*, Cambridge, 1955, pp. 21–23.

[5] Perhaps even the setting of the poem, a wood, is meant to hint at the *silva dicendi* or *silva rerum* (see Lewis and Short, *sub voc.* B. II)—the raw material of themes and ideas on which the ancient orator and poet drew.

[6] I believe that the last three lines of this poem

> '. . . *tu labor aeternus; quod petit illa breve est.'*
> *mota dedit veniam. teneri properentur Amores,*
> *dum vacat. a tergo grandius urget opus.*

were transmuted by Marvell's subconscious mind into the famous passage from the poem *To his coy Mistress*

> But at my back I alwaies hear
> Times winged Charriot hurrying near:
> And yonder all before us lye
> Desarts of vast Eternity.

[7] To bring out this lyrical quality one can employ a typographical device and write the elegiac couplet as a quatrain, e.g.

> *Verba puellarum,*
> *Foliis leviora caducis,*
> *Inrita qua visum est*
> *Ventus et unda ferunt . . .*
> *At vos, qua veniet*
> *Tumidi subsidite, montes,*
> *Et faciles curvis*
> *Vallibus este, viae.*

> (*Am.* 2. 16.45–46, 51–52)

It is worth noting that Horace's famous lyric *Diffugere nives* (*Odes* 4.7) has a metrical scheme in which the dactylic hexameter is followed by the second half of an elegiac pentameter.

[8] I have chosen to quote these stanzas from *The Baite* in modernized spelling because in the original spelling their psychological effect is somehow different and, it seems to me, less Ovidian. On the other hand, I have kept Dryden's spelling; to my mind it has no such disadvantage. Were one to archaize Graves's spelling, this poem of his could be passed off as late seventeenth century.

In quoting these poems as Ovidian I do not wish to imply that Donne or Dryden or Graves is imitating Ovid here.

[9] To my mind the successful poems in Book 2 are these: 1, 7, 8, 12, 15, and 17.

[10] Seneca the Elder, *Controversiae* 9. 5.17 and 2. 2.12.

Texts used: J. P. Postgate, *Tibulli Carmina*, Oxford, 1924; E. A. Barber, *Sexti Properti Carmina*, Oxford, 1957; Franco Munari, *P. Ovidi Nasonis Amores*, Florence, 1955; Theodore Redpath, *The Songs and Sonets of John Donne*, London, 1956; John Sargeaunt, *The Poems of John Dryden*, Oxford, 1910; *Robert Graves: Poems selected by himself* (Penguin Books), London, 1957.

Once or twice in the poems quoted from the *Amores* I have adopted a reading different from Munari's.

ROMANAE FIDICEN LYRAE:
THE ODES OF HORACE

R. G. M. Nisbet

THE criticism of Horace's Odes is unusually difficult. They cannot be understood without some knowledge of their literary antecedents; fortunately this is now obtainable from Professor Fraenkel's important book. Their technical excellence encourages indiscriminate appreciation, though in thoughtfulness and intensity of feeling they vary enormously. The poet's charm beguiles most readers; but he is a more enigmatic person than is sometimes supposed, and we should not be diverted from his poetry by our impression of his amiability. In this paper I have tried to suggest both the extent and the limits of his achievement, and to identify the important poems. I have expressed my value-judgements dogmatically, in the manner of critics, but I realize that other views are possible. If my readers are encouraged to justify their own preferences, no harm will have been done.

Everybody knows Pyrrha, so let us begin with her.

> Quis multa gracilis te puer in rosa
> perfusus liquidis urget odoribus
>   grato, Pyrrha, sub antro?
>   cui flavam religas comam
>
> simplex munditiis? heu quotiens fidem
> mutatosque deos flebit et aspera
>   nigris aequora ventis
>   emirabitur insolens

qui nunc te fruitur credulus aurea,
qui semper vacuam, semper amabilem
   sperat, nescius aurae
     fallacis. miseri quibus

intemptata nites. me tabula sacer
votiva paries indicat uvida
   suspendisse potenti
     vestimenta maris deae.   (1.5)

What thin boy drenched with liquid scents presses you, Pyrrha, among many roses in welcome grot? For whom do you bind back your yellow hair with dainty artlessness? Oh he'll often weep for promises and fortune changed, and stare surprised at calm waters ruffled by black squalls, who now credulously enjoys your goldenness, who hopes you will always be free, always lovable—ignorant of the wind's tricks. Unhappy those to whom you glisten untried. Me the sacred wall with votive plaque declares to have hung up my wet clothes to the potent goddess of the sea.

This poem is remarkable for its formal perfection. The word-order of the first line and the last stanza would have been impossible in the spoken language, and gives an aesthetic satisfaction unknown in English. The rigid metrical pattern imposes difficult problems (there is only one place in the stanza for a word like *potenti*), but their solution gives the ode an appearance of inevitability. The concentration of the poem is astonishing, even for Latin: *miseri quibus intemptata nites* is only an extreme instance of a general tendency. Most important of all, the structure of the whole is skilfully organized: Horace wrote not by the line or the stanza but by the poem. Those brought up in a non-classical tradition tend to undervalue structural coherence.

The vocabulary of the ode is plain. The Roman poets dignified their work by using a specialised poetic diction, and by avoiding words regarded as prosaic. Horace does not carry these tendencies so far as his contemporaries. Bertil Axelson[1] has pointed out words in the Odes which occur seldom, if at all, in the highest kinds of poetry; they include *cena, comis, condicio, delectare, mundus* (adj.), *negotium, pecunia, peritus, praesidium, studere*. In our poem *gracilis* is more prosaic than the English 'slender'; *simplex munditiis* is almost as austere as Milton's 'plain in thy neatness'; *amabilis* is not found in Virgil, Propertius, or Tibullus; *vestimenta* is not used at all by other poets. Besides being plain the diction is clear and precise. Horace hits the centre of the target every time with impressive efficiency. His ambiguities are clear-cut puns; unlike Virgil he does not contrive oblique allusions and evocative nuances. He heightens his verse by compression, hyperbaton, and the eccentric tilt of his syntax. The result is an artificial and original style such as nobody but a poet could have achieved.

The formalism of Horace's style is matched by his urbanity, realism, and wit. The Pyrrha ode is remote from the lush effusions of modern translators, an anthology of whose futilities has recently been published. The young man is depicted in slightly satirical terms, Pyrrha without sentimentality. The maritime metaphor of the second stanza is ingeniously sustained in *aurae fallacis* and *intemptata nites*. The reader will have noticed with surprise that I have accepted Zielinski's emendation *deae*, where the manuscripts read *deo*. But an allusion to Venus (as in 3.26.5) is much wittier than an allusion to Neptune. The goddess of love was born from the sea, and the epigrammatists of the Greek Anthology make play with her two spheres of influence (5.11, 5.17, 10.21). It is sometimes argued that *potenti maris*, 'powerful over the sea', can only refer to Neptune, but there is no need to take these words together. *deae* suits both the character of the poem and the convention of the genre, and if Horace did not write it he must have been less than usually alert.

The ode lacks nothing except seriousness and involvement. There was no grot, no sleek young man, no Pyrrha. One does not believe in her even as a composite or symbolic figure. The poem is suggested by poetry, not by real life; even Horace's protestations of disillusionment are artificial. Propertius offers a striking contrast:

> ecce coronatae portum tetigere carinae,
>   traiectae Syrtes, ancora iacta mihi est.
> nunc demum vasto fessi resipiscimus aestu,
>   vulneraque ad sanum nunc coiere mea.
> Mens Bona, si qua dea es, tua me in sacraria dono:
>   exciderant surdo tot mea vota Iovi.   (3.24.15 ff.)

See, the beflagged ships have made harbour, the Syrtes are passed, my anchor is thrown. Weary with the wild surge, now at last I come to myself; my wounds have now healed. Sane Mind, if there is any

such goddess, I dedicate myself in your chapel; for my many vows
to Jupiter rebounded from deaf ears.

These verses are less economical than Horace's, and artistically
less perfect (the fourth line disrupts the metaphor). They may not
even be literally autobiographical, for Propertius is not always
spontaneous. But they are written with an earnestness and
intensity that seem to be derived at least partly from real life.

None of Horace's love-poems (if that is the right name for
them) reaches the first rank. When Lydia praises the waxen arms
and rosy neck of Telephus, the poet's reaction is remarkable:

> tum nec mens mihi nec color
> certa sede manet, umor et in genas
>   furtim labitur, arguens
> quam lentis penitus macerer ignibus.   (1.13.5 ff.)

Then my head reels and my colour changes, and furtive tears glide
down my cheeks, showing the slow fires that waste me within.

Improbable confessions of this kind are disastrous, and one need
not contrast Sappho or Catullus to prove the point. The Lalage
ode (1.22) is a much better poem because its exaggerations
are deliberate and humorous. Yet, though perfect of its kind, it
is completely irrelevant to anything that ever happened or might
happen; whatever Horace was doing when he met the wolf, if
he met the wolf, he was not singing about Lalage. *extremum
Tanain* (3.10) is an agreeable variation of the lover's lament.
Horace describes his imaginary experiences with more verisimili-
tude than usual, though the poetical colour is scarcely serious.

> audis quo strepitu ianua, quo nemus
> inter pulchra satum tecta remugiat
>   ventis, et positas ut glaciet nives
>   puro numine Iuppiter?

Hear how the door rattles, and the grove planted amid the fine
buildings groans in the wind, and Jupiter with serene influence freezes
the lying snow.

In other 'love-poems' Horace does not even pretend to be per-
sonally involved; they are not any the worse for that reason.
Lydia dic (1.8) is one of the best of the kind, gay, vivid, and short.
nondum subacta (2.5) is a masterpiece of compact and tasteless

ingenuity, such as nobody but Horace could have achieved. The
Neobule ode (3.12) is an amusing exercise in *ionics a minore*:

> simul unctos Tiberinis umeros lavit in undis
> eques ipso melior Bellerophonte, neque pugno
> neque segni pede victus.[2]

But we are looking for something more than metrical acrobatics.

One of the odes to one of the Lydias is a particular favourite of
those who like Horace for the wrong reasons. This poem (3.9)
has a certain languid charm, but the contrast with Catullus's
Septimius and Acme (45) is too damaging. Horace says to Lydia:

> donec gratus eram tibi
> nec quisquam potior bracchia candidae
> cervici iuvenis dabat
> Persarum vigui rege beatior.

While I was welcome to you and no more favoured youth gave his
arms to your white neck, I flourished more blest than the King of
Persia.

Septimius says to Acme:

> ni te perdite amo atque amare porro
> omnes sum assidue paratus annos,
> quantum qui pote plurimum perire,
> solus in Libya Indiaque tosta
> caesio veniam obvius leoni.

If I'm not madly in love with you and amn't ready to go on loving
you all the time for ever and ever as much as the biggest lover of the
lot, then alone in Africa or burnt India may I come across a green-eyed
lion.

Horace's sentiment is conventional without being true to life,
and his phraseology, though mellifluous, has been too much
processed and denatured. Septimius, on the other hand, talks real
Latin, a better language for his purpose than readers of the
Augustan classics might think. In spite of all his elegance Catullus
preserves the vocabulary and movement of speech, and hence
something of the feeling as well. His only specifically poetic
touch is the green-eyed lion, which is worth much more than the
King of Persia. Ancient critics would no doubt have said that the
Horatian passage was written in a higher style. If they thought

it was better poetry that would explain much about the decline of Latin literature.

In fact, Horace wrote a much better Lydia ode, though the anthologists do not think so.

Parcius iunctas quatiunt fenestras
iactibus crebris iuvenes protervi,
nec tibi somnos adimunt, amatque
    ianua limen,

quae prius multum facilis movebat
cardines; audis minus et minus iam
'me tuo longas pereunte noctes,
    Lydia dormis?'

invicem moechos anus arrogantis
flebis in solo levis angiportu,
Thracio bacchante magis sub inter-
    lunia vento,

cum tibi flagrans amor et libido,
quae solet matres furiare equorum,
saeviet circa iecur ulcerosum,
    non sine questu

laeta quod pubes hedera virenti
gaudeat pulla magis atque myrto,
aridas frondis hiemis sodali
    dedicet Euro.   (1.25)

Not so often do the eager young men shake the fastened shutters with repeated throws. They do not take your sleep away any more, and the door hugs the threshold which many a time used to move compliant hinges. You hear less and less now 'While I your love die long nights, Lydia, can you slumber?' You will lament in turn the arrogance of wenchers, a slight old woman in a deserted alley, while the Thracian wind revels more wildly as the moonless nights draw near. Then the burning passion and lust that maddens the dams of horses will seethe round your ulcerated liver, and you will whine that exuberant manhood takes more pleasure in green ivy and dark myrtle, but consecrates withered leaves to winter's comrade, the East wind.

The opening is effective. The scene is set not in a grot this time, but in a street. The rattle of the pebbles on the shutters is represented by the hard clatter of the c's. The third and fourth lines with their m's and n's are rightly smoother. Horace, unlike Virgil, could not write convincing descriptions of things he had not seen. Here he knows what he is talking about.

In the second stanza the familiar laments of the excluded lover, usually so lengthy, are ingeniously compressed in seven words. What follows is more pungent. Realistic descriptions of ageing beauties were a conventional type of poem, but they consist too often of tasteless catalogues of the details of ugliness. Horace concentrates on what matters, and with a few expert strokes draws a vignette worthy of Catullus. He visualizes the Thracian wind as a Thracian bacchanal; allusions to bacchanals in Latin poetry usually bring out the stalest conventions, but not this one. Bentley asks with eighteenth-century common sense why Lydia had to go out on such a windy night, but Horace's evocation of atmosphere, though untypical, is wholly admirable.

The fourth stanza is remarkable for its concentrated venom; again one may note the alliteration of the c's (*circa, iecur, ulcerosum, questu*). The metaphor at the end of the poem refers to garlands, which were regularly worn by party-goers. Such garlands could be dedicated to Venus; so *dedicet* has more point than might appear. Winds are elsewhere described as companions of the seasons, but *sodali*, 'boon-companion', is livelier than *comiti*. The last word of the poem is *Hebro* in the manuscripts, but the Thracian river has no place here; the scene is set in a city, and the withered garlands are thrown in the street for the wind to play with.[3] In his handling of his metaphor Horace shows not only his usual ingenuity but also unexpected imagination.

This ode to Lydia should be compared with the ode to Lyce (4.13), which handles a similar theme. The earlier poem is more concentrated, its images are stronger, and it is better in every way. Horace predicts Lydia's future ugliness, but in the other poem he is exultant because Lyce has turned ugly; the latter situation is not only more disagreeable, but also less plausible. The Lyce ode, it is true, strikes a more serious note when the poet laments for vanished beauty:

> quo fugit Venus, heu, quove color? decens
> quo motus? quid habes illius, illius
>   quae spirabat amores,
>   quae me surpuerat mihi.

Where has the charm fled, oh where the complexion? Where the graceful movement? What have you left of her of her who breathed love, who had stolen me from myself?

But such sentimental regrets do not blend with virulent gloating. Psychologically the poem rings false; the unmitigated ferocity of the Lydia ode may be just as conventional, but it is much more convincing.

The Lydia ode, needless to say, is not a favourite with Horatians: 'The poem has no merit,' says T. E. Page, 'and may be omitted with advantage.' This is a lamentable verdict, typical of the Victorian attitudes which have stifled the understanding of Latin poetry, but we must not lean too far in the other direction. Intensity and imagination are rare virtues, but in the best poetry humanity is also an asset.

Many of the odes profess to describe symposia. The appurtenances of a Horatian party are only too familiar, flute and flute-girl, nard and garlands, Caecuban and Falernian. In spite of Horace's own warnings (*Epistles* 1.19), some readers find these features particularly characteristic of our author, yet they tell us less about his own tastes than about the conventions of his genre. When the modest poet contrasts his *vin du pays* with the cellar of his patron (1.20) the touch seems agreeably Horatian; yet Philodemus had said much the same when inviting L. Piso to his frugal supper (*Anth. Pal.* 11.44). We hear a snatch of dialogue from a symposium formalized with skill and charm (1.27), but the setting is Greek and the element of reality negligible. There is a lack of arresting visual detail, particularly in the invitation poems: it is difficult to be graphic in the future tense. It is seldom that one meets a sentence like '*sordidum flammae trepidant rotantes vertice fumum*'[4] (4.11.11–12). To catch the atmosphere of a real party one must try Propertius instead:

> Nile, tuus tibicen erat, crotalistria Phyllis
> (haec facilis spargi munda sine arte rosa),
> Magnus et ipse suos breviter concretus in artus
> iactabat truncas ad cava buxa manus.   (4.8.39 ff.)

The flute-player was Egyptian, Phyllis played the castanets (artlessly neat she was, and ready to be showered with petals). Lofty in person, bunched up in his short body, wagged the stumps of his hands to the hollow box-pipe.

Horace's convivial poems are only important when they sound a serious, Epicurean note. Reflections on the brevity of life were a commonplace of the genre, but here, at least, Horace persuades us that his imitations are not simply external. The Soracte ode (1.9) is the best of the category:

> Vides ut alta stet nive candidum
> Soracte, nec iam sustineant onus
>   silvae laborantes, geluque
>   flumina constiterint acuto?
>
> dissolve frigus ligna super foco
> large reponens atque benignius
>   deprome quadrimum Sabina,
>   o Thaliarche, merum diota.
>
> permitte divis cetera, qui simul
> stravere ventos aequore fervido
>   deproeliantis, nec cupressi
>   nec veteres agitantur orni.
>
> quid sit futurum cras fuge quaerere et
> quem Fors dierum cumque dabit lucro
>   appone, nec dulcis amores
>   sperne puer neque tu choreas,
>
> donec virenti canities abest
> morosa. nunc et Campus et areae
>   lenesque sub noctem susurri
>   composita repetantur hora,
>
> nunc et latentis proditor intimo
> gratus puellae risus ab angulo
>   pignusque dereptum lacertis
>   aut digito male pertinaci.

See how Soracte stands piled white with snow, and the straining woods no longer bear the load, and the rivers are halted by the piercing frost. Melt the cold, laying logs plentifully on the fire, and draw more generously, o Thaliarch, four-year wine from Sabine jar. Leave all else to the gods; when they have laid the winds that battle on the seething seas, neither cypresses are shaken nor ancient ash-trees. Do not ask what will happen tomorrow, and every day that fortune gives place to your account, nor spurn sweet loves when young nor the revel, while your sap is green, while grey and captious age is far away. Now seek the park and the piazzas, and soft whispers in the evening at the time arranged, now the agreeable laugh from inmost corner that gives away the hiding girl, and the token tugged from arm or from unreluctant finger.

This poem is formally modelled on a drinking-song by Alcaeus, but Horace has blended with it elements of very different provenance. Monte Soratte is a familiar landmark, visible from Rome. The rivers are invisible, and come from Alcaeus; in their scene-painting the ancients wrongly aimed at general effects rather than literal accuracy. *diota* is a Greek word for a two-eared wine-jar and is found hardly at all in Latin; but in spite of its name this jar comes from Horace's favourite countryside. 'Thaliarchus' is another Greek word translated by editors 'prince of good cheer': the artificiality is strange by modern standards, but the ode would be no better if it were addressed, like others, to some unscrupulous contemporary statesman. The central theme, stated as often in the middle, is Epicurean in spirit, though *lucro adpone* hints at the prosaic tones of the Roman businessman. The last two stanzas may have been influenced by Hellenistic epigram, but one suspects that they are not entirely derivative. The scene is set on home ground, and *Campus* is the Campus Martius, the Park of Rome. The reminiscences of Alcaeus's light-hearted song were ornamental and deceptive: Horace has taken varied strands from reading and experience and woven out of them a serious and original poem.

Horace's language is remarkable for its terseness and precision. *stet, laborantes, acuto, dissolve* (to go no further) are exactly right, and not easily translated. *alta* is usually rendered 'deep', which is unsatisfactory: you only think of the depth of snow when you are close to it, usually above it. But though we translate 'altus' sometimes as 'high', sometimes as 'deep', there is only one Latin word meaning literally 'nourished', and hence 'built-up'. Dryden saw the point:

> Behold yon' Mountains hoary height
> Made higher with new Mounts of Snow;
> Again behold the Winters weight
> Oppress the lab'ring Woods below:
> And streams with Icy fetters bound,
> Benum'd and crampt to solid ground.

But though Dryden is not a diffuse writer he takes 34 words to Horace's 17.

The end of the poem is as memorable as the beginning. The intricate word-order produces effects of balance and contrast impossible in an uninflected language. The concentration of the expression increases the vividness of the scene. Yet there is no prettiness or sentimentality: the tones are those of a detached observer. Critics complain that the weather is too frosty for the Campus, but there is no inconsistency. *nunc* means 'while you are young'. A modern poet might have given advice for today, but Horace is as indifferent to the details of time as he was to those of place. Of course, the ode veers somewhat: in A. Y. Campbell's phrase, it describes not a circle but a parabola. But its formal unity remains unimpaired and the vignette at the end provides an artistic contrast with the landscape at the beginning.

'*Hübsche Verse*', says Wilamowitz, '*aber noch kein Gedicht.*' If this is not a poem I do not know what is.

The ode to Leuconoe (1.11) may be less elaborate in texture, but within its limits it is also an impressive poem:

> Tu ne quaesieris, scire nefas, quem mihi quem tibi
> finem di dederint, Leuconoe, nec Babylonios
> temptaris numeros. ut melius quidquid erit pati.
> seu pluris hiemes seu tribuit Iuppiter ultimam,
> quae nunc oppositis debilitat pumicibus mare
> Tyrrhenum, sapias, vina liques, et spatio brevi
> spem longam reseces. dum loquimur, fugerit invida
> aetas. carpe diem, quam minimum credula postero.

Do not ask, we may not know, what end the gods have given me, what end to you, Leuconoe, nor meddle with astrologers' arithmetic. Better to accept whatever happens. Whether God grants other winters, or this the last, which now tires the Tuscan Sea with a barrier of rock, be sensible, filter your wine, and cut back long hopes within short limits. While we talk jealous time will have run. Pluck the day, trusting the morrow as little as possible.

Leuconoe is an imaginary person with a Greek name and the astrological interests of some Roman ladies. The sentiments of the poem are also conventional, but Horace's treatment is original, serious, and apparently sincere. The evocative picture of the Tuscan Sea is not an irrelevant piece of local colouring: the poet contrasts the unending strife of the elements with the brevity of human life and happiness. The rapidity of the choriambs and the shortness of the sentences alike suggest that there is no time to lose. 'Carpe diem', however hackneyed, remains a brilliant expression. Horace nowhere expresses his scepticism with greater energy and concentration.

The ode to Postumus (2.14) is even more pessimistic, and offers no temporary consolations. The first half of the poem falls short of greatness, for though the words are solemn and sonorous they make no clear pictures. The last three stanzas are very different.

> visendus ater flumine languido
> Cocytus errans et Danai genus
>   infame damnatusque longi
>   Sisyphus Aeolides laboris.
>
> linquenda tellus et domus et placens
> uxor, neque harum quas colis arborum
>   te praeter invisas cypressos
>   ulla brevem dominum sequetur.
>
> absumet heres Caecuba dignior
> servata centum clavibus et mero
>   tinget pavimentum superbo,
>   pontificum potiore cenis.

Black Cocytus must be viewed, winding with sluggish stream, and the sinful daughters of Danaus, and Sisyphus Aeolides, condemned to long labour. Land must be left and house and agreeable wife, and of the trees you tend none will go with you, their temporary owner, except the grim cypresses. Your more deserving heir will use up the vintages guarded by a hundred keys, and will splash the tiles with a proud wine that is better than a pontiffs' feast.

The Cocytus is described in four words, each with a visual appeal. Sisyphus is much more interesting than the mythological personages at the beginning of the poem: the grandiloquent *Aeolides* and the euphemistic *longi laboris* both provoke the imagination. The domestic scene, with its Lucretian reminiscence, is drawn with admirable restraint; the reader is left to fill in the details from his own experience. The cypresses can also be visualized, at least on the most poetical interpretation; for one would like to think that Horace is referring to trees round the grave rather than to branches round the pyre.[5] In yet another vivid picture, Horace imagines the spendthrift heir splashing the mosaics with hoarded vintages. *dignior* gives an unexpected and satirical twist, and A. Y. Campbell's emendation *degener* is dull by comparison. The compressed allusion to priestly banquets makes a brilliant climax. In this rich and imaginative poem Horace has transferred Greek pessimism to a Roman setting.

Horace wrote other fine poems on pessimistic themes, but they cannot all be discussed here. The ode to Dellius (2.3) is almost as good as the ode to Postumus, though its imagery is less vivid. The ode to Torquatus (4.7) is also impressive, and was regarded by Housman as the most beautiful poem in ancient literature. Yet it might be argued that the earlier ode to Sestius (1.4) shows greater concentration and variety:

> Solvitur acris hiems grata vice veris et Favoni,
>   trahuntque siccas machinae carinas,
> ac neque iam stabulis gaudet pecus aut arator igni,
>   nec prata canis albicant pruinis.
> iam Cytherea choros ducit Venus imminente luna,
>   iunctaeque Nymphis Gratiae decentes
> alterno terram quatiunt pede, dum gravis Cyclopum
>   Vulcanus ardens visit officinas.
> nunc decet aut viridi nitidum caput impedire myrto
>   aut flore terrae quem ferunt solutae;
> nunc et in umbrosis Fauno decet immolare lucis,
>   seu poscat agna sive malit haedo.
> pallida Mors aequo pulsat pede pauperum tabernas
>   regumque turris. o beate Sesti,
> vitae summa brevis spem nos vetat incohare longam.
>   iam te premet nox fabulaeque Manes
> et domus exilis Plutonia; quo simul mearis,
>   nec regna vini sortiere talis,
> nec tenerum Lycidan mirabere, quo calet iuventus
>   nunc omnis et mox virgines tepebunt.

Bitter winter dissolves at the welcome succession of spring and zephyr.
    Dry boats are dragged down on rollers.
Beasts now huddle no more in the steading or the farmer by the fireside.
    The grass with grey frost no longer whitens.

Under a looming moon Cytherean Venus leads the dances,
  And hand in hand with the nymphs the smiling Graces
Beat on the ground with rhythmical kick after kick, while fiery Vulcan
  Tours the heavy Cyclopean forges.
Now is the time to entwine on a shining head the verdant myrtle,
  Or flowers that the loosened earth gives birth to.
Now is the time in shadowy woodland to sacrifice to Faunus
  The lamb he asks, or a kid if he prefers one.
Ghastly death impartially kicks at the cottages of poor men
  And kings' castles. Greatly blessèd Sestius,
Life's short total forbids the forming of long-term aspirations.
  Soon night will cramp you and the shades of story
And the incorporeal halls Plutonian, whither when you journey
  You'll not be chosen king of the wine by dice-throw,
Nor will you then admire young Lycidas for whom the men are hot now
  And girls will begin to grow warm soon.

The metre of this poem is vigorous and distinctive; by comparison the ode to Torquatus is a little tame (*'diffugere nives, redeunt
iam gramina campis/arboribusque comae'*). The pictures of the earlier
poem are more lively: in the first few lines we see the launching
of boats in the spring, white frost on the fields, Venus dancing
under a hanging moon (when the Graces dance in the other ode
there is no moon). The ode to Sestius covers wide ranges of emotion, gaiety and hope at the beginning, then the startling kick at
the door, the matter-of-fact assessment of the human condition
in line 15, hints of a transitory hedonism at the close; on the other
hand the ode to Torquatus is written in a melancholy monotone.
The proper names in our poem show the range of Horace's
thought. Venus's dance seems to be drawn from some Hellenistic
Primavera, Vulcan is at once Venus's husband and a grim Roman
manufacturer, Faunus suggests the simple pieties of the Italian
countryside, Sestius (consul 23 B.C.) the secure and successful
contemporary world, *Plutonia* the sphere of epic and tragedy (the
adjective is more grandiose than the genitive *Plutonis*), Lycidas
the fantasies of Greek symposiastic verse. To cover ground is a
merit in a poet, and the ode to Sestius is one of Horace's masterpieces.

The elegy on Quintilius Varus (1.24) is a serious poem of a
different sort. The first two stanzas show both the merits and the
defects of Horace's formal manner:

Quis desiderio sit pudor aut modus
tam cari capitis? praecipe lugubris
cantus, Melpomene, cui liquidam pater
vocem cum cithara dedit.

ergo Quintilium perpetuus sopor
urget. cui Pudor et Iustitiae soror,
incorrupta Fides, nudaque Veritas
quando ullum inveniet parem?

What shame or measure should there be in grief for one so dear?
Lead the mournful strain, Melpomene, to whom the Sire gave with
the cithern the voice of clear tone. So then the sleep which knows no
waking lies heavy on Quintilius! When shall Modesty find again his
peer, and stainless Faith, own sister to Justice, and naked Truth?

(Wickham)

The opening sentence is admirable for its gravity and restraint,
but Melpomene fails to satisfy; the allusion goes on too long,
and does not help to convince us that Horace is in earnest. The
second stanza again begins well, but the rest is vague and exaggerated. The abstractions tell us nothing about Quintilius, and the
rhetorical question might have been asked in almost any Roman
obituary. Horace goes on to say that Quintilius is mourned by all
good men, and especially by Virgil, but we are not told why these
people liked him. Callimachus does better in his classic epigram
on Heraclitus, so diffusely mistranslated by William Johnson
Cory; he says nothing about the dead man's moral qualities, but
seizes on the essential and convincing circumstance: ἐμνήσθην
δ᾽ ὁσσάκις ἀμφότεροι/ἥλιον ἐν λέσχῃ κατεδύσαμεν, 'I remembered how
often we both had sunk the sun in conversation.' It is particulars
like these which give a poem life and authenticity.

In the fourth stanza Horace returns to mythology:

quid si Threicio blandius Orpheo
auditam moderere arboribus fidem,
num vanae redeat sanguis imagini . . . ?

What if more winningly than Thracian Orpheus you played a lyre
to which the trees listened, would the blood return to the hollow shade?

These serene lines suit the character of the dead man (Quintilius
was a poet), and Horace's own scepticism about an after-life. Yet

the story about Orpheus and the trees is too fanciful and too trivial for the context. When Catullus writes about his brother (who had died near Troy) he uses mythology with much more originality and intensity (68.89 f.):

> Troia (nefas!) commune sepulcrum Asiae Europaeque
> Troia virum et virtutum omnium acerba cinis.

Troy (abominable), the common grave of Asia and Europe, Troy, the untimely dust of all true men and manliness.

But the last two lines of Horace's poem are excellent:

> durum: sed levius fit patientia
> quidquid corrigere est nefas.

Hard, but what cannot be put right becomes lighter by acceptance.

Here we have no elegant allusions or conventional hyperboles, but a rational remark which suits the poet's own view of life.

Some of Horace's most attractive, though not his greatest, odes are concerned in whole or part with the placid scenes of the Italian countryside. These poems seem to reflect a genuine facet of his personality, and therefore deserve serious consideration. More than most ancient poets Horace localizes his affections in a specific area, and such particularization is always gain. His Sabine valley seems agreeable to the sentimental modern pilgrim, but contemporaries must have thought it remote and uninteresting, much like many other valleys. Yet Horace talks about this obscure district as if it would be as important to his readers as it was to him; his poem on the fashionable neighbourhood of Tarentum (2.6) is dull by comparison. It is the mark of a poet not to defer too much to other people's preconceptions, but to make us look at the world through his eyes.

Yet though the place-names are precise the scenery is vague and undefined. Horace enjoyed the peace of the countryside (some of the time), and his own status as a proprietor, but he was not a countryman. He had no interest in the details of agricultural activity or animal life; Virgil's loving portrayal of ants or irrigation was beyond his range. As a painter of landscapes he is greatly inferior not only to Virgil but to Ovid and Statius. It may be relevant that he suffered from *lippitudo*, a complaint of the eyes which in some of its forms affected the vision; but whether he was shortsighted or not, flowery descriptions might have seemed too affected and Alexandrian to his classicizing tastes. He can describe a slow-moving river in memorable terms (1.31.7 f. *'non rura quae Liris quieta/mordet aqua taciturnus amnis'* 'Not the fields which the Liris erodes with its quiet waters, a silent river'); but one expects no subtle observation of shadow and reflection in the manner of Ausonius's Mosella. His pictures are a blurred background to human activity or inactivity:

> purae rivus aquae silvaque iugerum
> paucorum et segetis certa fides meae
> fulgentem imperio fertilis Africae
> fallit sorte beatior. (3.16.29 ff.)

The man who is splendid with authority over fertile Africa does not understand that a stream of pure water, a wood of a few acres, and the sure reliability of my cornfields are the happier lot.

Such verses are pleasant to read, but they make no strong appeal to the imagination, and cannot be regarded as poetry of the first rank.

The richest poem of this whole group is the Lucretilis ode (1.17). Lucretilis was an unimportant mountain near Horace's farm, but here it appears, side by side with the Arcadian Lycaeus, as a haunt of Faunus. The peace of the Sabine countryside is suggested in a few simple strokes:

> impune tutum per nemus arbutos
> quaerunt latentis et thyma deviae
>   olentis uxores mariti,
>   nec viridis metuunt colubras
>
> nec Martialis haediliae lupos
> utcumque dulci, Tyndari, fistula
>   valles et Vsticae cubantis
>   levia personuere saxa.

Straggling at large through the protected wood the wives of the smelling he-goat look for lurking arbute and thyme, and the kids are not afraid of green snakes or the wolves of Mars whenever with sweet pipe, Tyndaris, the valley and smooth rocks of sloping Ustica resound.

On top of his realistic scene, with its smooth rocks and straggling goats, Horace has superimposed features derived from the imaginative world of Greek poetry. Ustica was an insignificant place in the Sabine valley; Tyndaris, on the other hand, was neither a local shepherdess nor a visiting artiste, but an invention of the poet's brain. Horace goes on to describe the bounty of nature in genuinely Italian terms, but then Tyndaris appears again singing of Penelope and Circe. Finally the poem goes off on another tangent with a scene from urban night-life portrayed in the manner of Hellenistic epigram. We have come a long way from those goats, but the variety is typically Horatian.

The Lucretilis ode is curiously artificial by modern standards, but one must make distinctions. When a poem has no bearing on life it can hardly be placed in the highest class. But provided that it reflects in some sense the real world and the poet's genuine interests, then there is a place for artistic fantasy. Other people besides Horace owned goats near Ustica; other people read about Penelope and Circe; but nobody else did both. In that way the poem is not only sincere but individual.

The ode to the fountain of Bandusia (3.13) has probably more admirers than the Lucretilis ode. It is overrated. After telling us that the spring is clearer than glass Horace announces that he is going to kill a goat in it, and he visualizes with aesthetic relish the mingling of the cool water and the red blood. The Romans were an unsentimental people, accustomed to slaughter in the arena and at religious ceremonies; but when assigning a value to their poetry, while we should be aware of their own standards, we must not surrender our own view of good taste. In any case, Horace's behaviour was strange even by ancient criteria. As A. Y. Campbell asks with admirable forthrightness, 'Who wants a drink out of the fountain of Bandusia after that?'

The value of the poem depends almost entirely on the last stanza:

> fies nobilium tu quoque fontium,
> me dicente cavis impositam ilicem
> saxis unde loquaces
> lymphae desiliunt tuae.

You too will become a famous fountain because I speak of the oak perched over the cavern from which your waters leap down chattering.

Every reader must be charmed by the clarity and simplicity of the picture, and the agreeable onomatopoeia at the close. Yet the poem is not just a pretty picture of a country scene: its main subject is Horace himself. It belongs, in fact, to the large group of odes (2.13, 3.4, and 3.30 are the best) which deal in whole or part with the poet's own art and aspirations.

It will be convenient now to mention some miscellaneous odes based on Greek models of several types. The hymn was a familiar category, but Horace's imitations fail to reach the first rank. The ode to Mercury (1.10) is charming and serene; but though a rationalist might be moved by the old legends, he could hardly write a major poem on such outmoded themes. The ode on Bacchus (2.19) has some artistic descriptions, but they are completely derivative. Horace's shouts of 'Euhoe' are embarrassing, and though he claims to have seen the god singing in the mountains, posterity has remained incredulous. The ode to Diana and Phoebus (1.21) is too formal and involved to create any clear picture:

> vos laetam fluviis et nemorum coma
> quaecumque aut gelido prominet Algido
> nigris aut Erymanthi
> silvis aut viridis Cragi.

Sing the goddess who rejoices in rivers and the foliage of the groves whatsoever is prominent on cold Algidus or the black woods of Erymanthus or of green Cragus.

H. A. J. Munro admirably compared Catullus's less pretentious hymn:

> montium domina ut fores
> silvarumque virentium
> saltuumque reconditorum
> amniumque sonantum.   (34.9 ff.)

That you might be mistress of the mountains and the flourishing forests and the secret clearings and the sounding rivers.

One may endorse Munro's verdict: 'If Catullus does not surpass Horace here alike in the simple vigour of the thought and the majestic march of the rhythm, then I confess myself to be no judge of Latin or any other poetry.'

The hymn of Fortuna (1.35) is equally disappointing. As he looked back at the vicissitudes of his own career, the sceptical poet might have found some interesting ideas about the goddess of Anzio. Instead we are offered conventional platitudes and blurred images:

> te Spes et albo rara Fides colit
> velata panno, nec comitem abnegat,
> utcumque mutata potentis
> veste domos inimica linquis.

Thee Hope waits on and Faith so rare, clad in white garments, nor does she leave thee companionless whensoever with changed garb thou desertest in displeasure the homes of the great. (Wickham.)

The ode on Jupiter is much more vivid and sensible:

> valet ima summis
> mutare et insignem attenuat deus,
> obscura promens; hinc apicem rapax
> fortuna cum stridore acuto
> sustulit, hic posuisse gaudet.   (1.34.12 ff.)

God can change the lowest with the highest, reducing the illustrious and bringing the obscure to light. With a shrill whirring of her wings thieving Fortune has lifted the crown from here, and here has gleefully placed it.

Elsewhere Horace wrote even better lines on Fortuna. If the reader has forgotten them he will find them later in this essay.

Horace also tried his hand at less important types of poem. The ode on Virgil's departure for Greece (1.3) is a so-called *propempticon*; nobody could like it much unless his aesthetic perceptions had been blunted by a prolonged classical education.

> illi robur et aes triplex
> circa pectus erat qui fragilem truci
> commisit pelago ratem
> primus, nec timuit praecipitem Africum
> decertantem Aquilonibus
> nec tristis Hyadas nec rabiem Noti . . .

He had oak and triple bronze round his breast who first trusted a frail boat to the rough sea and feared not the headlong Afric wind struggling with the North, nor the gloomy Hyades nor the rage of the South wind.

Navigation in the ancient world was more dangerous than it is today, but Horace's sombre musings on the audacity of man go far beyond anything which the occasion justifies. *O matre pulchra* (1.16) is another frigid attempt at a minor genre, this time the palinode. When Horace wrote such poems he was not stirred by any actual event, but decided in cold blood to imitate a conventional category. Unfortunately one is not interested in pretended reconciliations, after fictitious feuds, with imaginary women.

The purely mythological odes are not much more satisfactory, even though they contain some memorable phrases. The poem on Paris (1.15) does not even pretend to have contemporary relevance. The poems on Hypermestra (3.11) and Europa (3.27) are more complex, but the Lyde and the Galatea who introduce them are as artificial as the heroines themselves. Horace could not re-create the conditions of the early fifth century, when mythology still had contact with life. He could not rival the Greek lyric poets in splendour of language, or in their power to paint a rapid series of strongly imagined scenes. He might have tried something more modern, but modern tastes were frivolous and uncongenial. Ovid wrote a sprightly narrative on Hypermestra (*Heroides* 14), but Horace aimed at greater concentration. The Alexandrian Moschus had visualized Europa on the bull's back with purple frock billowing, while dolphins somersaulted, Tritons trumpeted, and serried Nereids rode their sea-beasts. The unromantic Horace ventures nothing more picturesque than *scatentem beluis pontum*, 'the sea swarming with monsters'. Europa's psychology would have intrigued some of the neoterics, but Horace had no imaginative sympathy with desperate heroines, or any women for that matter. So we are fobbed off with conventional rhetoric:

> quae simul centum tetigit potentem
> oppidis Creten 'pater, o relictum
> filiae nomen, pietasque' dixit
>   'victa furore!
>
> unde quo veni?'

As soon as she touched Crete, powerful with a hundred cities, 'Father!' she said, 'name abandoned by a daughter, and duty overcome by madness! Whence, whither have I come?'

Virgil could do that sort of thing better.

The Archytas ode (1.28) seems also to be modelled on a Greek original, but it is much more successful than any of the poems just mentioned. In his boyhood Horace may have been set thinking by the great mathematician's tomb on the Apulian coast; certainly he communicates a feeling which does not seem to be second-hand.

> Te maris et terrae numeroque carentis harenae
> mensorem cohibent, Archyta,
> pulveris exigui prope litus parva Matinum
> munera, nec quicquam tibi prodest
> aerias temptasse domos animoque rotundum
> percurrisse polum morituro.

You who measured the sea and the land and the unnumbered sand, Archytas, are hemmed in near the Matine shore by the patch of dust allotted to your grave. It does you no good to have climbed the halls of heaven or to have traversed the sky with a wind that had to die.

There follow references to famous figures who were wrongly thought to have escaped death; the indirect use of myth is much more effective than straightforward narrative. The last of the list is Pythagoras, who is described with a pleasing mixture of grandiloquence and satire. Romantic poets may write in a single key, but readers of Horace must be alert to subtle shifts of style.

The structure of the poem is unusually obscure for Horace: it is not even agreed whether it is a monologue or a dialogue. The problems cannot be debated here, but one point should be made: in spite of its great difficulties, perhaps partly because of them, the Archytas ode seems one of the most imaginative in the whole collection. Another quotation may show something of its quality:

> me quoque devexi rapidus comes Orionis
> Illyricis Notus obruit undis.
> at tu, nauta, vagae ne parce malignus harenae
> ossibus et capiti inhumato
> particulam dare: sic, quodcumque minabitur Eurus
> fluctibus Hesperiis, Venusinae
> plectantur silvae te sospite, multaque merces
> unde potest tibi defluat aequo
> ab Iove Neptunoque sacri custode Tarenti.

Me too the South wind, the tearing companion of setting Orion, overwhelmed in Illyrian waves. But as for you, captain, do not grudgingly refuse a grain of drifting sand to my unburied bones and skull. If you do as I ask, whatever the East wind's threats against the western waves, may you be preserved while the woods of Venusia suffer, and may great profits be lavished on you, as they can, by a beneficent Jupiter and Neptune, the guardian of sacred Tarentum.

The first two lines are unusually 'poetical', rather in the manner of Propertius or some other 'Alexandrian' poet. The rolling sentences that follow are quite unlike the poet's usual congested style. The dactylic rhythm allowed him to express fluctuations of feeling with the ease of conversation: it is significant that some of his best poems are written in simple 'epodic' metres. Horace evokes with particular effect the wind beating on the woods of his native Venusia. Such a touch helps to give the ode authenticity: though as artificial in conception as any in Horace, it alludes, however obliquely, to real life and real emotion, which the Europa ode does not. And though the poem may contain reminiscences of Simonides, it is not archaic in spirit. However much Horace talks of his debt to the old lyric poets, he was writing for a sophisticated age, and his best poems, like this one, were inspired primarily by Hellenistic influences.

We turn now to the national and political odes.[6] Here the poet's sincerity, or at any rate involvement, has been called in question, and some distinctions must be drawn. It would be absurd to suppose that Horace was a secret scoffer who sold his poetry for a Sabine farm. However, that does not settle the matter. Maecenas did not befriend Horace simply for cultural reasons, and Horace owed him not only moral encouragement but a secure and comfortable mode of life. It is difficult now to understand patronage; the eighteenth century knew more about these things. Under such a system an intelligent and tolerably honourable poet may flatter an unworthy patron in the most unrealistic terms; what is worse, he may mean what he says. In semi-feudal societies men feel loyal to their superiors, and the Romans set a high value on *fides*. When the two parties are people of subtlety and charm they may become friends, as Horace and Maecenas no doubt did. A poet of servile origins might feel particular gratification at the attentions of the great, and when he spoke of his patron and his patron's causes his consciousness of his own virtuosity would give added impetus and warmth to his writing.

In fact, when we examine Horace's political poetry we find some discrepancies with the rest of his work. Youthful republicanism is not inconsistent with a change of heart, but this change of heart is too complete. Elsewhere Horace has a sceptical turn of mind, and a gift for deflating pomposity: here he supports the most exorbitant pretensions of the new order. His Epicurean hedonism (not to mention Maecenas's) does not suit his proclamations of a revived morality. He treats private emotions with restraint, but discusses national issues with enthusiasm. His attitudes conform precisely and predictably to the ethos of the régime, and even his exhibitions of independence are calculated and innocuous. Political naïveté is not surprising in Virgil, but if Horace had been left to himself he might have been more detached and wary.

But the sincerity of dead men cannot be calculated; a more objective test should be applied. When a poem makes what profess to be serious statements about the political world, if these statements are palpably untrue or show no signs of genuine reflection, it cannot be regarded as completely successful. The poet's sincerity is immaterial here: it does not matter whether he says what he does not think or does not think what he is saying. It is illuminating to compare Horace's political poetry with Marvell's Horatian Ode. Marvell's metre and diction are less impressive than Horace's, but he has one great advantage: he talks about politics like a rational man.

> For 'tis all one to Courage high
> The Emulous or Enemy;
>   And with such to inclose
>   Is more then to oppose . . .
>
> Could by industrious Valour climbe
> To ruine the great Work of Time,
>   And cast the Kingdome old
>   Into another Mold.
>
> Though Justice against Fate complain,
> And plead the antient Rights in vain:
>   But those do hold or break
>   As Men are strong or weak.

These lines are as applicable to Augustus as to Cromwell, but while Marvell sums up like a historian, Horace exaggerates like an orator. Only in the ode to Pollio (2.1) does he achieve comparable objectivity:

> Motum ex Metello consule civicum
> bellique causas et vitia et modos
>   ludumque Fortunae gravisque
>   principum amicitias et arma
>
> nondum expiatis uncta cruoribus,
> periculosae plenum opus aleae,
>   tractas, et incedis per ignis
>   suppositos cineri doloso.

The upheaval that began with Metellus' consulship, the causes of the war, its faults and phases, the whims of Fortune, the disastrous coalitions of great men, the weapons smeared with blood that has not yet been expiated, these are the themes of your history, a work full of dangerous hazard, and as you walk across the treacherous crust of ash, the fire below still smoulders.

But Pollio was a historian and a neutralist, and the change in tone was appropriate.

The most dramatic of the political odes celebrates the death of Cleopatra in 30 B.C.

> Nunc est bibendum, nunc pede libero
> pulsanda tellus, nunc Saliaribus
>   ornare pulvinar deorum
>   tempus erat dapibus, sodales.
>
> antehac nefas depromere Caecubum
> cellis avitis, dum Capitolio
>   regina dementis ruinas
>   funus et imperio parabat
>
> contaminato cum grege turpium
> morbo virorum, quidlibet impotens
>   sperare fortunaque dulci
>   ebria. sed minuit furorem
>
> vix una sospes navis ab ignibus,
> mentemque lymphatam Mareotico
>   redegit in veros timores
>   Caesar ab Italia volantem

remis adurgens, accipiter velut
mollis columbas aut leporem citus
    venator in campis nivalis
        Haemoniae, daret ut catenis

fatale monstrum; quae generosius
perire quaerens nec muliebriter
    expavit ensem nec latentis
        classe cita reparavit oras;

ausa et iacentem visere regiam
vultu sereno, fortis et asperas
    tractare serpentis, ut atrum
        corpore combiberet venenum,

deliberata morte ferocior,
saevis Liburnis scilicet invidens
    privata deduci superbo
        non humilis mulier triumpho.   (1.37)

Now let us drink, now stamp the ground with foot unfettered, now
'tis already time to array the gods' cushions with Salian banquets,
friends. Before this it was a sin to bring out Caecuban from ancestral
cellars, while the Queen prepared mad destruction for the Capitol
and death for Roman power, with her tainted tribe of degenerate 'men':
she was demented enough to hope for anything and drunk with sweet
success. But her madness abated when scarce a ship survived the
flames; though her brain was crazed with Mareotic, Caesar reduced it
to realistic terror when he closed on her with his galleys as she sped far
from Italy. He was like a hawk pursuing soft doves or a swift hunter
a hare in the plains of snowy Thessaly; for he was eager to enchain the
fatal prodigy. But she with lordlier spirit preferred to die, and did not
shrink women-like from the sword, nor sought an unseen shore with
her swift ships, but was ready to look on her stricken palace with serene
gaze, and had the courage to handle rough snakes, in order to drink their
black poison with her body. Made more ferocious by her design to die,
she evidently grudged one victory to the fierce Liburnian galleys: she
that was no mean woman refused to be led in the proud triumph like a
private person.

The first stanza is exultant, and sets the key. Horace imitates
Alcaeus's ode 'Now we must drink since Myrsilus is dead'; so the
literate reader understands from the start 'the tyrant is dead'.

libero means not only 'agile' but 'free from enslavement'. Next comes an allusion to Roman religion: Octavian claimed to be defending Italian piety against Oriental superstition. Whether we like Horace's sentiments or not, there can be no doubt about his mastery of his medium; by comparison the ninth epode, which deals with the same subject, seems dull and diffuse.

In the next stanzas word after word is charged and loaded. Caecuban is a vintage wine from the reassuring countryside of Latium. *cellis avitis* suggests a proper respect for ancestors, and the stable inheritance of property. The Capitol, with its temple of Jupiter Optimus Maximus, was the most sacred site in Rome; and Cleopatra had said, or was believed to have said, that she would make laws there. *regina* to Roman ears is even more sinister than *rex*, and is effectively placed next to *Capitolio*. *contaminato, grege, turpium,* and *morbo* are offensive, and *virorum* ironic. *ebria* is used metaphorically, but the sympathetic reader will think of real orgies. Mareotic was a sinister Egyptian drink, quite unlike Caecuban.

The battle of Actium is described in a single vivid line. Antony is conspicuously ignored; it suited official policy to maintain that the civil war was directed against foreign enemies. The celestial phenomena invented by other poets would not suit Horace's realistic manner. It was alien to his purpose, as well as beyond his powers, to attempt the picturesque metaphors of Propertius (4.6.25 f.):

> tandem aciem geminos Nereus lunarat in arcus,
> armorum et radiis picta tremebat aqua.

At last Nereus had arched the battle-lines into two crescents, and the shivering water was painted with the rays of arms.

The account of the pursuit must have surprised contemporaries, as nearly a year passed between the battle and Cleopatra's death. The simile of the hunter is both trite and arrogant. Compare Virgil's subtle lines where the Nile (river-god blended with river) receives the crippled fleet in the secret reaches of the Delta:

> contra autem magno maerentem corpore Nilum
> pandentemque sinus et tota veste vocantem
> caeruleum in gremium latebrosaque flumina victos.
>
> (*Aen.* 8. 711 ff.)

On the other side the Nile, grieving with great body, and opening the folds of his bosom, and calling with all his cloak to his green recesses and secret reaches the defeated.

Horace was never a poet that way.

The ode's greatest strength lies in its powerful close. Propertius might describe the snakes more poetically, but Horace maintains his realistic note: *asperas* means not only 'fierce' but 'rough to handle'. The prosaic words *privata* and *deduci* confirm the serious and political tone of the poem. *non humilis* is a superb litotes, and just. Propertius is petty in comparison (4.6.65 f.):

> di melius! quantus mulier foret una triumphus
> ductus erat per quas ante Iugurtha vias!

Heaven forbid! What triumph would one woman be, in the streets where Jugurtha had once been led?

Yet Horace's magnanimity should not be exaggerated: the third stanza is more abusive than anything in Virgil. Cleopatra is a magnificent animal who will die rather than be caged, and her very ferocity increases the glory of the victor. Her disastrous life ends in bizarre suicide, the perfect confirmation of her enemies' assessment. One would never guess from the Augustan poets that she was a Greek princess and the mistress of Julius Caesar, or that the war would have taken place even if she had never lived. Horace may have been carried away by the enthusiasm of his milieu; yet if a poet writes as a partisan, committed to and sustained by one political group, there is a risk that his views may seem inadequate to future ages. The Cleopatra ode is a splendid paean of victory, which actualizes an important historical event, but it shows no real compassion or understanding. Elsewhere Horace is more sensitive:

> qui gurges aut quae flumina lugubris
> ignara belli? quod mare Dauniae
>   non decoloravere caedes?
>   quae caret ora cruore nostro?   (2.1.33 ff.)

What flood, what rivers know nothing of dismal war? What sea has Italian slaughter not discoloured? What shore is without our blood?

The six odes at the beginning of the third book are too readily taken together. They all deal with national themes, their language is uniformly magnificent, they are written in the Alcaic metre; yet they vary greatly in poetic merit. To discriminate among them it is necessary to look at more than the resonance of the rhetoric. We shall be impressed especially by the poet's originality and imagination, his ability to communicate emotion, and the sense and importance of what he says.

The first of these poems (*odi profanum*) is an attack on the materialism of the age. The theme suits the poet's personality, and may therefore be taken seriously (as in the excellent short poem 2.15). The imagery is most successful when Horace transfers Hellenistic moralizing to a Roman setting (the candidate in the Campus, the urn of necessity). The account of luxury building is particularly striking:

> contracta pisces aequora sentiunt
> iactis in altum molibus; huc frequens
>   caementa demittit redemptor
>   cum famulis dominusque terrae

> fastidiosus: sed Timor et Minae
> scandunt eodem quo dominus, neque
>   decedit aerata triremi et
>   post equitem sedet atra Cura.

The fish notice the contraction of the sea when piers are sunk in the deep water. Here loads of rubble are dumped by contractor and slaves and the proprietor who disdains the land. But Fear and Forebodings climb out the same way as the proprietor. Black Care does not come off the brazen schooner, and sits on horseback behind the Knight.

The combination of prosiness and grandeur, realism and abstraction is characteristic of our author. The poem may seem rather cold and formal, but in the last stanza Horace hints at a more personal feeling:

> cur invidendis postibus et novo
> sublime ritu moliar atrium?
>   cur valle permutem Sabina
>   divitias operosiores?

Why should I erect a high hall in modern fashion with doorposts for men to envy? Why should I exchange my Sabine valley for the greater troublesomeness of wealth.

The second ode is less satisfactory. Horace encourages the young to learn endurance in military service, but the subject does not seem to spring from his own deepest convictions. His description of warfare is absurd, with his king's daughter sighing from the ramparts. Horace had fought in the most horrible battle of the age, and for concentrated slaughter a big ancient battle surpassed modern efforts; yet the unmilitary Virgil describes war in much more convincing terms. 'dulce et decorum est pro patria mori' is a famous line, engraved on many war-memorials; but Horace should not produce elevating maxims for others while seeking *otium* so sedulously himself. In the last two stanzas Horace advises against careless talk with superfluous eloquence; the passage is suggested by a line of Simonides which appealed to Augustus, but it is not integrated with the rest of the poem.

Iustum et tenacem (3.3) has good moments, but much of the poet's energy is misdirected. When Horace sets Augustus among the demigods the fantasy is bad enough; when he imagines him drinking nectar with bright lips the precision is intolerable. There are more difficulties to come. Most of the ode consists of a long speech by Juno, who warns against rebuilding Troy; but the transference of the capital to Troy, even if it was the subject of uninformed rumours, was certainly never a political issue. Some scholars have supposed that Troy symbolizes the dead Republic, but the allegory would be impossibly obscure. One is left with the conclusion that Horace has revived a legend which is totally irrelevant to the mood and needs of the day. If that is so, the ode lacks something.

On the other hand *descende caelo* (3.4) is a subtle and complex piece of work which no summary can adequately expound.[7] The central theme is the power of literature to civilize the world, but the poem owes much of its effect to the personal element. The essentials of Horace's own career and interests are all included: the unimportant villages of his Apulian childhood, his Sabine farm, the rout at Philippi, even his accident with the tree, his admiration for Augustus, his love of Greek poetry. Horace transfers Pindaric motifs to Latin with surprising success:

> vis consili expers mole ruit sua:
> vim temperatam di quoque provehunt
>   in maius; idem odere vires
>   omne nefas animo moventis.

Strength without mind collapses from its own bulk. Strength when controlled is exalted by the gods themselves. But the gods abhor the strong when they plot every abomination.

The myth at the end is also Pindaric. The giants of the First Pythian symbolized Hieron's fallen enemies, but Horace's contemporaries could give the story a more topical application. When Horace applies his imitations of Greek poetry to a concrete situation the formula usually succeeds.

The Regulus ode (3.5) is rightly admired, though its admirers sometimes forget how it begins. Some of Crassus's soldiers, taken prisoner by the Parthians a quarter of a century before, had settled down with barbarian wives; and Horace's indignation is the professed occasion for the poem. He might have shown more sympathy with these unhappy men, the victims of an unnecessary campaign, but his severity no doubt reflects official attitudes. To illustrate his point he tells the story, or rather myth, of Regulus. The last stanzas, describing Regulus's departure for Carthage, are extraordinarily impressive: after talking in grandiose generalizations he here states the situation of an individual in the most direct terms:

> atqui sciebat quae sibi barbarus
> tortor pararet; non aliter tamen
>   dimovit obstantis propinquos
>   et populum reditus morantem
>
> quam si clientum longa negotia
> diiudicata lite relinqueret
>   tendens Venafranos in agros
>   aut Lacedaemonium Tarentum.

And yet he knew what the barbarian torturer was getting ready for him. But he moved aside the relatives in his path and the crowd that hindered his return just as if he had adjudicated an action of his clients and was leaving their tiresome affairs on his way to the Venafrum countryside or to Tarentum that the Spartans built.

The prosaic terminology of Roman business is more moving than any poetical periphrasis, and the conventional epithet in the last line gives the ode a typically peaceful ending.

The sixth poem also begins badly:

> Delicta maiorum immeritus lues,
> Romane, donec templa refeceris
> aedesque labentis deorum et
> foeda nigro simulacra fumo.

You will suffer undeservingly for the sins of your fathers, Roman, until you renew the temples and the gods' falling shrines and the images that are filthy with black smoke.

Horace could not be indifferent to Roman religion, which was inextricably bound up with the Roman State, yet one cannot suppose that he is speaking from the heart when he makes this fantastic statement; the sentiment is entirely suggested by Augustus's repair of eighty-two temples in 28 B.C. The central theme of the ode, the degeneration of national morals, is likewise inspired by Augustus's moral legislation. But when Horace turns to particulars the poem becomes quite different. The adulteress and the salesman ('dedecorum pretiosus emptor') are depicted with forceful realism. There follows an equally vivid picture of former manners, when stalwart Sabines fetched wood for their mothers till the sun went down. The sentiment of the last stanza is modelled on some indifferent verses by Aratus, but is stated here with a concentrated pessimism worthy of a historian:

> damnosa quid non imminuit dies?
> aetas parentum peior avis tulit
> nos nequiores, mox daturos
> progeniem vitiosiorem.

Ruinous time impairs everything. Worse than our grandfathers our parents produced us more worthless than themselves, soon to yield a progeny more degenerate.

In other political odes Augustus himself is the central subject. *Iam satis terris* (1.2) is a conspicuously unattractive poem. It begins with a lively account of the storms which have afflicted the city; Horace pretends to regard them as a sign of divine disfavour, but his mythological fancies do not suit his serious subject. Worse follows. The poet seeks a god to save the falling state, and he imagines that Mercury may be disguised on earth in the form of Octavian:

> sive mutata iuvenem figura
> ales in terris imitaris almae
> filius Maiae patiens vocari
>   Caesaris ultor.

Or perhaps assuming the form of a young man, thou wingèd god hast come disguised to earth, the son of kindly Maia suffering to be known as Caesar's avenger.

This way of talking was an offence to Roman tradition, and went against one of the dominating themes of classical Greek literature; it may be partly explained, but ought not to be excused, by allusions to Hellenistic ruler-cult and Alexandrian court poetry. As for Horace's talk about the avenger of Caesar, one can only ask him 'What were you doing at Philippi?'

As Augustus's position grew stronger he pretended to revive Republican forms, and the poets with their usual percipience moderated their eulogies a little. *Quem virum aut heroa* (1.12) reflects the change. The poem begins with a Pindaric reminiscence ('What man, what hero, what god shall I sing?'), but Horace's short sentences and Sapphic stanzas fail to reproduce the roll and rhythm of his model. The catalogue of gods and men is perfunctory and conventional; contrast the muster in the Sixth Aeneid. The best part of the ode comes in the prayer to Jupiter at the end:

> te minor laetum reget aequus orbem;
> tu gravi curru quaties Olympum,
> tu parum castis inimica mittes
>   fulmina lucis.

Under thee he will rule justly a rejoicing world: thou wilt shake Olympus with heavy chariot, and hurl unfriendly bolts at polluted groves.

The words are eloquent, but what do they mean? Did Horace really think this way?

Divis orte bonis (4.5) is a much better poem, but here, too, the poet's intelligence does not seem to have been fully engaged.

lucem redde tuae, dux bone, patriae:
instar veris enim vultus ubi tuus
adfulsit populo, gratior it dies
et soles melius nitent.

Give back the light, good Leader, to the land. For when your face
has shone like spring upon the people, the day goes more pleasantly
and the sun beams brighter.

This is conventional panegyric, and has nothing to do with the
way people behave: one may feel temporary exhilaration as the
Head of State goes by, but the mood soon vanishes. Horace next
compares Italy's longing for Augustus with the feeling of a
mother who scans the sea for her absent son; the image is not
drawn from life, is too sentimental for a political poem, and does
not fit the facts. It was one thing to believe that the safety of
Augustus was the best guarantee of political stability, another to
feel positive misery when he was out of the country. The picture
of rural peace which follows is wholly charming, the account of
Augustus's moral legislation less so. But the rest of the ode is as
serene and mellifluous as anything in Horace:

condit quisque diem collibus in suis,
et vitem viduas ducit ad arbores;
hinc ad vina redit laetus et alteris
te mensis adhibet deum.

Each man sinks the day among his own hills and leads the vine to
the unwed trees. Then he goes home glad to his wine, and at the end
of the meal invokes you as a god.

Yet in spite of what many critics say, our view of a poem cannot
be completely separated from our view of its subject-matter.
Every reader must judge for himself whether he finds this stanza
acceptable.

Horace's best panegyrics are the ode to Lollius (4.9), the ode
to Augustus on Tiberius (4.14), and best of all the ode on Drusus
(4.4). In this last-mentioned poem Horace transfers to Latin
something of the grandeur of Pindar; the explicit imitations of
1.12 and 4.2 are much less successful. The opening period lasts
28 lines, but Horace never loses control (though the excursus on
the weapons of the Vindelici is a mistake). The spirit of the ode

is Roman and republican, and the argumentation as rational as
the genre permits. The vigour of Hannibal's speech is brilliantly
suited to the subject:

> gens quae cremato fortis ab Ilio
> iactata Tuscis aequoribus sacra
> natosque maturosque patres
> pertulit Ausonias ad urbis,
>
> duris ut ilex tonsa bipennibus
> nigrae feraci frondis in Algido
> per damna, per caedis, ab ipso
> ducit opes animumque ferro.

The race which strong from the pyre of Troy, tossed in the Tuscan
seas, brought its sacred objects and sons and aged fathers to the cities
of Italy, like an oak lopped by the hard axe on black-leaved Algidus,
amid slaughter and disaster draws resources and spirit from the very
steel.

The ode has become the glorification not just of an individual
or a family but of a nation. If poets must write panegyrics this
is how to write them.

I have left to the last the great Ode to Maecenas. Horace's
other poems to his patron are not outstanding, but *Tyrrhena regum
progenies* (3.29) is a different matter. Horace combines in this ode
many of the most characteristic elements of his poetry, and that
is no doubt why he put it at the end of his first collection of lyrics,
before the epilogue. The poem's appeal is not immediate, and it is
perhaps less popular than it should be;[8] yet Dryden wrote a fine
translation which contains something of the 'noble and bold
Purity' which he recognized in our author. He dedicated it to
Lawrence Hyde, Earl of Rochester, with the comment "Tis his
Darling in the Latine'. The Earl of Rochester knew what he was
talking about.

The first half of the poem contains characteristic phrases on a
wide variety of topics. Maecenas's Etruscan ancestors, Horace's
drinking party, the waterfalls of Tibur, the troubles of the rich,
the peace of the countryside, and the anxieties of foreign policy
are all brought in somewhere. One sentence makes a particular
appeal to the imagination: *omitte mirari beatae/fumum et opes
strepitumque Romae* 'Interrupt your admiration for the smoke,

wealth, and noise of prosperous Rome'. But the poem is half-done
before it reaches greatness. With a magnificent spate of rhetoric
Horace compares the stream of time with the Tiber in flood, then
with contrasting simplicity he states the Epicurean position:

> ille potens sui
> laetusque deget, cui licet in diem
> dixisse 'vixi: cras vel atra
> nube polum Pater occupato
>
> vel sole puro; non tamen irritum
> quodcumque retro est efficiet neque
> diffinget infectumque reddet
> quod fugiens semel hora vexit.'

> Happy the Man, and happy he alone,
> He, who can call to day his own:
> He, who secure within, can say
> To morrow do thy worst, for I have liv'd to day.
> Be fair, or foul, or rain, or shine,
> The joys I have possest, in spight of fate are mine.
> Not Heav'n it self upon the past has pow'r;
> But what has been, has been, and I have had my hour.
>
> (Dryden)

Here there is no ornament, none of the appeal to the senses which
we have noted as characteristic of the better odes (so difficult is it
to generalize about poetry). The words are ordinary and the
thought unoriginal, yet the statement is definitive.

There follows an impressive passage on Fortuna:

> Fortuna saevo laeta negotio
> ludum insolentem ludere pertinax
> transmutat incertos honores
> nunc mihi, nunc alii benigna.

Fortune exulting in cruel officiousness, tenaciously enjoying an
arrogant amusement, redistributes her unreliable prizes, kind now to
me, now to another.

Every word is edged and felt, but the concentration is achieved
without any strain. The poem ends, as often, on a quiet note; the
storm may howl, but Horace will row his own lifeboat[9] under the
benign protection of the Dioscuri:

tunc me biremis praesidio scaphae
tutum per Aegaeos tumultus
aura feret geminusque Pollux.

Then through the heaving Aegean, safe in the protection of my two-oared dinghy, I shall be borne by the breeze and the Heavenly Twins.

Horace is nowhere more personal or more universal.

The Odes could only have been written by a poet of unusual energy and intelligence. Horace created a style which was both original and inimitable. He covered a far wider range than most lyric poets. He transferred the metres and the themes of Greek poetry to an alien setting, and somehow gave them a genuinely Roman quality. Yet his limitations must be acknowledged. His high standards of technical perfection brought a loss of spontaneity: only those who write fast can express all the shades and subtleties of thought. He lacked style and grace of the Catullan sort (his social origin may be relevant here); he had no appreciation of certain sorts of beauty; he was unusually self-conscious, for a poet, about expressing emotion. When he turned to public subjects he could not speak as an autonomous agent; and freedom to conform is not enough for anybody who is any good. Yet the Odes are much more than a triumph of technique; Horace is not just a civil servant who applied a talent for organization to the writing of poetry. In spite of the constraints imposed by his art, temperament, and society, he talks often enough as a real person. The Odes are most successful when they reveal something of the poet's own humanity and scepticism.

NOTES

[1] *Unpoetische Wörter* (Lund, 1945), pp. 98 ff.

[2] An *ionic a minore* is ‿‿ − −. The rhythm is more important than the sense.

[3] Cf. *Anth. Pal.* 12.107.3 f. μύρτον ἕωλον ἐρρίφθω ξηροῖς φυρόμενον σκυβάλοις ('let him be cast aside like stale myrtle mixed with dry refuse').

[4] *The flames flicker agitatedly and whirl a spiral of dirty smoke.*

[5] I have sometimes wondered whether *sequetur* could have a semi-legal tinge, as in the formula *hoc monumentum heredem non sequitur*, 'this tomb does not pertain to the heir'. By Roman law a grave became the property of the Di Manes (F. Schulz, *Classical Roman Law*, Oxford, 1951, p. 342.)

[6] I should warn the non-professional reader that the views expressed here are very controversial.

[7] For details see the illuminating discussion by Fraenkel, *Horace*, pp. 273 ff.

[8] See, however, the notable appreciation by Fraenkel, *Horace*, pp. 223 ff.

[9] A *scapha* was a small dinghy, towed at the stern of a ship, to which one resorted in emergencies: see E. Zinn in *Festschrift für H. Hommel* (Tübingen, 1961), pp. 185 ff.

INDEX OF NAMES

INDEX OF PASSAGES